Awed, Amused, and Alarmed

Fairs, Rodeos, and Regattas in Western Canada

Faye Reineberg Holt

DETSELIG
ENTERPRISES LTD

Faye Reineberg Holt

Awed, Amused, and Alarmed

National Library of Canada Cataloguing in Publication Data

Reineberg Holt, Faye

Awed, amused and alarmed: fairs, rodeos and regattas in Western Canada/Faye Reineberg Holt

Includes bibliographical references and index.
ISBN 1-55059-249-1

1. Fairs--Canada, Western--History. 2. Rodeos--Canada, Western--History. 3. Exhibitions--Canada, Western--History. I. Title.

GT4813.A3W4   2003   394'.6'09712   C2003-910491-5

210-1220 Kensington Rd. N.W., Calgary, AB T2N 3P5

Phone: (403) 283-0900/Fax: (403) 283-6947

E-mail: temeron@telusplanet.net

www.temerondetselig.com

We acknowledge the financial support of the Government of Canada through the Book Publishing Industry Development Program (BPIDP) for our publishing activities. We also acknowledge the support of the Alberta Foundation for the Arts for our publishing program.

ISBN 1-55059-249-1

SAN 115-0324

Printed in Canada

COMMITTED TO THE DEVELOPMENT OF CULTURE AND THE ARTS

Frontispiece: Viola Dana, from Hollywood, along with Ormer Locklear, treated Calgary audiences to a unique, comical aviation act in 1920. Courtesy of Glenbow Archives, NA 1258-23.

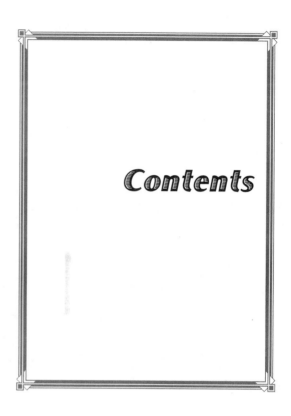

Contents

Full version of photo from the frontispiece: Viola Dana, from Hollywood, along with Ormer Locklear, treated Calgary audiences to a unique, comical aviation act in 1920. Courtesy of Glenbow Archives, NA 1258-23.

Dedicated with love to my husband Walt
Without whose love, support,
and endless patience
This book would never have been completed.

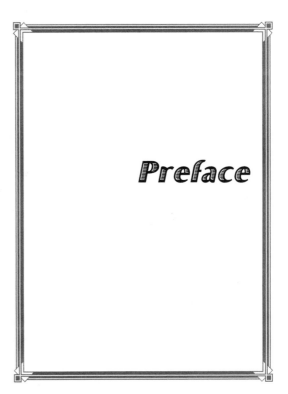

Preface

Initially, the popular culture of fairs, rodeos, regattas, and circuses seems inconsequential compaired to the history of Canada's involvement in two world wars and the Depression, but that pop culture supported government effort and encouraged people during those trying times. Throughout the world and here at home in western Canada, such pop culture affected individuals and communities. In fact, a rich and diverse history awaits the simply curious, as well as serious social historians. Discovering its "truths" may be even more difficult than deliniating political and economic history. So much must be based on conflicting newspaper accounts. So much was never reported because hard news was the priority. Much must be based on vague memories, some transformed into myth. Then again, I decided, those myths were important, too.

The annual festivals of summer reflected the many ways people enjoyed themselves, but they also reflected prejudices and injustices of the time. Many of those stories are challenging to tell, especially in today's social climate, where even writing some words in the context of serious discussion could result in criticism. I believe we must explore the real past – not an idealized or sanitized past. We need to do that both in oral discussion and in print. To me, it is better to use the words that were used then, rather than rephrase them in academic "equivalents." At the same time, words are like swords. They can be very hurtful. So, I have tried to walk that fine line, exploring what really happened, what was printed about it, and what was expressed orally. I have tried to be honest without incurring needless harm or excessive sensationalism, and I hope I have been able to do that.

This book was certainly the most overwhelming I have ever written. To a large extent, that was because there is such a wealth of material available. It was not possible to tell all of the fascinating history related to the special summer events in a community. Although most people's memories are generalized and fond, many of the "stories" had a serious side. In the end, I looked for stories that represented the larger picture or gave a glimpse of the smaller one, too. As well, I wanted to show some of the links between the many festivals, but in no way could I present all the fine accomplishments of competitors, organizers, and volunteers. There were so many, and I could explore only a few. Nor could I present this history chronologically. Various large and small, isolated and urban communities did share similar experiences, but these may have happened decades apart.

Another problem was terminology and common usage. As a result, I have used the words *fair* and *festival* to represent the overall classification for exhibitions – whether industrial or agricultural – as well as to encompass rodeos and regattas. Of course, some communities named their most important summer gathering "the fair," and so the word is used to represent specific fairs, too.

I want to express a very special thanks to Oney and Doug Martin, Russ Overton, John Thurston and Conklin Shows, Ron Getty of the Calgary Exhibition and Stampede Archives, Norman Cook, the Willis family, and Gerry and Leona Mann. In addition, my thanks to the many, many others working in museums and libraries, who gave me invaluable assistance and permission to publish photos.

Also, special thanks to my publisher Ted Giles and editor Linda Berry for their phenomenal patience and support.

Faye Reineberg Holt

Nothing Like a Show

"Incidents that left the great audience breathless, incidents that were a powerful stimulant to heart action and some that were intensely amusing marked the third day of the Stampede. There was enough excitement crowded into four stirring hours to send the red blood racing through the veins of the most confirmed dyspeptic," claimed a reporter for the *Manitoba Free Press* when describing the 1913 Winnipeg Exhibition and Stampede.[1]

Chapter 1

Days of Delight

Exhibitions, stampedes, pow-wows, regattas, circuses, and horse races have long been the highlight of the summer for countless western Canadians. Almost every community staged a festive summer event, one that recurred each year and was more important than all other community celebrations. Those wonderful days of delight share a tangled but fascinating history.

Whatever the annual event was called, whatever its primary focus or featured entertainments, the crowds gathered from nearby and from hundreds of miles away. Usually, the most important summer event centred around

Bucking horse. Courtesy of Stockmen's Memorial Foundation, CHRA 037-Vol. 1.

four themes. They involved competition, educational displays or events, entertainment opportunities, and local culture or identity.

To foster education, they presented the latest and greatest from industry and technology, new farming techniques, successful livestock breeds, as well as gardening, homemaking, and artistic skills. The events encouraged competition – local, provincial, national, or international – in very diverse fields. They acknowledged the importance of entertainment and pleasure for its own sake, and they celebrated the history and background of the people. Making that happen was a monumental task – much of it volunteer – but it generated thousands of dollars in business.

The annual summer festivals were the most significant form of popular culture in western Canada prior to the 1950s. Prior to settlement days, First Nations people held sporting events. Too, there have long been forums for conveying agriculture priorities, industrial developments, education, and culture. Having a good time was nothing new. It was the combination of all these as priorities during one day or week that made the festivities the best in pop culture, even after other forms of entertainment arrived, such as television.

Nellie McClung wrote, "A Fair is a cross-section of life. If you had only one day to spend in a country, you would be well advised to go the Agricultural Fair if you wished to find out about the people....You would be able to see something about the people's way of living and their ideas of beauty."[2]

Inevitably, concerns arose. Even in 1907, one fair visitor voiced criticism. "Our people are more interested in the Vaudeville and the horse racing attractions than in the progress of the country as emphasized by its products." One prairie writer admitted, "it takes lots of different people to make a world, so does it take a variety of objects and subjects to make a fair, and what

Simple costumes transformed children and adults into clowns for this Kelowna parade. The wool, ribbon, or strips of old cloth used as decoration made the carriage worthy of a parade too. Courtesy of Kelowna Museum Archives, PC 439-50.

one comes to see, the other does not, so in order that all shall see something and we can obtain a crowd, we must have an exhibit of general interest."

One of the worst problems about attending the fair, the visitor dared to add, was that "the welcome is so extensive [and] entertainment tendered precludes the possibility of someone doing justice to what there is to see, and the constant flow of invitations also interferes with sleeping...."[3]

Yet, for those few wonderful days sometime between spring and fall, that didn't seem to matter. Work was put on hold while families attended local events or the festivities in other communities. There were displays and competitions. Individuals submitted their handiwork, baking, produce, and livestock, but communities also displayed their own strengths, and they advertised and competed for newcomers.

The season for such festivities opened in May. By late October, even the fall fairs had ended. National or provincial holidays were great days for the events. Still, settlement culture, local situations, and the touring schedules of fair-related businesses helped dictate which dates worked best for each community. Spring or fall fairs were perfect where the weather was perfect, but farmers had little to exhibit at spring fairs, and even in late fall, they might be busy with harvest.

In 1941, during the Kelowna Regatta, Okanagan water-skiier Bruce Paige was towed by a launch at a speed of 50 miles [80 km] per hour and successfully made an eight-foot [2.4 m] jump, then the highest-known water jump. Courtesy of Kelowna Museum Archives, 667.

Winter carnivals were popular in snow-bound Canadian communities, especially communities like Banff with a strong tradition of outdoor winter sports. Some competitions were based on Aboriginal skills. Others evolved from the blending of traditions. Yet, in most western Canadian communities, the winter festivals never attracted the crowds of the summer events. Brandon, Manitoba, developed a very successful winter fair, but it held a summer fair, too. The Royal Winter Fair in Toronto would draw hundreds and hundreds of exhibits and agricultural competitors from western Canada, but at home, the summer festivities were the highlight of the year.

The tradition of fairs and festivals was rooted in similar events staged in Britain, Eastern and Western Europe. Immigrants carried those expectations with them to Canada. Soon after the first settlement in North America, summer fairs became part of culture. Among the first on the continent was the fair at Windsor, Nova Scotia, in 1765. The idea quickly took root across the country.

There were many early festivals in Victoria. Given the number of American prospectors headed to the Fraser River in search of gold during the late 1850s, the community celebrated the Fourth of July in grand style. The city was named after Queen Victoria, and Victoria Day became the community's biggest and best celebration. Like its sister city New Westminster on the BC mainland, Victoria claimed to have held its first fair in 1861.

Those early dates did not automatically grant Victoria or New Westminster the honors of the first agricultural fair in Western Canada.[4] With its earliest European settlers arriving in 1855 and its agricultural society formed in 1861, the community of Saanich, about 16 miles [26 km] from Victoria, has determined that its 1868 fair was the first "continuous agricultural fair in western Canada." For New Westminster, the problem was continuity. For Victoria, the focus was not primarily agricultural, since it was held on Victoria Day.

Manitoba fairs began early and had strong agricultural components. Unfortunately, the threat of the Fenian raids led to problems and partial cancellation of the first planned agricultural fair in Fort Garry [Winnipeg] in 1871. In 1872, the agricultural society at Portage La Prairie, which had a population of only 300, attracted about 400 entries for its first fair. By hosting fairs each year thereafter, it became the first permanent fair on the prairies. Also early on the scene were St. Boniface and Brandon in Manitoba, which could boast 17 towns hosting fairs within a decade.[5]

Not far behind Manitoba fairs was the one held at the Hudson Bay's Fort Edmonton on 15 October 1879. True to the booster spirit of fairs, later-day Edmontonians bragged that theirs was the first in the Northwest. Geographically speaking, it was the first in the North West Territory that became Alberta and Saskatchewan. Also true to the booster spirit, the Edmonton fair's aim was to "manifest to the World and ourselves"[6] that the community could produce the finest agricultural products. For the 300 people living at the fort, the fair was a hit.

Cowboy and western traditions were destined to become part of the fairs, too. Closely linked to ranch history in the United States as well as Canada, rodeos built on the even longer tradition of summer gatherings amongst the indigenous people. In the far west and the Okanagan, traditions of competitive war canoe races were an early part of community celebrations. On the prairies, another kind of First Nations gatherings had an impact. Powwows were steeped in spiritual meaning, and through rituals and dancing, First Nations people sought spiritual strength, especially in time of war. Oneness among humans, nature, and the great spirit was central to the powwows, but so were the secular good times of a community gathering together.

Throughout the world, horse races were another popular entertainment. In western Canada, horses and riders were an everyday sight. All that was needed was a track. In a pinch, a stretch of prairie or a town's main street would work. With excellent riders amongst the First Nations, both men and women were keen entrants into horse races. Their involvement led to specialty

This finely-dressed First Nations contingent in the 1913 Winnipeg Stampede parade continued an already-established tradition of participating in community parades and rodeos. Courtesy of Archives of Manitoba, Winnipeg Stampede 1913 6.9.

races, limited to indigenous people. In them, First Nations women were the earliest and most serious female competitors at racing and rodeo events.

Certainly, history and the "spirit of ancestors" was an important theme for many fairs and festivities. The national roots of immigrants became apparent in traditional costumes, dances, music, and food at both large and small community celebrations.

Still, few of the events staged in western Canada were truly unique. Chautauqua originated in New York State, but the travelling show stopped in communities from BC to Ontario and further east. It first appeared on the Canadian circuit in 1917 in Alberta, and for the summer engagements, a huge tent was raised – often at a community's local fairgrounds. Organizers provided financial guarantees and sold tickets.

In the four to six days of the engagement, Chautauqua brought a festive atmosphere. Young performers presented vaudeville, musical, and magic acts, and people loved them. Offering a break from work, a cultural experience, and social opportunities for local people, towns welcomed the shows. In the interests of education, there were informational and uplifting lectures. Where a sports day or cowboy competition offered nothing cultural, Chautauqua seemed a lifeline to the world. The tours were successful in western Canada until the mid-30s.

Children and adults eagerly awaited the arrival of the big tent and travelling performers. Sometimes, they journeyed significant distances to fill seats. Yet, Chautauqua was different from local fairs. There were no farm exhibits and agricultural homemaking competitions, no sporting competitions or industrial displays. However, once the days of small, tabletop fairs had faded into history, the entertainment at local fairs was similar to Chautauqua.

In 1948, Penticton held its first annual Peach Festival and Rodeo. Here movie star Alexis Smith (right) and the festival's first queen enjoy the fruits of the Okanagan. Courtesy of Penticton Museum, 2000-005-07.

Local people and their communities had their own "take" on the best type of festivity to stage. In some villages and towns, the fairs had more in common with church picnics, Farmers' Day, and informal cowboy contests than with the industrial exhibitions that developed in large cities. These didn't offer the more unique pleasures of the carnival midway, circuses, or full-fledged regattas, rodeos and agricultural fairs, but locals loved them.

Geography played a role in this evolution of events. In ranch country, rodeos captured the imaginations of audiences. For communities located on lake shores or near rivers, the popular summer festivals often specialized in water sports and became regattas. The type of regional agriculture or industry dictated the types of competitions and displays. Also, the background of the local labor force played a role in selecting the date and shape of events.

Festivities attracted crowds to the fine parades, amusements, exhibits, and competitions. With awe, children in large and small communities watched races and performances. Some dreamed of becoming world-class competitors or stars. Some did, but occasionally, horses and bulls became more famous and awe-inspiring than their riders.

Airplanes and roller coasters wowed crowds. Elephants escaped their custodians. Planes crashed. Balloons burst. Men and animals died, and rides were smashed by high winds.

Those weren't the only difficulties. Finding money to stage the events was not easy. Seldom would the gate cover all the expenses. Civic governments, departments of agriculture, and

For the Hazelton Agricultural Fair of 1916, a display tent held photos and lumber samples from British Columbia Forestry Service. Courtesy of British Columbia Archives, NA-04474.

wealthy individuals made donations. Volunteers held raffles and bake sales, and local talent or theatre groups sometimes performed for free.

Still, decade after decade, people spent months organizing the festivities. Crowds flocked to the events, and most people left with powerful memories. The fairs of western Canada did not exist in isolation from the rest of the world. Instead, they were ways in which the world came to small and large communities, and they remain central to the histories of leisure, sports, agriculture, women's studies, business, industry, and community development.

Evolution New Westminster Style

Which day was the right day for the community's biggest shindig? What kind of event should it be? The question was never decided on one day for all time. Instead, the festivals evolved. Often, they began as tabletop fairs – small agricultural competitions with little or no entertainment. Samples and displays were then submitted to other community fairs, and boosterism took hold. Somewhere along the line came the sporting competitions as well as the festival or carnival-style parades, midways, and other entertainments.

The date and type of the most significant celebration usually reflected the personality of the community and even its politics. May Day, Victoria Day, Coronation Day, Empire Day, Dominion Day, Labour Day, and Canada Day were just a few of the names for some important, recurring festival dates that were tied to the national and world community. Other celebrations were local and specific to the area. Eventually, one celebration became most important. Usually, such an event appeared early in the community's fair or festival history, and it survived to the present day. The name might change, but the activities remained similar.

However, some such events have very specific beginning and endings. New Westminster's story captured the ups and downs of summer fairs and festivals.

May Day at New Westminster, BC, encouraged the participation of local children and garnered huge crowds. Courtesy of New Westminster Public Library, 1757.

The history of The Royal City, a name given to it by Queen Victoria, dated to the earliest settlements on the west coast mainland. Eventually, the community became part of the metropolis of Vancouver. Having an early and clear sense of self, by 1861, New Westminster citizens decided they would send a display to the great Industrial Exhibition in London, England, planned for the next year. Other west coast communities were joining together to send exhibits, but given the boosterism in The Royal City, New Westminster erected a building to prepare and house its planned exhibits for overseas.

With all the excitement, the locals wanted to see the exhibit for themselves. A promotional pamphlet was prepared, and the community held its first agricultural fair from the 13th to 15th of November. By 1867, the agricultural society, eventually the fair's sponsor, was founded to hold annual events.

The fair grew rapidly. The name of the society changed to Royal Agricultural and Industrial Society of British Columbia, and that new name reflected the increasing interest in industrial development. A natural area was chosen for staging events. By 1889, after six months' work on grounds and buildings, the new site was ready for the exhibition. Called Queen's Park, there were livestock pens, a grandstand, race track, athletic field, and a main display building.

The fair wasn't the only event that meant a great time for the people of New Westminster. With better weather than most areas of Canada, the coastal community could host events with outdoor activities throughout much of the year.

The most dramatic early moment in the fall fair's history came in 1894. A highlight for the 11 October fair was the flight of a "dirigible balloon."

The reputation of the dirigible preceded its arrival. These nonrigid, cloth airships were powered by small steam engines, and made their debut in 1852 in France. Not surprisingly, they were a hit at fairs, and crowds gathered at the New Westminster fair to see the technological wonder.

The aeronaut who brought and flew the dirigible was Professor Soper. In Los Angeles, he had hired a helper named Charles Marble for $10. Once the dirigible was high above the crowds, the 26-old was to parachute from its platform and land on the opposite side of the Fraser River.

The airship rose 1500 feet [457 metres], and audiences thrilled at the sight. Marble jumped from the platform. His parachute opened, and he floated downward but veered towards the river. He splashed down, headfirst in the middle of the Fraser. Far from watchers on the banks, the balloon enveloped him. Tangled in the chute, he couldn't struggle free, and no one could reach him in time. The young man drowned, the first death related to a lighter-than-air machine in Canada, but not the last.

Other developments for the fair were positive. In 1910, Vancouver had staged its first fair, but New Westminster's was the showcase event on the coast. By 1912, organizers and citizens could boast that community's premier event had been granted the status of provincial exhibition, making it the most important fair in the province. As well as the agricultural competitions and exhibits, that year, it featured the World's Lacrosse Championship. Organizers had garnered the two games for $7000. They were pleased to offer fair visitors the chance to watch the west coast's Salmonbellies vie for the Minto Cup in the national game of the dominion.[7]

By September, 1922, enthusiasts could watch their sports heroes play lacrosse or compete in the provincial track meet championships. "A striking feature is the honey exhibit comprising tons of the product of the busy bee," claimed *The British Columbian* newspaper of the six-day fair. "Band competitions, balloon ascensions, Magnificent Daylight Fireworks and Nocturnal Pyrotechnical Display. Agricultural, Horticultural, Industrial and Livestock Exhibition, Junior Stock Judging Competitions. All the Fun of the Fair....A Full Week of Education and Entertainment...Perfect Days of Enjoyment."[8] What more could a fair-goer ask?

The Indian exhibits were exactly what the national Department of Indian Affairs wanted from indigenous people. Overseeing the display was John Smith, Indian agent at Kamloops. Shuswap Indians from four reserves were exhibiting vegetables, grains, and fruits. Impressive handcrafts – including basket work, buckskin, beaded buckskin moccasins and gloves – from First Nations women were on display.

By 1923, with a 45-year history, Toronto's Canadian National Exhibition set an attendance record of 1 493 000. That was 120 000 more than the previous year. No community in western Canada could achieve those numbers, but the New Westminster fair, celebrating its 44th birthday, certainly did offer a big bang for the buck.[9]

Then in 1929, things went wrong. Disaster hit Queen's Park.

"New Westminster lost practically all of its Exhibition buildings...when the fire fiend swept through Queen's Park to destroy the Agricultural, Women's and Manufacturers' [buildings], the Arena and the Poultry and Industrial buildings inside the short space of one hour and ten minutes."[10]

Only the stock barns remained.

Winston Churchill had been invited to open the fair. Volunteers erected tents. The fair, like show business, must go on, but the cost of rebuilding would have been astronomical.

New Westminster decided to amalgamate its fair with the Vancouver event. The community's fairs had to evolve but festivities continued. With the boosterism attitude that makes for success, organizers now claim the May Day celebration is "the longest continuing celebration of its kind in the Commonwealth."

Vancouver's Pacific National Exhibition proved to be successful and enduring. The importance of fun is conveyed in this photo from the 1927 Exhibition. Courtesy of City of Vancouver Archives, CVA 180-296.

Grabbing Attention

During the entire history of festivals in western Canada, organizers have realized the value of promotion. They have handled it in thousands of ways, with thousands of pictures, and hundreds of thousands of words. Purple prose filled columns in newspapers, and the language of boosterism became the language of fair advertising.

Organizers never lacked imagination or walked away from silly or risky promotional stunts. Motorcycles raced through rings of fire. A number of cities held ski jump competitions to advertise summer exhibitions. In 1921 at Calgary, a ski jump was erected over the grandstand building, but the promotional stunt fizzled when, ironically, a warm Chinook wind brought uncooperative weather.

When it came to ideas for promoting events, it didn't matter how small the community nor how outrageous the idea. Someone came up with an idea; others thought it hilarious or sure to

capture imaginations. Then, someone or some group of people had the jam to carry out the stunt.

One of the funniest, most dangerous, and most outrageous came out of the Big Gap Stampede in the Neutral Hills, near Consort, Alberta. The event had started as a round-up and community get-together. The surrounding hills provided a stunning environment, and a beef barbecue meant plenty of food. In 1915, the grounds were designated by the hills and a circle of cars and buggies. The stampede competitions were always a hit, but local ranchers wanted an even bigger hit.

Why not give the folks a homegrown, real wild west show, someone suggested.

So they added re-enactments of cowboy and ranching history. Local cowboys became Billy the Kid, and they found themselves in sketches called "The Gold Rush," "The Whiskey Trader," "The Indian Massacre," or "The Stage Coach Robbery."[11] People loved it.

The shows attracted people from as far as 50 miles [80 km] away. Still, there might be others who wanted to join in the good time – if they knew about it. Likely, Edmontonians would enjoy the Big Gap Stampede.

Free publicity was the key. Why not do something in a big way, something to surprise everyone, something no one could ignore?

Why not rob a bank? Rancher Bert Coffee suggested in the spring of 1919. That would grab people's attention.

Bert was a friendly, big cowboy who wouldn't hurt a flea and loved to have a laugh. All the boys were good at playing roles, so pretending to be bank robbers would be easy for Bert and his ten compatriots, including Bert's brother Carl.

They planned for a rootin' tootin' style robbery. They would dress in cowboy duds, and carry guns – loaded with blanks.

They decided having an insider at the bank was best. So, they enlisted the manager of the Merchants Bank. The ride to Edmonton was too far to be realistic. They needed mounts from a source in the city. Horses were still common, even in the city, but getting them all at one location would be easiest. The cowboys approached the RCMP, and the Mounties agreed to lend the necessary mounts. The robbers were ready.

The day of the robbery, they travelled to Edmonton and saddled up. The cowboys rode along Jasper Avenue until they were close to the bank. Suddenly, they broke into a gallop, drew their guns, and started shooting.

People ducked for cover.

Nine cowboys dismounted and rushed the bank, but Bert rode right through the door, across the marble floor, and up to the wicket.

With his gun drawn, Carl covered the shocked customers.

Bert's mount skidded, the steel of its horseshoes hard on the marble. Bert was unfazed.

"This is a stick up," he yelled, repeatedly firing his gun. "Hand over your money and don't try any funny stuff."[12]

Customers stood frozen and watched as the teller handed over bags of money. A female customer pulled out the bills for the robbers. Then, hands still in the air, she broke into tears.

For his getaway, Coffee reined his horse in a sudden turn. The horse skidded and stumbled to the marble.

"Help," the woman wailed and fainted.

"Come here," Carl yelled to his brother. "The old gal's fainted."

Quickly, Bert dismounted and went to check her pulse. He directed the teller to bring water. When the customer recovered, the cowboys reassured her it was all a publicity stunt.

But the unfortunate incident wasn't the worst in their day. A second robbery had been planned to guarantee even more publicity. The cowboys returned the horses to the RCMP and set out.

On the outskirts of Edmonton, the robbers once again headed to a bank. Again, they had contacted the bank manager, but they hadn't announced the gag to the public. Nor did an ex-Mountie living in the area know about it.

With guns blazing, the cowboys hit the bank.

The ex-Mountie, who owned the nearby creamery, heard the shots. Worried, he went for his service revolver. He only had two rounds in the chamber. From the creamery, he took aim at the robbers.

Bert came running out of the bank with bags of money. The ex-officer took aim and fired — with live ammunition.

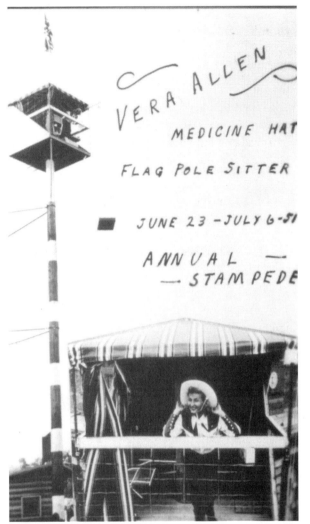

To generate interest and garner free publicity, the 1951 Medicine Hat Exhibition and Stampede organizers hired 29-year-old British-born Vera Allen to sit at the top of a flag-pole. For 13 days, Vera lived on the platform at the top of the 45-foot [14 m] pole. Nights were spent in her 6 x 7 foot [1.8 x 2.1 m] penthouse or roost. During the day, she waved to visitors, modeled bathing suits, sunbathed, and responded to telephone interviews, many of which were printed in international newspapers. Food, water, and other necessities were delivered via a pulley system. Medicine Hat Museum and Art Gallery, 2403.

What a show! thought Bert. He ran towards the gun-tooting officer. The ex-Mountie backed away and prepared to fire again. Just as he was about to shoot, he fell over cream cans. Running and laughing, Bert continued to the officer.

What a great show! What a great joke!

The ex-Mountie was not impressed and didn't laugh. If he had had six bullets instead of two, Bert might have laughed his last laugh, claimed the Mountie – all in the interests of publicity for the Big Gap Stampede.

Associations and Circuits

The wonderful, annual celebrations of summer were not only great times. They were business, and they were hard work. Festivities did not begin on opening day or with the traditional parade. Long-term and careful planning was important in the late 1800s but even more so when festivities grew from a few hundred people to crowds of thousands, hundreds of thousands, or even over a million. The big events required countless individuals and groups working together.

Given Canada's weather and the agricultural base for much of western Canada, the season for festivities was short. Summer gatherings proved best in terms of attendance, but produce and fat stock weren't ready for display or competition until fall. If a community waited too long, an early winter might cancel the show. Too, touring sports competitors, midways, and performance companies were on the road from late spring to early fall. Dozens of far-flung communities wanted to book the best among them, making travel and schedules difficult. Cost was another crucial factor. Small towns could not afford to invite pricey guest performers or make large financial guarantees to travelling companies.

Loosely-knit groups had organized the first May Day and Victoria Day celebrations. Local agricultural societies, farmers, and ranchers launched the first agricultural fairs. Too, businessmen and charities were involved in local festivals. Even inventors, manufacturers, machinery distributors, and the CPR wanted in on the action. Then, too, there were all the touring groups to organize.

Volunteers and their communities realized that organizing into even larger societies – ones representing many communities – would bring greater opportunities and successes. Banded together, the communities could offer one big contract, and in doing so, get the best financial deal. Together, as a lobby group, they had a louder voice when approaching the federal government for grants or the railways for transportation subsidies. Also, for exhibitors from different communities to compete against each other – whether with their grain, livestock, handicraft or cooking – standardized categories and rules made everything easier. Numerous fair associations developed to help organizers handle the multitude of details involved in hosting a large fair. Committees within the associations heard the pitches of travelling shows, set up schedules, and made hundreds of decisions.

Community individuals continued to do endless hours of volunteer work, organizing everything from raising money, preparing food, and entering competitions to judging and performing themselves.

Increasingly, fair associations made decisions about who to hire for the midway, concessions, free shows, and grandstand shows. They offered one contract to cover everyone's print materials, fireworks, and sound systems.

Some communities did decide not to join the associations. When advance men for performers showed up, some small towns booked their own entertainers and midways. Because they could afford less, their events and entertainments included more simple pleasures. Needle and thread, sack, egg, tennis ball, and stick and ball races were popular. Ball games drew crowds, and horse races – even if the horses and riders came from the nearest ranch – were always a hit.

Still, the movers and shakers wanted more. Fair associations and staff became increasingly large and powerful. Names and priorities constantly changed, and as a result, members grouped and re-grouped but, always, the intent was to create the best festivity possible. Communities on the Pacific Coast worked towards shared objectives, and the British Columbia Fairs Association was formed. On Vancouver Island, in the lower mainland, and the Okanagan, where fruit, vegetables, and flowers played such an important role at exhibitions, the horticultural societies had significant influence, much more than elsewhere in western Canada.

Geographically, it made sense for fairs on the prairies to work together. In 1911, at the first joint meeting of western Canadian fair managers, held at Regina, representatives from Winnipeg, Edmonton, Brandon, Prince Albert, Calgary, Lethbridge, Saskatoon, and Regina formed the Fair Managers' Association.

Another group, including fair organizers and turf or horse racing clubs from Calgary, Edmonton, Saskatoon, Yorkton, and Moose Jaw formed the Western Canada Fair and Racing Circuit. By 1915, the Fair Managers' Association amalgamated with the fair and racing circuit, and the enormously powerful organization negotiated fair-related contracts and established racing rules.

Because of size and the different needs and budgets of the large and small fairs, once again, the association had to be re-shuffled in 1923. The Western Canada Association of Exhibitions – commonly called the Class A Fairs or the A Circuit – served the five large fairs of Edmonton, Calgary, Regina, Saskatoon, and Brandon. Initially, Winnipeg had opted out of the circuit, but by 1929, it applied for membership. The Western Canadian Fairs' Association became the representative of smaller fairs and was known as the Class B Fairs or the B Circuit.

Over the years, the Class A cities burgeoned in size, but the Class B association faced a very different problem. Soon, there were simply so many communities, hundreds of miles apart, staging short two or three day fairs, that negotiating for all of them became unrealistic. It had become difficult, if not impossible, for one contractor to handle all routes and stops in the tight timeframe. In 1926, when Conklin & Garrett All-Canadian Shows won the bid for B Circuit midways, the tour included short stops in Carmen, Portage La Prairie, Dauphin, Yorkton, Melfort, Estevan, Weyburn, Red Deer, Camrose, Vegreville, Vermilion, Lloydminster, North Battleford, and Prince Albert.[13]

Other small towns wanted into the circuit. Finally, in 1929 the Western Canadian Fairs' Association made a practical decision. It split the Class B fairs into an eastern and a western circuit.

Issues were complex, but they were common to the fairs and exhibitions across the entire nation and continent. Already, in 1917, W.J. Stark, manager of the Edmonton Exhibition, was one of two Canadians named to the Program Committee of the American Association of Fairs and Expositions. The association addressed the problems, entertainment needs, and financial issues affecting fairs throughout North American. In 1923, fairs across Canada organized to address national issues, and fair representatives from all across the nation met. By 1928, for the Toronto meeting of the Canadian Association of Exhibitions, there were about 30 delegates representing 18 fairs.[14]

Other lobby groups and associations played roles in fair-related business. In summer, wild west shows, rodeo companies, rodeo competitors, circuses, and midways criss-crossed the continent. They were subject to as many pressures as the fairs and fair associations. Not surprisingly, they formed associations, too.

Competitors, rodeo companies, horse race owners, midways, and circuses wanted profitable routes. All might accept work anywhere, if enough money was offered, but they and their associations established procedures, preferences, rules, and lobby positions.

Showmen with large midway operations became members of professional and support organizations. On Canada's west coast, two associations were helpful to the owners of the travelling shows: the Pacific Coast Showmen Association, which usually met in Los Angeles, and the Showmen's League America (SLA). The SLA was comprised of showmen from across the continent, and many of their businesses worked in western Canada. For a time, Patty Conklin, of Conklin All Canadian Shows and one of the best known Canadian showmen, was president of each of the associations. In the position, he influenced those bringing shows into Canada, and he lobbied on issues related to transportation, border crossing regulations, and customs.

To assist in the organization of fairs, many associations developed quite naturally out of need. The work required to stage successful events was often monumental. Much of it was volunteer, and communities across the west benefited from the thousands dedicated to the events.

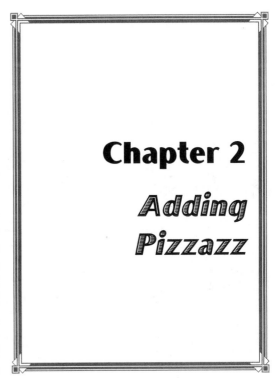

Chapter 2
Adding Pizzazz

Attracting Attractions

Fairs, rodeos, and festivals needed pizzazz, and hiring the best attractions was serious work. Smart fair organizers from BC to Manitoba didn't simply look to the talented in their own communities. They advertised and scouted North America for acts that would impress audiences. In very small communities, the net was not cast far, but in larger communities, exhibition association committees did their homework when it came to finding top acts. Associations that represented a large geographical area could offer more engagements, which meant more work and higher incomes for the independents or the performance companies.

From the early days, the various fair-related associations recognized that hiring great attractions was central to their business. What good were fine displays and educational exhibits if nobody came to see them?

The simple truth was that larger audiences were attracted by what was unusual and exciting compared to their everyday lives. For many, day after day was filled with work, and often, the break for the fair was a much needed respite. Very young children had a good time simply by riding the ponies or merry-go-rounds. Some, especially young men, enjoyed the arcade games and gambling concessions. More wanted a theatrical show for their dollar. They yearned for a kind of posh or polished entertainment that allowed them to forget work or money problems, even if only for a few hours.

Pizzazz was the answer. Smart organizers booked acts that were daring, exciting, unusual, glamorous, or just plain funny. Some events turned into serious sports competitions. Horse races were an early part of the scene. Both running races and harness races were enormously popular and remained popular into modern times. Chariot racing, an earlier form of harness racing, was also booked by attraction committees. The excitement of harness and chariot-style races, when combined with ranching traditions, contributed to the birth of a new style of race, the chuckwagon race. At first, it was featured as a spectacular exhibition of wagon driving and racing horses. Later, the competitive aspect was as important as it was in harness racing.

Many wild west show companies presented performances based on cowboy skills. The acts inevitably impressed audiences, but some fair visitors bought tickets specifically to watch the cowboys and cowgirls.

Some stage and platform shows featured local talent. The Golden Girls in this 1939 photograph were from the Swift Current, SK, area. Courtesy of Swift Current Museum.

Other fair-goers wanted unusual acts, music, dance, and theatre. They expected circus acts with exotic animal and trapeze performers, but large circuses did not often find their way to small town fairs in western Canada. However, theatrical touring companies featured wonderful dog and pony shows, high wire acts, platform show extravaganzas, bands, and wacky comedians.

In contrast, working together, the fair associations, especially for the A Circuit or in the lower mainland, were big enough and had enough

Not only was she an excellent standing rider, young Daisy Parsons performed a suicide drag at the Calgary Stampede in 1919. Courtesy of Stockmen's Memorial Foundation, SFL 40-14-003.

money to hire circuses or large touring companies for their fairs. Before booking the shows, committees heard presentations by representatives of the bidding companies, many of which had their headquarters in large American cities. In addition to booking one of the major companies, the associations or individual communities often added to their roster. Sometimes, major fairs made independent bookings with a second or even third company. Sometimes, they simply added an act that seemed outstanding.

In contrast, smaller towns depended on home-grown entertainment. Local bands and theatre groups pleased the audience because the performers were part of the community. Too, the acts worked well in the fair budget. They could be booked for token payment or for free, and the bookings supported local talents and interests.

Talented kids were the most popular of the local acts. People loved seeing children who were amazing performers. Sometimes, it was their single moment in the limelight, and they went on to live ordinary lives. Local children were often outstanding fancy or trick riders. In the Calgary area, Daisy Parsons performed a suicide drag and Roman riding to thrill her audience. Ad Day Jr. was another young talent from Medicine Hat. Dubbed Boy Day, he had been riding since he was a tot. At age 11, he performed at Winnipeg in 1913. In one trick riding act, he and Peter Bray did acrobatic stunts on the back of a horse. Later, the renown cowgirl competitor and performer Tillie Baldwin stood on the back of a horse and rode with Boy Day high on her shoulders.

Other young stars were the sons of Peter Welsh, who owned the Alberta Stampede Company, which travelled and staged rodeos in western Canada in the mid-twenties. For the 1926 stampedes, Welsh promoted 18-year-old son Alfie as the youngest trick rider in the world. He announced 16-year-old son Louis as the youngest trick roper in the world. By then, they were old pros. Both had also already made names for themselves in the world of show jumping. However, like other local performers – whether adults or children – some outstanding acts were never fully appreciated until years later or until they made big names for themselves elsewhere.

By the 1950s, the festivity organizers could brag of booking big name entertainers but they had to pay big name prices,

At the 1913 Winnipeg Stampede, Horace Day, three years younger than Ad Jr., performed with Tillie Baldwin. She travelled with the 101 Millers Brothers' Wild West Show. Courtesy of Glenbow Archives, NA 1029-21.

Alfie Welsh travelled and performed with his father's show. Here, he rides Madamoiselle. In 1917 at Edmonton, nine-year-old Alfie and Madamoiselle made a record jump of 6 ft. 10 in. [over 2 m]. The feat spoke volumes about the horse's character – it was 23 years old at the time. Courtesy of Glenbow Archives, NB 16-475.

too. Still, audiences went home happy and intent on attending the show the following year. Usually, fair committees tried to make each year even bigger and better.

The booked attractions were enormously varied. Some performances generated fear in audiences. In fact, many of the acts – performed by both humans and animals – would never be allowed today. Safety and fire regulations are well defined, including for the entertainment industry. The possibility of accident would be too great and the cost of insurance prohibitive.

In 1912, an American woman named Miss Carver and her horse dived 50 feet [15 metres] into a tank of water 10 feet [3 metres] deep for an exhibition performance at the Calgary Exhibition and Stampede. The same year, she also performed a similar stunt at the Lethbridge fair. For that event, the tower with the diving platform provided a 30 foot [9 metre] drop. In 1934, another diving horse appeared at the Edmonton exhibition. Despite phenomenal success with such acts, diving horses are a thrill of the past. Today, some acts do remain dangerous, but, generally, they do not go beyond what laws, insurance, safety precautions, and modern equipment make reasonable.

The stage acts have always been important, too. Many of the theatrical performances were surprisingly extravagant. Costumes were elaborate. Props and backdrop created exotic worlds. Performers were numerous. Mood and content was upbeat, and constant energy and movement captivated audiences. With engaging music and impressive lighting effects, the biggest and best could compete with theatrical shows of today.

Early western Canada was happy to import entertainment. World renowned shows that made their way across the border included wild west shows, the Barnum and Bailey Circus, and the Sells-Floto Circus. All appeared at fairs and stampedes.

Homegrown touring companies also made their way around the local circuits. Some graduated from the B Circuit to the A Circuit. One of the homegrown travelling shows that was invited to tour internationally and represent Canada was the great RCMP Musical Ride.

Usually, the travelling shows were very happy to have bookings that coincided with local fairs. That meant crowds in town for their shows, and large audiences translated into higher gate receipts. Extensive advertising meant more bookings for the future, too. Better railway rates for both the show company's transportation and for out-of- town visitors could be garnered, once again boosting profits. However, some shows required financial guarantees. Generally, the fair committee put up the guarantees, but sometimes well-off residents had to back the shows.

Most of the larger travelling shows were American. They left their home base early in the spring and returned late in the fall. Compared to American circuits, the western Canadian circuits had more unpredictable weather, worse roads, and smaller audiences than even North Dakota, Montana, and Washington. Although sometimes nicknamed the "Death Circuit," the route still paid off for selected companies.

Because of the ethnic and settlement heritage of different communities, some entertainments became more appealing than others. Preferences embedded in the community culture led to specialization. The Okanagan wanted great diving acts. Ranch country wanted trick ropers. Big cities wanted Las Vegas-style shows, but everyone wanted to be impressed.

Not Just a Fair but a Circus

Audiences loved circuses. Performers and performances were exotic, so different from the lives of first settlers and townspeople in western Canada. The elephants, snakes, and lions were fascinating, both to the adults and children who had never seen such animals as well as to those who had immigrated from lands where travelling circuses were part of summer life.

In a surprising number of communities, the fair was a circus – or at least, the circus came to town when the fair was in progress. The Edmonton Exhibition of 1910 had it all – agricultural exhibits, home craft displays, races, and the circus. It didn't just feature a few independent circus acts. Edmonton hosted the outstanding Al G. Barnes Big Three Ring Wild Animal Circus. The show was a major American one, and it brought together all that any circus lover could want.

The city had never been a slouch when it came to holding grand exhibitions, but the 1910 effort was an outstanding one. In preparation, work on the grounds had been fast and furious in July. The exhibition manager, A.G. Harrison, oversaw construction of a 500 seat dining hall, a new grandstand, horse show building, and a dog and poultry building. About 400 feet [122 m] of water pipe was laid to serve the grounds. Like other big exhibition managers, Harrison had thousands of details regarding exhibits and races to address in order to make the fair a success.[1]

The arrival of a circus meant a chance to see the exotic. Usually, the event (sometimes independent, sometimes part of a fair) began with a parade down main street. As well as elephants, this circus brought two-humped camels to Prince Albert, SK. Courtesy of Saskatchewan Archives Board, R-A 4382.

Yet most memorable of all that year was the circus featured at the fair. What more could a child ask? Thousands of adults were just as thrilled with the range and standard of performers.

A smaller tent show, Downie's World's Best Dog, Pony and Trained Wild Animal Shows, featured fine performers and animals. The show displayed a flying machine, with a design based on the Wright brothers' plane, and Professor De Goshen gave lectures on how it worked. Downie's show held its own parade and was on the grounds during the fair, but it was not the biggest show in town for the Edmonton Exhibition. That honor went to Al Barnes and his three ring circus, which had arrived in 20 double-length railway cars. With it came a big top, smaller tents, a monster Ferris wheel, a magnificent merry-go-round, an international reputation, and international stars. Daily ticket holders held their breaths in worried anticipation when a circus performer defied fate. They laughed uproariously at clowns and monkeys, and the show went on – rain or shine – from August 23-26.

"Martha Florinne, a diminutive bit of Dresden doll-like femininity enters the enclosure with a number of beautiful spotted Persian leopards and South American panthers, one of the most treacherous and least dependable animals known in the annals of animal mastery," a journalist for the *Edmonton Bulletin* wrote about one of the exceptional acts.[2]

In the steel cage with her jungle animals, the young Swiss woman seemed unconcerned. She walked among them and stroked their fur while they hissed and snarled. Outside the cage stood armed attendants who never took their eyes off the cats and Miss Florinne. The performance was enough to amaze and impress any audience, but there were 20 other wild animal acts in the show billed as "The Only Real Wild Animal Circus on Earth."

Children and adults marveled at African lions, Royal Bengal tigers, and pumas. As expected, elephants performed, but for the first time in their lives, ticket-buyers might see Burmese camels, kangaroos, hyenas, and elephants. As advertised, Barnes had a brass show band, and Dixieland minstrels. One of his fun factories was the Australian Wonderland. Lolo, the Daughter of the Nile and Nettie, the Mastodonic Fashion Plate were two of the human performers with exotic names and acts.

One of the most popular performers was Big Dick. He was seven-years-old, an outstanding show talent, and a sea lion. Over five years, he had been "educated to a degree of proficiency unequaled in the animal kingdom."[3] Big Dick played the guitar, harmonica, and French horn.

He waltzed in perfect time to music, juggled, and played handball with his trainer. The finale for his act was even more impressive. First, he climbed on the back of a horse. The horse started running. Precariously, Big Dick stayed aboard, and while the horse galloped around the ring, the star sea lion balanced a ball on his nose. Edmonton audiences loved him.

By the end of the exhibition, people also raved about the fine exhibits and livestock. The stock parade and entries that year eclipsed all others ever held in Edmonton. The 2585 pound [1173 kg] Hereford bull, imported from England, winner at English exhibitions and owned by a Brandon farmer, was the talk of farmers. The bull had never been beaten in the show ring and claimed the local title. Yet for others, the most vivid memories were of the Al. G. Barnes Three Ring Circus and the show's outstanding human and animal performers.

Sells-Floto was popular at fairs. This circus ad appeared in the Vernon News in 1905. Greater Vernon Museum & Archives, Circus Clipping Files.

Other circuses appeared at fairs or annual festive events. Sells Floto was another of the great names in American circus, and it made repeated engagements in many western Canadian communities. Its circus wagons were colorful and attracted attention. Much-loved, they were added to the annual parade or became a parade on their own. The pre-show, teasers outside the tents, were freebies intended to sell tickets, and they worked.

But by 1928, some predicted that circuses would not continue to play fairs. The attractions were too different from the fundamental purpose of fairs, which might curtail government funding. From the circus owners' viewpoint, few fairs attracted large enough audiences to generate the kind of income a big circus needed.

The love of circus remained. Complete three ring attractions became less likely to play at fairs, rodeos, and regattas. Instead, circus performers travelled with the many other midway and show companies. A few continued to book independently with fairs, but eventually, most of the circus acts that came to western Canadian fairs were components of larger shows.

Money and the Depression

In 1936, western Canada was deep in a depression. Despite the lack of money, the major rodeos and fairs wanted to set the stage for a wonderful time. That year, competition for the show contracts with the Western Canadian Association of Exhibitions was stiff. Still, the list of bidders was long.

A number of smaller companies offered a variety of show to the association that year. All the shows had strengths but the real battle, the two real competitors, were the Barnes and Carruthers Fair Bookings Association from Chicago and the Ernie Young Show, also from Chicago.[4]

M.H. Barnes made the pitch for Barnes and Carruthers, which had 65 people in the touring company, including performers, stage hands, wardrobe mistress, and musicians. They offered an outstanding show called "Soaring High." Nothing could compare

The talented Roy Seward was really from Golden, BC, but he was known as Calgary Red on the exhibition circuit. Shown here at age 21, performing his slack rope act, he was a hit at rodeos and exhibitions. Courtesy of Golden Museum, P0136.

with the Barnes-Carruthers show, insisted Barnes. Acts were outstanding, including a modern age dance review, opera, circus, clown, teeter-board troupe, 3-elephant act called Big Burma, Zeigfield-style Follies, and royal naval holiday performance. "A special feature is the shooting from the mouth of a naval-type cannon for a distance of 60 feet, of little Bobby Jeanne, the Rocket Girl, she being caught in the arms of her two male partners who are costumed as navy officers, and making a strong finale to a sensational show."[5]

The cost would be $27 500, without loud speaker, for five weeks. Exhibitions would have to provide electricity, eight extra stage hands, and labor to handle the portable stage. The show carried its own revolving stages, with lots of chrome and lights. Since the set had already been paid for by American midwest and southern fairs, the company was offering a very good deal and reasonable price to western Canada fairs.

In making his pitch, Ernie Young came with a model to illustrate stage setup and design. The price was $4500 for a production at one location or $22 500 for the five communities. If that price was too steep, some of the acts could be dropped.

What did Ernie Young offer the audiences of the Depression? His show was quite Canadian – at least in terms of theme and approach. Called "The Passing Parade," the show provided glimpses of the culture of foreign countries and the culture at home.

One act, "Winter Time in Banff," had both imitation skis and girls that wore bells. Each bell rang out a different note. In fact, the American company had performed this same number during two consecutive years for the Chicago World's Fair, and it had been a hit. "Mardi Gras Ball in Montreal" showcased acrobatic French clowns. "The International Five" was a Japanese-style performance.

A number called "Tom-Tom" re-created British Africa, and it included a hunter dance. "Eton at Play" brought together the greatest troupe of dancers ever presented in Canada at any time, or so Mr. Young claimed. "An English Pantomime" was a truly unusual act. There would be 20 girls, costumed and painted so as to appear as if there was a man between each pair of girls. Performing with them would be Large and Margner, the only "team of one-legged dancers on earth, one man having lost his left leg, and the other his right leg. They do a hand-balancing routine, and the act has a sensational finish."

The finale for the "Passing Parade" was called "The Canadian Royal Mounted," and it introduced a flaming neon gun.

"The girls do a fast military march, concluding with a bombardment of shells, the lighting of a flag in fireworks; the girls form the word "Canada," and as the fireworks die out the guns are slowly turned off, "taps" is blown, and ....this finale was the most impressive ever attempted by any producer and without doubt the most elaborate and pleasing...."[6]

Also, Young's show had wandering musicians to perform in exhibition buildings during the afternoon. He had the greatest dog act in the world, a girl and cannon act, and bicycle-on-wire act. His musicians would work with local musicians, and he had his own platform, stage hands, carpenter, and electrician.

With reasonable ease, the association limited the finalists to Barnes & Carruthers and Ernie Young, who had bid on the circuit in 1935 but not won it. Saskatoon delegates definitely wanted a change from the last year's company. It had promised an Arab Troupe and another act, which had not been forthcoming. Then, when the company's prima donna had been injured during the Brandon show, other exhibitions had been shortchanged, too. Both Barnes-Carruthers and Young were good possibilities, but when it came to money, the Saskatoon delegate didn't feel the Barnes-Carruthers show was $5000 better than the Young show.

P.W. Abbott, manager of the Edmonton Exhibition, wanted more comedy than Young was offering. The previous year there had been too much dancing. Barnes-Carruthers seemed to have less dancing. Guy Herbert, a delegate from Calgary, agreed.

The committee recalled Young, asked more questions, and gave more directions about what they wanted. Young offered to co-operate with service clubs, do a 30 minute radio broadcast about the show, make substitutions, and ensure there was adequate comedy.

Barnes was recalled and cross-examined on the comedy issue.

Oh, he reassured, there were the funny penguins, the pantomime, a comedy knock-out act, actors falling into pails, and the elephant, Big Burma, did a shimmy and carioca.

Calgary and Edmonton wanted Barnes-Carruthers. The rest decided it just wasn't worth the extra $5000. They wanted Young.

There was only one solution. All would go with the majority decision. Then the two communities would add more independent acts. In the end for the Dirty Thirties on the prairies, the $27 500 had been too much money. The association opted for the Ernie Young Agency out of Chicago.

More Funny Men Required

Laughter was high on the list of priorities. Fairs wanted to give people an escape from everyday responsibilities and problems. Both for afternoon or evening shows, clowns were a must, and not just for the kiddies. Comedians entertained both children and adults, and usually, a variety of comedy acts were added to the summer events.

As vaudeville began to disappear and be replaced by movies, many clowns who had travelled the vaudeville circuit joined the circuses and midways. They performed alone or as part of an act. Imparting jokes long before loud speaker systems were as sophisticated as today, they relied on mime for much of their humor. Some clowns were talented as tumblers; others had animal partners or wacky jalopies; and still others were willing to taunt bulls.

Many of the best known and most loved of the clowns who worked in western Canada achieved their fame in the rodeo infield. Unlike circus clowns who might not re-appear in communities for years, if ever, many rodeo clowns returned year after year to the annual stampedes. The athletic men, wearing wigs and sporting giant noses, could run and pivot on a nickel – with a bull charging the seat of their big, baggy pants. Their props included gag explosives to create a big bang just when no one expected it, back-firing and bucking cars, as well as trick ropes and tires. The funny men made people laugh while they waited for the next cowboy and his mount to lurch from the chutes, and they knew how to make the local circumstances humorous, whether it was sweltering hot or pouring rain.

For rodeo clowns, a knack for pantomime was crucial. Voices were not easily heard by the distant audiences, but announcers helped out, repeating words, offering cues, and acting as the comedian's straight man.

Comic responses to the unexpected were certainly part of the job, but their work life had as much to do with fearlessness as with humor. A 1500-1800 pound [680-816 kg] bull would buck and spin. Even when the cowboy was thrown from his back, the belligerent bull was just as likely to gore the cowboy as head back to a corral. The job of the clown was to distract him. Any method would do, but the audience had to be laughing as it held its breath in fear – for the cowboy and clown.

Rodeo clowns incorporated props and stunts in their shows, but when it came to dealing with bulls, they tended to be barrel men, who wanted the bull to charge a barrel, or bullfighters, whose intent was to get close to the bull and distract it with a cape. One clown might be both barrel man and bullfighter, or two clowns might work as a team, one in the barrel and the other distracting the bull. No matter what the approach, bravery was a prerequisite.

Not surprisingly, at one time or another, most rodeo clowns left the infield with battered bodies. Bulls rammed them against barrels, bruised them against corral railings, gored them, kicked them, or stepped on them.

During the 1960s, John Robertson of the *Winnipeg Tribune* wrote about the life of the rodeo clown. Gene Clarke was one of his subjects. Unlike most cowboys, Clarke took home a salary rather than a cash prize, but his career choice meant he also took home injuries. In his polka dot shirt, to the crowd, he looked like he was grinning, but often, he was gritting his teeth. Everyone thought he was funny except his wife. So that they could have a family life, she and the kids often travelled with him, but when he was in the arena, she buried her face in her hands, and prayed while Clarke competed with bulls, not simply to win, but for his life.

"A brother of mine has made a mistake or two in this game," Clarke admitted. "He didn't get penalized a yard or two in this game. The price he paid was a broken neck, two broken legs, a fracture of every rib and a broken thumb."[7]

But Clarke knew that clowns were to cowboys what a life jacket was to someone who was drowning. A clown's job, he claimed, was to jump in and say, "Hey bull, hit me instead."

All the while, Clarke and other rodeo clowns kept the crowds laughing. Others among the world's great rodeo clowns who made appearances on the western Canadian rodeo circuit

G-64   CALGARY   STAMPEDE
BUDDY HEATON AND A BRAHMA BULL

Although physically a very large man, rodeo clown Buddy Heaton was able to move fast enough to dodge bulls, despite his baggy trousers. Faye Holt Collection.

included big names such as Hank Mills, Buddy Heaton, and Slim Pickens. As well, Benny Bender, with his mule Joe Lewis, made crowds gasp in fear and roar with laughter.

With one of the greatest stampedes in the world, Calgary was able to attract and pay super clowns such as Buddy Heaton. Originally from Kansas, Heaton weighted about 240 pounds [109 kg], and in his baggy pants, he looked even bigger – but still no match for the big bulls! Often, Heaton wore his hair down his back, sported a handlebar moustache, and worked with his pet buffalo. Great at improvisation, he had a reputation as a wild man.[8]

Between the late 1940s and the 1960s, Slim Pickens was another of the famous rodeo clowns to appear on the Canadian circuit. Born Louis Lindlay and growing up in California, Louis started ed riding calves at 11 and entered his first rodeo at the age of 12. At 15, he was competing in and winning bareback and steer riding. His father didn't approve, so he competed under pseudonyms such as Slim Oak from Texas and Slim Pickens from Oklahoma.

In 1948 at age 28 and weighing 217 pounds [98 kg], Slim decided he was over the hill when it came to competing, but he chose not to leave the world of rodeo. Instead, he put on his funny face and funny clothes and stepped into the infield to fight bulls and save cowboy contestants. The first time he worked as a rodeo clown, he made $5. By 1949, he could made $100-$200 a performance. In terms of rodeo clowns, he was a hot commodity.

Here Slim Pickens wears a matador costume for his bull fighting act. Faye Holt Collection.

For some shows, Slim partnered with Judy, a mule that was half Shetland-pinto and half Spanish burro, and a character in her own right. But Judy did not belong in the arena with bulls, so just as often, Pickens stepped into the arena in the costume of a matador. Wearing black stockings and toreador pants trimmed with gold, he captivated audiences with the grand style of the Spanish and Mexican bullfighter. Still, surprise was sometimes the best defense against a bull. Sometimes the brave Pickens dropped on all fours, began pawing the dirt and moving toward the bull. With Pickens on the prowl, bulls backed away – one as much as 100 yards [91 m].

Rodeo work was highly unpredictable and dangerous. In Vancouver in 1949 working for the Marpole Rodeo with good friend Herman Linder, who produced the show, a bull horn had pierced skin on Slim's chest, and another bull stepped on his chest. At the time of the Marpole appearance, he was the highest paid rodeo clown in the business, but the movie business became even more attractive, and eventually, he made an even bigger name for himself starring in westerns and as a comedic performer.[9]

The most famous rodeo clowns on the continent thrilled western Canadians, but some local fellows really warmed audiences. Watching one of their own bring tears of laughter to the eyes of crowds was truly a pleasure.

Ralph Overton was one such talent, and he was deeply rooted in the small town life of Alberta and BC. Born at Erskine, Alberta, in 1906, Ralph and his family lived in Hanna and Alliance before moving to Chilliwack. In BC, as a young man, he worked in logging camps and sawmills, eventually spending time on Vancouver Island and at Fairview, Keremeos, Hedley, and

Okanagan Falls. The sports days in nearby Oliver got him hooked on rodeo. By 17, he did some steer riding, but he also began his career as a rodeo clown.

At 5 feet 8 inches [172 cm], Ralph wasn't a big man, but he was as agile as a cat. According to his brother Russ Overton, Ralph was self-taught, but he was a natural clown and a talented musician who could play just about any musical instrument. In fact, he created some of his own novelty instruments, including a cigar box mandolin.

When Ralph became better known as a clown, invitations to work rodeos came from farther and farther away, and he got paid more and more. For his act, usually, he wore jeans, a big plaid shirt and running shoes, but sometimes, he chose a more interesting costume. For his Nancy the Clown act, his donning of women's clothes brought laughter, but for the most part, it was simply his sense of fun and his spontaneity that worked. Eventually, he found a good partner for his act, too.

Not only did he buy a ranch in the Okanagan, he bought a donkey, who he named Honest Abe. Ralph trained the 350 pound [159 kg] animal to do tricks. For one rodeo in Kamloops, Ralph had Abe in the ring, and the act began as expected.

"The donkey was trained that when Ralph crawled underneath him and touched him in a certain place, the donkey would drop onto Ralph's back and just lay there. This day, he did this and Ralph was screaming and kicking and throwing dirt in the air and pretending to be in trouble. The donkey never moved," remembered Russ.[10]

The audience loved it, but again, spontaneity brought the best laughs.

A big, heavy man who was slightly inebriated came to the rescue.

"When he got close enough, Ralph's hand shot out and grabbed the fellow by the foot and pulled him down on his back," remembered Russ, "and at the same time, he flipped the donkey over onto the man's stomach and chest….Ralph was on his feet, and the donkey never batted an eye. Then Ralph was pulling the man's boots and hat off, pretending he was trying to get [his rescuer] out from under the donkey."

After a few minutes, Ralph signaled Abe. The donkey stood up.

"The man who was the brunt of the trick got to his feet, dusted himself off and left the arena," remembered Russ. Another show had gone well.

Not only did Ralph perform in the BC interior, he took his show into the northern states and continued the career for almost two decades. In his late thirties, married and with a family, Ralph left his clowning career behind. He and his brothers had contributed to rodeo in other ways, too. Knowing the challenges of rodeo life and cowboy competitions, in their local community, Ralph and his brothers pushed for a rodeo association, and 1941, they were successful. Still, being a fearless funny man was one of his greatest successes. He had brought laughter to thousands.

By the late 1960s, more western Canadian funny men were entering the rodeo arena. Wayne Hale and later Jason Hale from Bassano captivated crowds. For a few years, Dave Parsons, from south of Red Deer, performed as a clown and bullfighter. In the late 1970s, Kelley LaCoste, from Medicine Hat, became a bullfighter and barrel man. Western Canada was cowboy country. Small and large stampedes needed clowns, and no matter how big the name of other rodeo clowns, local crowds always loved the hometown boys the best.

Balloons & Planes

Hot air balloons, airships, and planes became very popular at fairs. From early on, they most certainly meant excitement and drama. German-born Count von Zeppelin designed the first rigid dirigible, which had an internal skeleton and was safer than the non-rigid type of earlier times. The Zeppelin had its inaugural flight on July 20, 1900, and it was not affected by the cool temperatures of high altitudes. In 1903, the Wright brothers beat the odds with a heavier-than-air flying machine. Like many fairs in western Canada, in 1906, the New Westminster fair planned for action in the air. To the crowd's dismay, the balloon didn't get off the ground. The next year, another balloon flight was scheduled with an aeronaut named Brooks.

At about 5:00 in the afternoon, the cords anchoring the huge balloon to the ground were cut. On board was Brooks and his parachute. The plan was for him to make a parachute jump from the balloon.

The balloon rose about 3000 feet [914 m] above the ground. Although high above their heads, the crowds could make out Brooks' movements, gymnastic feats that he seemed to perform with ease as he made himself ready for the plunge.

Suddenly, he jumped from the sky-high platform. Brooks was in free-fall. The crowd gasped, stared, waited. After a drop about 100 feet [30 m], the parachute finally opened. Brooks began to float, for a while remaining almost stationery.

Seated on a bar beneath the parachute, Brooks began more gymnastics. He leaned backwards, so far that the bar slipped along his legs, and he seemed to be holding on only by his feet while his head dangled towards the ground.

Like a trapeze artist, he came up and grasp the bar with his hands. His slow decent to the ground became an acrobatic performance unlike anything the crowd had ever imagined, let alone witnessed. As the ground came closer, he dangled by his hands, twisted, turned and somehow guided the parachute. His final landing was only about 100 yards [91 m] from where the large balloon had first risen.[11]

The audience could not have been more impressed, but the aeronaut had other acts, too, including taking a dog up in his balloon and returning safely.

By 1906, even around Calgary, the skies were dotted with flying apparatus of different shapes and designs. For the 1907 local exhibition, Calgarians had been thrilled when a large hot-air balloon drifted over the fairground, and flights by an airship were contracted for the city's 1908 Dominion Exhibition.

Airplanes created an equal, if not louder buzz, than the dirigibles. People had a sense of how a balloon worked. That a heavier-than-air machine could take to the skies was even more amazing and awe inspiring.

Everyone thrilled to see the first airplanes at the big summer events. Crowds gathered around the planes when they were on the ground and stared wide-eyed when the machines were over their heads. They even gathered in tents to hear lectures about planes and flying. Showcasing flight was a surefire hit with visitors at early fairs. With progress a perennially popular theme of fairs, air shows were easy to justify, and managers were willing to pay the price.

Especially after the First World War, returning local pilots were happy to perform. In 1919, audiences loved to watch war heroes and flyers like Fred McCall and Wop May. Some fair-goers bought tickets to ride as passengers, and that year, from McCall's plane, 50 visitors looked down on the Calgary Exhibition.

Other aerial performers brought truly amazing acts. Many of the acts went to all the cities on the western Canada A Circuit. In 1920, one such act in Calgary was by Omer Locklear from California. Changes in air regulations almost led to the cancellation of his daring act. An inspector enforcing the new regulations decided that, as a safety precaution, Locklear couldn't land his plane in front of the grandstand. The new landing spot took away some of the excitement but proved acceptable.

Another rule also determined his act was too dangerous. Locklear worked with two great pilots, and he had thrilled audiences across the USA by changing planes in mid air. Usually, he performed the feat at about 150 feet [46 m] above the ground. Because of the new rules, the planes had to be at an altitude of 2000 feet [610 m] before anyone jumped out of them.

The regulation didn't stop Locklear. In fact, the greater height made the stunt all the more thrilling and frightening for watchers and dangerous for Locklear. According to the 29 June *Morning Albertan*, he "dropped from the lower wings of his plane to the top of the other. A few minutes later...he caught a rope ladder after hanging in mid air by his knees for a breathless moment, clambered up into his seat again."[12]

To the disappointment of many, one part of his act did have to be cancelled. He wasn't allowed to make the high altitude plane change at night by flashlight.

Flying demonstrations at exhibitions continued to be popular through the 1930s, but enthusiasts in more and more communities organized flying clubs. More airstrips and hangars were built for airports. Also when flight companies began organizing and scheduling their own regional or national air tours, meets, flight circuses, and air pageants, the flying demonstrations moved from the exhibition grounds to the airports. Air shows became popular enough in many communities to garner crowds without having an association with the local fair. In Vernon, BC, by 1932, huge crowds gathered to watch 15 planes complete formation stunting, dog fighting, airplane races, and aerobatics. Flight had simply outgrown most fairs.

Yet, some pilots continued to barnstorm, and their stunts and passenger flights remained popular – especially at small town fairs far from communities with airstrips.

Two men who made names for themselves in the late 1930s and 1940s were from windy Lethbridge. The skies were blue, but locals knew that anyone braving the winds needed courage. Ernie Boffa was a mechanic and pilot, and Roy Lomhein was a local meat cutter. They began doing weekend barnstorming tours, and fairs became good clients. Pilot Boffa gave rides to paid passengers. Then, for their act, Lomhein parachuted from the plane, making his jump at about 2000 feet [609 m] in altitude. His parachute always opened but he cut it loose and allowed himself to free-fall. When he was ready, he opened a second chute. When winds allowed, he landed in front of the grandstand, but he made jumps even when the wind was 40-50 mph [64-80 km/hr]. In about 10 years, Lomhein made well over 300 jumps, many at small town fairs, others at air shows, or wherever else there was interest.

Always a Hit

The performers who offered specialty acts, elaborate shows, or unique and daring stunts were inevitably a hit with audiences. Too, they inspired future generations. One popular act was offered by American Bonnie Gray, who jumped vehicles while riding her horse. Such feats inspired young women and men with their daring.

A few of the specialty performers were from western Canada. From Raymond, Alberta, "Suicide" Ted Elder was especially popular. A multi-talented showman from the late 1930s, he toured North American fairs and rodeos. Like others from the area, he was an outstanding rider, and one of his best stunts involved Roman riding. He added challenge by leaping his galloping horses over a car while standing with one foot on each of the two horses' backs.

Some of those who toured western Canada returned, choosing to live here. Stastia Cross Carry, a one-time performer with Sparks Circus in the USA, also worked with Sells-Floto Circus. Stastia met Alberta rodeo performer Jim Carry. Known as Alberta Jim, he was an outstanding roper and performed with wild west shows in Canada and the USA.

They married, and together they started their own wild west show called A.J. Carry's Wild West Hippodrome Attractions. As performers, they accepted contracts with Alberta Stampede Company, which held contracts with many western Canadian cowboys. Between 1925 and 1927, the Stampede Company impressed thousands at performances from BC to Quebec and in the USA. In later years, the Carrys settled in Black Diamond, AB. There they trained their own race horses, which were booked on both fair and race circuits.

People loved the full range of shows, stunts, and outstanding performers. Many were equally thrilled with sports competitions, whether those were cowboy competitions, horse races, bicy-

For this 1924 photo, Stastia Cross Carry posed in one of her exotic working costumes for her performances with the Sparks Circus. At other times during her career, she had an elephant act and a cowgirl act. Courtesy of Glenbow Archives, PA 3457-34.

cle races, auto races, or motorcycle races. Some sports combined serious competition with daring or unusual stunts. Diving horses, but also something called auto polo, amazed crowds. Still, calmer entertainments were well-loved, too. Hearing the great John Phillip Sousa band warmed many a heart when it appeared in western Canada in 1919 and 1927. Whoever the performer, whatever the show or stunt, organizing spectacular entertainment was only one job among many in staging the festive events of summer.

Chapter 3

Putting Together the Pieces

Planning Festivities

The spring to fall events offered glimpses of the identity of individual communities. Most communities showcased livestock and produce, the physical prowess of young men and women, homemaking skills, and new agricultural practices and technology. In prairie communities, displays of grain were important. In other communities, such as those in the Okanagan, fruit farming took hold. Not only were there cherry blossom festivals but peach festivals. During the festivals and fairs, the world and neighbors saw the image the community wanted to project.

Some festivals, rodeos, fairs, and regattas were small town affairs, and locals were happy to keep them that way. In other instances, the festivities became huge financial ventures. They advertised internationally and drew international tourists. The volunteer hours committed to successful ventures were enormous, and increasingly, the exhibitions required numerous paid, year-round-personnel, but almost all festivals began with the work of volunteers.

Plans included countless details. Organizers needed to attract shows, midways, and competitors. They wanted to ensure that visitors would be entertained, but fair-goers also expected educational displays, and everything had to be advertised in a manner that attracted displayers and visitors, alike. As well, seating space, display space, and parking space had to be arranged.

There were basic human needs to be addressed. Visitors required food and beverage concessions. They needed toilets and a nurse or hospital tent available if someone was injured.

For out-of-town visitors and performers, fair associations had to address the issue of temporary housing. For some, hotel space was an expectation. Others were prepared to camp, but they still needed access to adequate sanitation and meals.

Politics entered the picture, too. Eventually, both regional and federal governments supported fairs through grants and legislation. Agricultural societies, those primarily responsible for early fairs, gained legal status within acts related to agriculture. The Act to Incorporate the Regina Agricultural and Industrial Exhibition clarified what was considered of value. Fairs had to provide opportunities to exhibit produce and various breeds of livestock. They had a mandate to encourage competition amongst farmers and homemakers, which in turn would lead to better livestock or seed choices. Exhibitions were to educate by demonstrating and providing information on both agricultural and homemaking skills, and they were to exhibit the latest technologies related to the home and farm.

That mandate re-enforced the work ethic. It acknowledged the need for continuing education for adults on farms and, most importantly, for the immigrant populations. Such a mandate was far-sighted and balanced in recognizing the needs of people. Hardworking and isolated populations benefited from relaxation, social opportunities, and entertainment! Fortunately, the governments didn't limit fairs to offering education and competition. The exhibition could be a place of wonder, fun, and indulgence, too.

For their annual festivals, communities highlighted the resources or skills of the area. This float was for the Steveston Salmon Festival. The community claimed to be the salmon capital of the world. Courtesy of City of Richmond Archives, 1985-68-35.

Fair organizers had to find money – when none seemed available. They recruited volunteers when everyone claimed to be too busy. They needed to plan for the worst. Fairs developed disaster plans and bought insurance. They arranged for a police presence to ensure safety, and at the same time, they wanted to showcase their communities and have the best entertainments possible. Organizers focused on strengths, many of which were rooted in the geography and heritage of their areas.

Proud Regina: Organizing for Success and Survival

Southern Saskatchewan became a land of grain, seed, and weed fairs. The people of Regina weren't the first to host fairs in western Canada, nor was the city one of the largest communities. Simple size made it harder for organizers to fund and attract major shows and midways. Becoming part of a large fair association helped, but long before that, Regina volunteers and organizers were prepared to do whatever hard work was necessary. They did it in a manner that built a solid reputation. Year after year, sometimes facing far worse problems than other fair organizers, they created great events.

By 1884, Regina sponsored a two-day fair in October under the auspices of Assiniboia Agriculture Association. As well as enjoying the foot races, horse races, and ox races, the 150 people who attended entered agricultural competitions and passed along information on prairie farming. The following year, the impressive prize list included a $6 rocking chair for the best Durham bull, and the owner of the best Berkshire boar won 1000 shingles.

Prize lists had to be planned and printed before opening day. This image was on the cover of the prize list for the Canadian Territorial North-West Exhibition of 1895. The graphics also acted as advertising for the province of Saskatchewan. Courtesy of Glenbow Archives, 630.9712.C2124c PAM

The first major indication of what Regina organizers were prepared to do to showcase their community and stage the best fair ever became clear in 1894. In order to host a great Territorial Exhibition in 1895, Regina citizens convinced the Canadian government to grant them $25 000. To fair coffers, they added $10 000 from the town council, and the territorial legislature chipped in $5000-10 000.[1] With the money, the association built a two-story display building, three other small buildings, and a 1000 seat grandstand. The grounds became the site of countless tents, and the fair was on.

Organizers knew that good prize money attracted the best competitors, so they offered prizes totaling $19 000. In the traditional manner of agricultural fairs, there were countless categories for livestock breeds and home skills. For exhibitors bringing horses, in addition to competition prizes, the NWMP promised to buy all mounts. Organizers made arrangements with the CPR to provide free transportation for exhibits, and show stock came from as far away as Ontario. With competition keen for the best horses, sheep, and pigs, the fair boasted 900 head of stock on exhibit.

Women showed their enthusiasm by submitting 8000 entries into the handicraft contests. At the time, the most Winnipeg had achieved was 3500 such entries.[2] School children rated their own categories, as did artists. Organizers created many other categories for competition. Prizes were generous for horse races, horse jumping, bicycle races, foot races, a boys' military drill, and girls' calisthenics exercises. There was a bagpipe competition, Indian and settler polo tournaments, and trap shooting competitions. Winnings ranged from $1 for placing third in the dog races to $80 for placing first in the 3/4 mile [1.2 km] horse race. Twenty dollar prizes were offered for inventions related to "irrigation as applicable to certain districts in the Territories" and "how best to destroy gopher pests."

Unlike many strictly agricultural fairs, the Territorial Exhibition invited prize winning inventions, a direction that anticipated the great industrial and commercial fairs in the west in later years. One prize offered the unusual and enormous amount of $500, which went to the inventor of the best fire extinguisher that could be operated on less than $3 per day. The huge amount suggested just how important fire extinguishers were at a time when a community might have only one and that a massive and complex beast.[3] Not surprisingly, the task of judging was onerous. However, in an attempt to ensure judges were fair, rules were published.

Also in preparation for the event, caterers were given directions. Accommodation issues were more difficult. With so many expected visitors, organizers stuffed sacks with straw for mattresses, and cots were set up in the town hall and the curling rink. Extra tents were erected, too. An information booth, telegraph, and telephone booth were made available on the grounds, and a "bus" carried people back and forth from town. Special railway rates were arranged. Most impressive of all was the electric lighting. In the evening, lights illuminated both the grounds and the interior of buildings.

High on the list of priorities was entertainment. Bands paraded and performed. As well as watching horse races, polo, and trapshooting, sports enthusiasts enjoyed football, tennis, and cricket tournaments. For the 25 cent gate ticket, they could watch Red River jig competitions, the North West Mounted Police musical ride, and cowboy sports.

A women's church group sponsored a National Fair on the grounds, which was a huge tent with booths representing many countries, including Japan, India, Turkey, Ireland, Scotland, England and the USA. There, shoppers could purchase curios, souvenirs, and handicraft items.

First Nations participation was encouraged and enthusiastic. About 1500 indigenous people attended, and hundreds of teepees were erected both inside and outside the exhibition grounds. As well as participating in the races, "a whole host of Indians, all in paint and fine fixings...ascended the platform in front of the grand stand and gave a grand pow-wow." Most Aboriginal exhibits were from the Regina Indian School, but exhibits also arrived from Indian schools at Qu'Appelle, High River, Battleford, St. Albert, Elkhorn, and St. Boniface. Many of their exhibits were related to agriculture, blacksmithing, horse culture, homemaking, and sewing, but drawing and carving were part of their cultural exhibit, too.

One of the First Nations chiefs to receive special notice at the fair was Chief Calf Shirt, who was not only a showman but an organizer. When Native people arrived for the fair, the Blood chieftain called them together and offered advice on deportment. He took a leading role in the Charcoal Dance that was staged for the grandstand audience, but he had other skills to demonstrate, too. The six foot tall individual [183 cm] had a talent with rattlesnakes. To the amazement of all, he carried one under his shirt and against his skin. The rattler was hypnotized, he claimed, but reporters eventually learned his bathing in herbs repulsive to the snakes was added protection against poisonous bites.

The range of showmanship on the grounds that year was impressive. One troupe that was especially popular was the Lilliputian Midgets, who had their own show tent. Among the troupe was Mrs. Tom Thumb. The group's afternoon and evening performances included dramatic sketches, singing, dancing, and comedic routines.

Dignitaries were in attendance, too. The governor general, the province's premier, and the lieutenant governor all made appearances. No matter how hard organizers had worked, some things were beyond control. A thunderstorm rolled in one evening, and flattened some tents. In one was a cranky, eastern reporter, and he wrote "if we ever get out of this infernal hole, we'll never come back."[4]

In fact, the exhibition was a resounding success. Still, the association shouldered debt. Fortunately, the federal government came to the rescue, erasing the $5000 shortfall.[5]

The effort required by organizers to host the event had been Herculean. In many ways, it was one of the finer moments for western Canadian fair organizers. However, given the debts, for three years, Regina did not hold a fair. By 1899, the fair association had been re-named as the Regina Agricultural Association. True to the concern over agricultural issues and with worries about the proliferation of noxious weeds, Regina hosted a Weed Fair and was back in business. By 1907, reflecting a new direction, the fair added "Industrial" to its name.

The road to success was not an easy one. In 1911, for the Regina Dominion Exhibition, rebuilding the grandstand cost $70 000, to put the capacity up to 4000. Too, because sporting events, and in particular racing, were so important, the organization built stables for 100 horses.[6]

Then, 30 June 1912, Regina was struck by a tragedy of historic proportions. Flags and bunting flew for the celebration of Dominion Day and the fair. Special guests had arrived in town by rail, and proud of the phenomenal building and progress in recent years, the mayor had just finished touring them around the community. It was 4:48 p.m. Suddenly, a cyclone tore at the city. The winds of the tornado flattened a three block wide area that stretched a couple of miles in length. Elevators and other buildings were toppled.

The disaster response was immediate. Workers shut off power to prevent the further spread of fires. Torrential rain limited fire threat but complicated other efforts. Twenty-eight died.

The festivities of Dominion Day and the fair were of no significance in the light of the human tragedies dealt by factors completely beyond control. Only the relief efforts mattered, and all able-bodied men helped in rescue and clean-up, while women cooked and cared for those in need. The numbers of homeless mounted to 2500. More than $1 million dollars damage per minute had devastated the community.

To offer what aid they could, other communities dedicated profits from their fairs to disaster relief in Regina. Helping a neighbor in need mattered more than saving profits to build a new race track, display building, or stage.

The next year proved a difficult one for the Regina exhibition and for the new fair manager, Dan Elderkin. A quiet and courteous man, he would be responsible for exhibitions until his retirement in 1942. At the time of his appointment in 1913, Canada was suffering from an economic depression, so money was tight. Then, 11 June 1913, prior to the fair, the grandstand burned. The fire spread to the Industrial and Agricultural Building. Once again, prospects looked gloomy. Somehow, the city and exhibition committee managed to repair and rebuilt enough to open the annual fair, but the challenge had been a difficult one. The damage had totalled about $70 000.[7]

Only four years later, another fire struck the grandstand. During fair week, 25 July 1917, the fire started when the grounds and grandstand were crowded. Fortunately, sound planning for such a disaster meant there were no serious injuries.

Facing fire losses and other problems was not easy for organizers, but other successes inspired Saskatchewan fair enthusiasts to persevere. Seager Wheeler, an English settler who farmed at Rosthern, SK, was one such source of inspiration. His first rung on the ladder to fame was his submitting a Marquis wheat sample that won at the Provincial Seed Fair at Regina in 1911. That same year, he made an entry into the World's Fair at New York, and he won the title World Wheat King. He won countless provincial and national honors, dominating the grain contests at western Canadian fairs for more than 15 years. Better yet, he won world championship titles

Seager Wheeler, of Rosthern, SK, won countless trophies and titles in competitions and became known as one of the great wheat kings. Saskatchewan Archives Board, R-B2946-1.

five times with his grain entries, making it clear that grain from western Canada was the best in the world.[8]

Those wins at international fairs sparked pride in grain farmers. Saskatchewan farmers knew how to grow grain – the best grain in the world. Their history of firsts was impressive. Usually, the anticipated initial step was to win at local fairs, then at provincial fairs, then nationally, and finally internationally.

Instead of bowing to disasters, the organizers for Regina fairs built on such successes. In the 30s, the city was to host the first world-class grain fair in western Canada. Ironically, it had been scheduled during a decade of the worst drought and farm condition the prairies had ever witnessed. With circumstances as they were, the World Grain Exhibition and Conference was postponed from 1932 to 1933. Somehow, a new building was erected to create three acres [1.2 hectares] of floor space, and the indoor walkway stretched for two miles [3.2 km]. The community was ready to greet international visitors.

The first day, the temperature soared over 100° F [37.7° C], but former Prime Minister Mackenzie King opened the fair. In total, 2700 entries had been submitted from 40 countries. Many were from the USA, but the show featured more rice exhibits than wheat exhibits.

Representatives came from as far away as Great Britain, Holland, Mexico, Spain, Hungary, Italy, Germany, India, British Guiana, Siam, Philippines, Rhodesia, and Australia. Canada won the hard, red spring wheat category and was among the top prize winners in other categories, too.

Although the international event was successful in terms of visitors, entertainments, entries, and world-class competition, the end result was a $120 000 loss at a time when the prairie city was in the midst of the Depression.

In later years, other problems followed, too. On 28 July 1942, another wind of cyclonic strength hit and damaged both the stadium building and the livestock area on the exhibition grounds.[9] Then, in 1955, the most spectacular and worst fire ever experienced on the grounds almost totally destroyed the huge display building erected for the World Grain Show.

However, for the Regina Exhibition Association, as it was renamed in 1959, no challenge proved too great when it came to hosting fair competition, fun, and a celebration of the community and its past. The organizers and volunteers in Regina simply refused to give up.

Today, the city hosts a number of fair and agricultural exhibitions. From early in the 1900s, Regina held winter fairs, largely devoted to livestock. By 1971, Regina area farmers realized the potential and value of having a major western stock show near the majority of stockmen. They wanted a show with a stature equal to that of the Royal Winter Fair in Toronto. The Canadian Western Agribition Association was formed around the stock and agricultural objectives of traditional agricultural fairs. Too, the Agribition became a market place that brought together outstanding livestock from across western Canada with potential buyers. The idea met with phenomenal success. Within 30 years, the Agribition could brag of being one of the best livestock shows in the world, a show attended by one third of all western Canadian farmers.

The summer fair remained an important draw for the community, too. Called Buffalo Days, today's exhibition provides excitement, midway fun, topnotch performers, and a celebration of pioneer days.

On Parade

Great parades were one way of ensuring success. They were free to the public; they showcased the community and visiting talents; they were entertaining for those who watched, and fun for those who participated.

Decorating vehicles was a pre-parade job, and children were often enthusiastic assistants. Decorated for the 1919 parade, this was New Westminster's first May Day car. Courtesy of New Westminster Public Library 2090.

For parades, children and adults had a chance to dress up. The community, too, dressed up and showed off. Although the parades were not the first activity held at fairs, exhibitions, rodeos, and the other festive days or weeks of summer, they were a great kick off.

Even adults or children who could not afford tickets to the exhibition grounds could have a taste of the big event. They could laugh at clowns, wave to neighbors in the parade, point at awe-inspiring floats, and enjoy the marching bands as they paraded along main street.

The intent of the parade was to draw attention to the upcoming events, but for thousands, the parade itself was worth the trip to town and standing for hours to ensure the best spot to view the passing spectacle.

Wild west shows and Chautauqua announced themselves by parading through the streets. But a special loyalty and appreciation developed for the annual parade of the community's fair, rodeo, or regatta.

Despite their geographical isolation in Canada's northwest, fur traders of Fort Edmonton recognized the value of the parade. By 1879, the community organized its first parade. With few years as exceptions, parades have been held annually. Both the fair and parade evolved. Today, the thematic focus is a celebration of the 1890s and the Klondike gold rush, a time when an endless parade of prospectors made their way to the city, packed wagons with thousands of pounds of supplies, and headed north in search of dreams. No contemporary Klondike Day parade along Edmonton's Jasper Avenue would be complete without a Klondike Kate and Klondike Mike wearing period costume and reminding the city of its special place in gold rush history.

From early in the 20th century, the parades for the Pacific National Exhibition, Winnipeg Exhibition, and Calgary Stampede experienced phenomenal success. Throngs of the curious lined the streets to enjoy the events. In 1912, 80 000 watched the two-hour Calgary Exhibition and Stampede parade in a community of only 63 305 residents.[10] As its theme, the parade celebrated the early days of the west. Organizers had brought together Mounties, 2000 First Nations and Métis people, and pioneer ranchers and settlers.

The chaotic process of getting a parade underway is conveyed in this photo of the parade at Stonewall, MB, in 1913. Courtesy of Archives of Manitoba, Foote 1919 N15832.

The parade had not gone without a hitch. It was the weekend of the annual Labour Day parade. Labour Day organizers were reluctant to give up their traditional parade or join the Stampede parade. Finally, they did for a price – $1500.[11] The local newspaper and organizers, given to boosterism, claimed the grand pageant was unequaled in history.

The scene was repeated over and over again in community after community. Crowds waited. Then, from a short way off, clanging cymbals, trumpets, a drum beat, the haunting pitch of bagpipes, or marching songs roused the crowd's anticipation level. Military bands, pipers, guitar and banjo-plucking country and western stars, school bands, and local dance bands were always popular. But the west played host to some of the best bands and orchestras in the world, including a women's band from New York, which appeared in a Calgary parade. Whoever the musicians, the streets needed music during a parade.

Wide streets were an advantage for parades. This band, followed by cars from the Automobile Club, makes its way through Red Deer, AB, in the early 1900s. Courtesy of Red Deer and District Archives, Mg 18-6.

Along the route, children tried to catch candy or knick-knacks thrown in their direction. People clapped and smiled and waved to those on parade. Fingers pointed at elaborately decorated floats.

Still, despite the crowd's pleasure, the purpose of most parades was advertising. In a picturesque way, the mounted cowboys and cowgirls announced that the rodeo or fair was about to begin. When brightly decorated wagons hauled circus and bears and tigers through the streets, everyone wanted to be part of the festivities.

A well-planned parade was a wonderful pageant that sold tickets to the main event. Entertainment companies and fair organizers did not want to find themselves in the red when everyone returned home. So, the parade previewed the special performers – whether human or wild animal – and the diversity of the show being staged.

Parades also advertised the merchandise of local vendors. That merchandise might be telephones or it might be real estate, but floats were sponsored and funded because there was money to be made. Especially during settlement days in western Canada, not everyone had access to a newspaper or could read. Radios were uncommon and many immigrants spoke languages other than English. But everyone could understand the advertising conveyed during the parade.

Parades served useful business purposes. This land company float, circa 1912, showed the confidence and optimism of the community while it advertised real estate services. Courtesy of Medicine Hat Museum and Art Gallery, PC 439-50.

Children wanted the balloons that clowns carried. Seeing striking teams of horses or the latest models of buggies and automobiles made many wonder how far their bank accounts could be stretched. Farm men and women eyed the steam engines and other machinery.

Too, the parade showcased the community itself. One wagon or float might carry beautiful women. Another might feature children in a 4-H club holding the reins of calves. Both said, "This is a great community. Buy your land or bring your business here," or "we are growing, getting better by the year, so be sure you and your family join us."

Some communities held a daily parade of bands, clowns, livestock, and performers. Usually, that route was along the race track in front of the grandstand, and when the event was about to end for another year, some organizers staged yet another parade of winners.

Vernon 1891: No Place too Small for Big Plans

The small city in the interior of BC was never one to think small. Some communities had a local fair; others presented an annual rodeo. At many, horses races were popular summer entertainments.

Over the years, Vernon organized and hosted them all. Just to make sure locals never got bored, energetic organizers held auto meets and, once airplanes took to the skies, the community held air shows, too. In 1891, early pioneers were proud to organize their first agricultural fair. Although the community numbered only about 500 people and the lack of transportation would limit attendance, there was nothing small time about the people who attended.

For the October 14th fair, the Honorable Mr. F.G. Vernon was first choice to officially open the event. An early and successful pioneer rancher in the area, he had been elected to the legislature. Commitments meant he declined the invitation. Next, the organizers set their sights on the newcomers who had just purchased Mr. Vernon's ranch. They were expected to arrive in town that fall, but even before their arrival, the couple was creating a stir. The Earl and Countess of Aberdeen were among the Who's Who of Britain. For Canadians, they were the next thing to royalty, and just two years later, the earl would become governor general of Canada.

Mail service was uncertain for travellers, and the Aberdeens had already left for western Canada. The Countess of Aberdeen's brother, who was the new ranch manager, had arrived in Vernon, and the fair's president asked him to convey the invitation.

Meanwhile, the Aberdeens had stopped in Banff before continuing to the Okanagan. There, they received a letter from Lady Aberdeen's mother in England. She mentioned a letter that she had received from Lady Aberdeen's brother. Something about a fair. Nothing was too clear about dates or times.

The Aberdeens tried to contact Lady Aberdeen's brother, and he had tried to reach them. But, there was only one phone in Vernon, and telegrams were handled through the railway office in Sicamous. When no one was at the Sicamous station to take a message, messages became lost.

The Aberdeens continued their trip and finally reached Sicamous. Track had been built from there to Vernon, but the CPR had not yet started passenger service. Not too happily, Lady Aberdeen envisioned travelling the last leg of the trip by handcar, whizzing along the track at 20 miles [32 km] an hour, wind blowing through her hair. Coming to the rescue, her husband paid for a special engine to make the journey.

To accommodate other passengers, the trip was delayed, and the delay made fair day a historic date. Launching their first fair meant a celebration. Also thrilling was the sight of the first passenger train to rattle into Vernon. Better yet, the regal couple, Lord and Lady Aberdeen, were on it!

Local citizens and the town band welcomed them. The mayor and town councilors had wired Vancouver for top hats, and whether the hats fit or not, representatives of the town greeted the train and the Aberdeens in grand style.

When Lord Aberdeen learned this was the day that he was to open the fair, he came up with the appropriate speech. Then the delegation made its way to the Kalamalka Hotel. Although under construction, it held the exhibits.

"...really magnificent fruits and vegetables shown – monster cabbages and melons and pumpkins and splendid apples," wrote Lady Aberdeen in her journal.[12]

At the other end of town, where the livestock was being shown, her husband bought a team of mares and colt for $135.

"The team promptly took a first prize immediately afterwards and one of the mares and her foal got another first in another class," she continued. "It was funny to see everything going on just like at home at one of the Shows – the ring and the judges and the animals being led about and the groups of people discussing things in general."

It was high praise for fair organizers in the ambitious little village.

Later in the day, the couple was anxious to go see their new ranch property, so they didn't stay for the dance. It lasted until about 9:00 the next morning, another instance in which the townspeople did things in a big way.

Women's Place at the Fair

Women were volunteer organizers, exhibitors, judges, and contestants. Both farm and town women took pride in their traditional homemaking skills, and they were willing workers at fairs so those skills could be showcased. Too, farm women felt a stake in the stock and produce raised on their farms.

Despite making very significant contributions to the first fairs, women were not on the early fair boards. Although a female goddess, draped in sheaves of grain, might be the symbol used on early fair programs, men from local agricultural societies and town councils claimed board positions. Wives of members were expected to help whenever needed, especially with women's competitions and displays, but fair decision-making was the men's domain.

After the very earliest fairs, women did chair or became stewards of the Ladies' Committee or Ladies' Department – when such committees were established. They organized contest entries and displays for handiwork, baking, canning, other homemaking talents, garden produce, flowers, and floral arranging. In fact, hundreds of women gave thousands of hours to fair activities. Sometimes male board members felt they could depend more on the women volunteers than on male volunteers assigned similar tasks but related to grain and livestock.

Some female volunteers had ties to no particular organization. However, organizations such as the Women's Institute and the United Farm Women were strong supporters of fairs and

Exhibition grounds were used for many important occasions. On October 2, 1906, at New Westminster, Governor General Earl Grey and Countess Lady Grey were greeted outside the Women's Building for a party in their honor. During many fairs, mothers were encouraged to take small children to the Women's Building, where physical examinations by nurses were available for free. Courtesy of New Westminster Museum & Archives, 70.

women's involvement at all levels. In BC, at Westbank, the Women's Institute organized the fairs. Also, in Peachland, the same organization conducted annual fairs for some years. Throughout the west, other women volunteered on behalf of local church groups and a variety of service clubs.

Still, for the most part, their contributions were seldom documented, even in later-day histories. Those few who were credited tended to be married to directors of the fair associations.

In western Canada, by the second decade of the 20th century, provincial governments – through their Department of Agriculture – supported women's involvement in fairs. As part of the educational component of the events, governments sponsored classes for women, usually in cooking or household arts. Too, women were encouraged to compete in the domestic arts and sciences. After all, by 1916, most women on the prairies had the vote, and fairs presented an easy way of supporting their initiatives. Communities such as Armstrong, BC, and Red Deer,

Alberta, reflect the common experience of western Canadian women when it came to helping make local fairs successful.

In Armstrong, even for the earliest fairs, women were very active volunteers. The community held its first table top fair in 1900. By 1904, there, like elsewhere, women from local churches were responsible for the food services. That year and in subsequent years, the women of the Presbyterian Church served home-cooked meals at the fair. During the 1920s, in an old skating rink by the fairgrounds, United Church women served meals to fair-goers. Not only was there meat, gravy, potatoes, other vegetables, bread, and deserts, women brought countless salads, too. Prior to the fair, they baked pies and cakes, and dozens and dozens of loaves of bread and buns. In 1933, the United Church dining room required 250 loaves of bread. The local mill supplied the flour; the local women did the baking. Light lunch service was available on the grounds, too, once again offered by church women. In a tent that year, Anglican Church women served sandwiches, tea, and cake. Finally, when the United Church dining room needed to expand, it was moved to under the grandstand, where visitors could more readily stave off hunger.

Although men did help with food services by peeling vegetables and serving patrons, community women shouldered most of the work. They even brought dinnerware and cutlery from home, usually indicating ownership with colored yarn. In addition, at a time before paper plates and plastic glasses and cutlery, they washed dishes for hours on end so they would always have clean dinnerware.

Without the women who provided food services, it would have been next to impossible for fairs to grow as they did. Families could and did bring picnic lunches if they were attending for a single afternoon. However, when organizers wanted fair gates open from early morning to late at night, and when exhibitions stretched over a number of days, fairs without food would have failed.

Many women volunteered so that other women could compete and show their work at the exhibitions. Members of the weaker sex did head the Ladies' Department Committees, and committee work was extensive. Politicians and male organizers encouraged them with comments such as "Where would the fair be without the ladies?" But generally, they paid only lip service and never invited or expected women to serve in leadership roles.

Centrally located in Alberta, Red Deer was very progressive in terms of women's involvement. In 1906, amazingly, the community's first exhibition association had two women shareholders, Mrs. H. Baird and Mrs. K.M. Byer. After all, money was money, whether it came from a purse or pocket, and it was essential to run a fair.

There, individual women and the Women's Institute were strong supporters for the Red Deer fair. Still, even for the Ladies' Department competitions and exhibits, women organizers did not receive the official designation as "stewards" until 1913.

By 1915, fair directors needed more help from women and approached the Women's Institute. Members served light lunches and refreshments at the fair and made $275 between

2:00 p.m. and closing. Given their contributions to the fair, not surprisingly, the membership lobbied to have two "lady directors" from the W.I. appointed to the board.

The lobbying was successful – perhaps aided by the fact that some women were married to fair directors. Still, the power of the weaker sex remained limited. As "associate directors," the women's opinions counted less than their male counterparts. Also, members of the ladies' committee answered to a man. "Perhaps to ensure that things didn't get too out of hand, however, a male director was assigned to oversee the ladies." *The Red Deer Advocate* reported, "Mr. McLellan was in charge of the ladies' work and domestic products...and what he said went."[13]

In the growing community, other women's groups – including the Women's Christian Temperance Union and the Anglican Church women – supported the local fair. The Anglican women split profits on food service with the fair board in 1918. Still, women's concerns were not always addressed in a timely fashion. In 1919, women wanted repairs to the display building used for their exhibits. Three women were on the fair's board of directors.

Additional influence came through Mrs. Tallman, very active in the household arts section and married to a member of the board. He presented the problem. There were 44 other members, and the majority decided to take no action. Instead, a new stock barn was constructed on the grounds. Finally, the roof of the women's building collapsed. It was too late to heed the women's warnings, but not too late to rectify the problem.

In reality, the Red Deer board was progressive. Initially serving on the 1919 board, some years later, Mrs. J.C. Houghton became the first woman with an executive role on a local fair board. Becoming second vice-president, she had an interesting background from which to draw. Her husband had been a bank manager before the couple decided to farm. With experience rooted in farm, social, and financial issues, she became deeply involved in promoting agricultural concerns.

Another farm woman and a good organizer, Rubye MacFarlane was a booster for her community. She worked for many clubs and boards, but two organizations in which she held memberships were strong supporters of fairs. The Alberta Women's Institute was one; and for a time, she served as its provincial secretary and treasurer. Also, she was involved in the Red Deer Agricultural Society, so her association with fairs was not surprising. By 1942, Rubye MacFarlane was serving on the fair board, and little stood in the way of the energetic woman. She served on the fair board for 17 years. Then, she made Canadian women's history.

In 1959, she became the first woman to be president of an agricultural fair in Canada. Her overall contributions to the Red Deer Exhibition Board, and in particular, her position as first woman president and female pioneer in fair leadership garnered her honors. In 1974, she was presented with the Western Fairs Association Blue Ribbon Award. Her bronze plaque read, "for achievement of the highest order, aiding progress through fairs, stimulating energy, enterprise, intellect, and the quickening of human genius."

Her response was true to her own hardworking, optimistic, supportive, and indomitable spirit.

"Please girls, get on with it," she said. "Show that women can do it. I would very much like to see another woman as fair board president."[14]

More than a Voice

When competitive sports were planned, festivities needed announcers. In the early days, announcers were community people who were good with crowds. They needed to know enough local history, conditions, or people to offer insider jokes and judge how far to press locals so as to make everyone laugh but without distressing anyone.

Early announcers were male boosters for the community. They encouraged tickets sales for fair charities and belted out competition information through megaphones or, in later days, microphones. Sometimes they acted as straight men for clowns. They announced lost children and lost wallets. Many were good at the job and returned to do it year after year.

Local auctioneers were great choices for announcer. The auctioneer knew the people, knew livestock, and was never speechless. In Calgary, Josh Henthorn had announced at the first Calgary Stampede in 1912. By 1919, he was a dance instructor in the city, and as a sideline, Henthorn announced at the city's Victory Stampede. That year, his best joke evolved when Henthorn was on mic.

Someone carrying a suitcase whispered in his ear,

"You're wanted. Your suitcase is leaking."

Assuming the man was serious, Henthorn made the announcement. The crowd roared. Whoever owned the suitcase must have filled it with bottles of booze.

Somehow, the same joke entertained people year after year.

Warren Cooper was another who found fame announcing for rodeos in southern Alberta, Saskatchewan, and BC. Born in Calgary in 1902, Warren was one of nine children. He was slow to find his niche in life, but then, he had a slow and easy-going personality. He became known as "Coop," to rodeo and auction mart patrons and got along with everyone. He was never in a hurry to get or finish a job, but, in reality, he was always busy. Yet the relaxed image was perfect for his job.

Nanton had become the family home, but his job took him around the country. He had taken an auctioneering course in Idaho and travelled cattle country doing sales. The experience refined his skill at getting the most out of a crowd – the most money and the most good will. Those traits led him to the announcer's booth at rodeos.

By 1961, Warren Cooper had announced at the Calgary Stampede for 15 years and handled the mic at Medicine Hat Stampedes for 14 years. At times, he travelled with Dick Cosgraves or Herman Linder on the rodeo train. Not only would he announce, but sometimes he was rodeo secretary, handling paper work such as entrance forms and fees, keeping track of competitor's points, and paying winning cowboys.

Always, he had the knack for telling a rodeo yarn. For western Canadian events, he found the perfect balance between folksy and friendly, information and boosterism. He was smart enough to announce details and rules for events, acknowledge the home communities of competitors, pump up expectations, play down failures, and do it all without stepping into the role that was designated to the rodeo judge.

It was a fine line to walk, but great announcers helped make great events, and organizers knew it. In Calgary and across the country, great announcers such as Ed Whalen became so closely linked with events, local audiences were deeply saddened by their retirements or passing away. But the shows went on, and new voices filled the silence.

Great Posters, Great Ads

Every fair needed to get the word out. Before the days of TV, events were advertised on radio, but great images were the best advertising. They were published in newspapers and posted on barns, telephone poles, and community notice boards. Posters and ads were contracted from printers in Vancouver and eastern Canada. Then along came Andrew King.

Born in Winnipeg in 1885, as a young man, King and his wife bought a newspaper business in Rouleau, SK, a village of about 800 people. Hardworking, open to new ideas, not afraid try new things, and willing to invest in people and technology, King quickly rose above limitations.

The printing of event-related documents and publicity happened long before opening day of summer festivities. This poster was printed by Andrew King. Courtesy of Estevan Art Gallery and Museum, Andrew King Print.

From youth, King had worked hard learning his trade as a newspaper man. Then he and his wife took a chance. Rouleau was small but growing. The community and weekly newspaper seemed right for them, so they bought the *Rouleau Enterprise* and a house.

Long days and hard work were standard. Then, one day in 1912, a stranger walked in the door. The theatrical agent was looking for a commercial printer who could handle posters. His order had not arrived from the USA. Timely publicity was the difference between a successful show and a failure.

King couldn't solve the agent's problem. However, over the next three days, while he waited for his order to arrive, the agent patiently explained the basics of the poster printing business and the needs of theatrical companies touring the west.

King's first ventures into the poster printing business were small contracts, which gave him time to learn the trade. He personally approached theatrical companies performing locally, and there were many criss-crossing the prairies. With the *Enterprise* winning about one contract a week, word spread. King continued publishing his newspaper, but income from the posters improved. When he won contracts with large companies playing in the cities, this income became more stable.

By 1914, King sent out a small catalogue to the organizers of sports days and fairs. Within two years, he had 75% of the fair and exhibition print business in western Canada.[15]

Buying stock art from a company in Vancouver, King found the art did not always meet the needs or preferences of his clients. He scouted for artists, but local artists did not use simple lines, figures, and primary color combinations to create the energy he wanted. Herb Ashley of Banff submitted a portfolio. Clearly, he was the right artist for the job. He completed a number of drawings, which King had transformed into wood blocks for prints. Some were for small posters, but others were huge. Seven foot [2.1 metre] billboards, made up of numerous 28 x 42 inch [71-107 cm] sheets, could be plastered on barns or other buildings. They were perfect for fair clients! By leaving blank areas for specifics of community and date, King was able to use the blocks again and again.

Then King began making Canadian print history by printing color posters. Ashley designed posters in five colors: red, orange, yellow, green, and blue. Carving one block for each color, with overlay techniques, King needed only the three primary colors to do the job.

In the meantime, when an opportunity came along to buy a larger newspaper in Estevan, SK, King and his family moved. The jobs kept coming, and to King's surprise, big companies brought business. He served the big names of circus and midway work, almost all of whom appeared at western Canadian exhibitions. They included Sells Floto, Johnny Jones, Clyde Beatty, Hagenbeck-Wallace, Coles Brothers, and countless others.

Patty Conklin was a regular customer until he moved his winter quarters east after contracting the Canadian National Exhibition in Toronto. He brought huge orders to King, so his bills were high. Receiving cash from carnival and circus operators was not unusual, and many of the bills were paid in person with cash. Collecting one bill, King had a surprise. Conklin was settling the amount owing on a full season of printing. As Patty stood by, the money was passed from his accountant to King. Roll after roll of coins was handed over – long before the loonie or toonie was part of Canada's currency. Conklin's partner had taken the paper money to the railway station to pay another bill, said the midway owner. And his eyes had twinkled.

Realizing the pleasure Conklin was having with his joke, King dutifully filled every pocket with the heavy rolls. Payment totaled 35 pounds [16 kg] of silver.

King also enjoyed the joke, even more so when he went to the bank to make his deposit. He pulled out roll after roll of coins from his pockets. Finally, the teller disrupted the staid atmosphere of the financial institution.

"Where the hell did you get all that?" he asked.

In all the years King had worked with fairs, circuses, and midways, when it came to settling the bills, honesty was never an issue. Sometimes King counted the money at the time payments were made. Sometimes he didn't, but there had never been a single error in terms of amount when the tellers at the bank checked his deposits.

However, there was one instance when his business missed out $90 000. His company just couldn't fill the order.[16]

When the agent for the Barnum and Bailey Circus of Ringling Brothers first discussed the huge contract with him, King thought it was a joke. The famous circus wanted to do all that season's poster printing with King. The company offered an above average payment when compared to most printing jobs in Canada.

The Barnum and Bailey agent had done his homework. Most of the year's shows were planned for the central and western areas of Canada and the USA. Given the exchange rate and cost of shipping, doing business with King would be advantageous for the company.

A small fortune was at stake, and King studied the feasibility of the project. He could get another cylinder to handle the actual printing of the job, but for a job that size, he needed more well-trained and capable tradespeople, too.

With no one available locally, he advertised in Vancouver. He offered above union pay rates and committed to providing railway tickets and subsidized room and board.

When no one responded, King had to turn down the biggest deal of his life.

Community Chautaquas Ltd., later part of Dominion Chautaquas, was another big client. With the Depression, Chautauqua disappeared, but exhibition boards became ever-more important as clients. King had not only made a good living, he had made printing history. All the while he had lived in Rouleau or Estevan. The Enterprise Show Prints, later known as the King Show Prints, had advertised fairs, exhibitions, rodeos, circuses, and sports days. In doing so, they enticed thousands to memorable events.

More Than Just the Basics

Attending to food, water, toilets, lights, buildings, grounds, maintenance, publicity, accommodations, protocol for special guests, and fire and accident insurance was essential. Also, organizers prepared for petty crimes, injury, and unhappy – even violent – fair visitors.

Contest entry forms, rules, prize lists, gate tickets and other forms must be prepared and printed. The organizers had to find capable judges for contests, which were as varied as knitting, bronc riding, and beard growing.

Transportation issues could become a nightmare. Routes for travelling companies needed co-ordination, so that a company wasn't expected to be in two locations on one date. Trains carried exhibits, livestock, wild west shows, and midways. Good organizers lobbied for reasonable transportation costs with the railway and were successful. In contrast, at the American or Canadian border, customs officers might hold up a travelling show or charge exorbitant duty on stock, and there was nothing organizers could do to prevent that problem.

However, they could plan for cars, cars, more cars, and campers! Even in the 1920s, fair visitors needed parking spaces. Also, some wanted to travel to the fair in their cars or trucks and pitch tents beside them. Although the City of Regina did have a campground, it could not accommodate all the fair visitors who wanted to camp. So, the exhibition association developed its own 12 acre [4.8 hectare] campground. It was well planned. Services were exceptional and by 1928, the campers had access to washrooms and showers with hot water.

Annual budgets were important. Planners prepared for growth and economic downturns. No matter how bleak the economic times, festival organizers had to find funds and hire staff to create pleasurable events for local and out-of-town visitors.

Exhibitions, rodeos, and regatta boards hired countless employees, and some with modest beginnings in the industry made long-term and important commitments. When Roy Beaver was in his early twenties, he and his partner had a snake show, which travelled with midways in western Canada and the USA. Roy sold hot dogs outside their snake show, but finally, he and his wife settled in Calgary. Even after he no longer travelled with the midways, the couple ran food booths at stampedes. Eventually, they became restaurateurs, but their sabbatical from midway food services ended in 1948 when Roy and his wife, Lina, became the official caterers for the Calgary Exhibition and Stampede. For 20 years, not only did they prepare and serve food on the midway, the Beavers catered for the special guests and other events of the Stampede board.

With changing employee-employer laws, hiring and firing practices were increasingly important. Even establishing pensions for employees became an issue. In the early 1940s, at Edmonton, how best to deal with pensions and retirement of long-term employees was still under consideration. Whether employees held long-standing contracts with fair boards or were temporary workers, employee relations, policies, and procedures had to be developed. Also, they had to keep pace with developments in both politics and the business world.

The planning around other areas was much more enjoyable. Eventually, contests offering cars and trucks had became the rage. Owning a car or a better car became such a commonplace dream that fairs organized draws for them, and in doing so, they raised money for good causes or future fairs. During the 1934 Regina Exhibition, all adults playing the games on the midway were given tickets on the draw for a car. To claim the prize, the winner had to be in the grandstand during the evening of the last performance. He or she had three minutes to present the ticket and be declared winner or another draw was made. Not surprisingly, the plan encouraged attendance and created excitement.

Traditionally, many large and small communities chose a queen for the annual summer event, and often, she represented the community and board to other communities.

The first rodeo queen for the Calgary Stampede was chosen in 1946. Shown here at the family ranch, Patsy Rodgers was a working cowgirl. Courtesy of Historical Committee, Calgary Exhibition and Stampede.

Choosing a queen generated public interest. May Queens were a well-established and long tradition. In Kelowna, Queen of the Lake was crowned each year, but rodeo queens were surprisingly late arrivals on the scene.

The first Calgary Stampede Queen was not crowned until 1946. In 1954, for the first time, a young indigenous woman became Calgary Stampede Queen. Nineteen-year-old Evelyn Eaglespeaker was taking a secretarial course in Calgary, but she had grown up south of Lethbridge. She had attended St. Paul's Indian School and then high school in Cardston. The year that she was Calgary Stampede Queen, she represented five First Nations tribes: the Blood, Peigan, Sarcee, Blackfoot and Stonies. In an elaborate ceremony, she had been named Princess Wapiti by them, so she travelled as a good-will ambassador in both roles. She made appearances at rodeos in Cardston, Coleman, Lethbridge, and Medicine Hat. Evelyn spoke Blackfoot and attracted attention, especially when she wore the outfit that had been tanned, beaded, and embroidered by her mother. She couldn't always answer all the questions asked about First Nations folklore, and she had youthful uncertainties about the speeches she was invited to make to service clubs, but she felt honored to represent both the Stampede and First Nations people. Yet another first happened when, a number of years later, a Chinese Canadian was made Calgary Stampede Queen.

The contests required organization on a local level, but in 1955, rodeo queen contests moved to the international stage. The International Rodeo Association decided to run a Miss Rodeo America contest, and it was serious business. Famous Alberta cowboy and rodeo producer Herman Linder was on the planning committee, which created guidelines for the first contest.

The organizers did not want a popularity or ticket-selling contest. Rules limited the contest to young women between 18 and 25, but both amateur riders and professional contract performers qualified. Points were allocated for horsemanship to be judged by horsemen; appearance to be judged by photographers; and personality to be judged by educators.

Operating under similar guidelines, the Miss Rodeo Canada contest got under way at the same time, and Linder encouraged rodeos throughout the country to sponsor contestants. In August of 1955, the first international rodeo queen contest, called Miss Rodeo America of the Rockies, was held at Casper, Wyoming. Representing Canada at the contest was Connie Ivans [Robinson] of Lethbridge, who was studying to be a medical technician.

The following year, in 1956, Mary Lynn Cook of Cardston, Alberta, was crowned as Miss Canadian Rodeo. At the Chicago Rodeo that year, she was named Miss International Ranch Girl, and in the Miss Rodeo America contest, she placed second.

Over the years, changing times meant new problems, new rules, and new opportunities. Beer tents and large-scale gambling casinos increasingly found their way on to exhibition grounds. More display buildings featured fine art, but next door, video games captured the attention of youth. Organizing fairs, rodeos, and regattas was an ever challenging task, but to organizers, visitors, competitors, and showmen, the effort and endless hours provided a worthy service to the community.

Chapter 4

Wild West Shows, Rodeo, and the Real West

World-class Cowboy Events

Western Canadians seemed destined to fall in love with rodeo and wild west shows. Cowboy culture, horse culture, and fairs became a formula for great times. Before cars, horses shaped everyday life. Horse races in Europe and America were common, so adding running, sulky, and chariot races to community picnics, sports days, fairs, Victoria Day, and Labour Day celebrations was a given. Horse races were traditional enjoyments for First Nations and Métis, too, and rodeos included races specifically for Indian men or women.

From the late 1870s, when ranching became the life blood of many in south and central BC, Alberta, and Saskatchewan, cowboy competitions were a sure-fire hit. After the spring and fall round-ups, riding and roping competitions were especially popular with the many American immigrants.

The first cowboy competitions happened on the ranches. When work was done, cowboys gathered around corrals.

"Bet you can't ride that horse," one would say.

"Bet I can," was a frequent reply.

Others wanted in on the bet. The contest was on. And soon the contests were being staged on fair day, too.

From South America to western Canada, great cowboys embraced the sport, and some went from ranch to ranch to compete. *Rodeo* was the Spanish for "going around," and in Mexico, its colloquial usage meant "round-up." In the USA, the cowboy competitions were billed as rodeos and round-ups, and with the waning of the frontier lifestyle, they became Frontier Days. Blending British and American heritage, in western Canada, some events which included American cowboy sports and polo were known as gymkhanas, too.

Held on ranches or fair grounds, the gymkhanas and cowboy sports were diverse. As well as bucking horse competitions and polo matches, there might be cowboys wrestling while on horse back. Spectators loved the range of sports, and a few events stretched into day-long rodeos.

The date for the first North American rodeo isn't readily apparent. Some Texans claimed, because they had wagers on bronc riders, roping contests, and horse races in the 1830s and 1840s, that their state held the first rodeos. For an 1844 Texas rodeo, the judges had awarded prizes – Spanish blankets, Bowie knives, and pistols. Detractors claimed the events were really part of a wild west show. A number of other places also claimed the honor of holding the first rodeo.[1]

This chuckwagon race photo from the Gleichen Stampede is dated 1912. Gleichen, AB, had strong and early rodeo roots. If this race was an official competition at the June, 1912, Stampede, the event predates the first Calgary chuckwagon races by 11 years. Courtesy of Stockmen's Memorial Foundation, SFL 40-09-001.

Canada's rodeo history began in 1891 at Fort Macleod, AB, and the events were held in conjunction with the fall fair. Cowboys from local ranches competed in bronc riding and steer roping. As early as 1893, for the summer agricultural fair in Calgary, a steer roping event was organized by George Lane of the Bar U Ranch. Competitors included Lane, Bill Todd, and John Ware. A black cowboy, Ware worked at the Bar U and was known as an outstanding bronc rider. In the steer roping competition, he roped and tied his steer in 51 seconds. That beat his boss's time by more than three minutes and Todd's time by two minutes, and the audiences loved him.[2]

With their successes, both Fort Macleod and Calgary continued to expand the cowboy competitions. In 1894, bronc riding had been added to the Calgary fair, and in July, 1895, the most significant Canadian fair west of Vancouver featured rodeo competitions. That year, Regina's great Territorial Exhibition included a "broncho-breaking" tournament and a steer roping tournament. Contestants came from far and wide. With a time of two minutes and ten seconds, Duncan McIntosh, manager of the Glengarry Ranch near Claresholm, won the steer roping.

In Alberta, in 1900, at the Medicine Hat fair, steer roping was billed as a rodeo event. With an early background in ranching, the community was a natural for the development of rodeo contestants, fans, and rodeo stock companies. By 1907, the community's rodeo attracted an audience of 1500.

The first rodeo in Raymond, Alberta, was in 1902 or 1903, and organized as a Knight and Day rodeo. In 1904, Lethbridge Exhibition featured rodeo events, as did Cardston. John Ware competed in steer throwing, and following the event was a Sun Dance at Standoff. Also in Alberta, Gleichen, Hand Hills, and Banff were early to embrace rodeo-style competitions. There were cowboy competitions at the Edmonton Exhibition long before the 1912 Calgary Stampede. Similarly, at very early dates, Saskatchewan ranches and communities staged cowboy skill events, including both competitions and demonstration sports.

Many rodeo events were to experience phenomenal success at fairs and stampedes. In the early days, for saddle bronc contests, even getting mounted was a challenge. It might take a "wild horse contest" between a horse and a number of cowboys just to saddle the animal. Then, the horse was snubbed against the saddle horn of a good rider and cow pony, the contestant managed to mount, and the bronc was released. To win, cowboys had to stay on the horse until it stopped bucking – however long the ride. Afterwards, no matter what the outcome, money seemed to change hands.

Although the early rodeos were successful, there were often long delays between events. Having corrals and chutes handy made sense. At first, in many communities, chutes and corrals were built and then torn down at the end of the rodeo. Eventually, in larger rodeo towns, they became permanent structures on the fairgrounds.

As well as making improvement to the grounds, rodeo managers improved their operations. Organizing the Rodeo Association of America in 1929, managers explored answers to problems. With ever-more informed fans and demand for fair competitions, it became essential to have competent judges and rules that everyone understood. Rodeo became more professional, yet the development of a professional rodeo association for cowboys did not materialize until 1936. Formed in Boston, the Cowboy Turtles Association included both American and Canadian cowboys. Although concerned with the welfare of cowboys, the association's name reflected the cowboys' recognition of their own slow pace in organizing. Canadian and world champion cowboy Herman Linder became the first vice-president. Like all organizations, it constantly adapted to meet new needs and conditions. Changing the name to Rodeo Cowboy's Association and then Professional Rodeo Cowboy's Association were steps towards professionalism. The formation of the Cowboys Protective Association, which also underwent numerous name changes until it became the Canadian Professional Rodeo Association in 1980, meant further addressing risks, concerns, standards, and rodeo conditions.

Not only did the various associations lobby, they were instrumental in making rodeo as professional as possible. No longer were the exploits of great competitors dependent on the memories of old cowboys and fans. The associations documented wins. Statistics determined who was eligible for national and world competitions. A world championship title meant the cowboy was truly a world champion.

Continuing the tradition of women rodeo competitors and shown here in 1969 at the Cochrane Stampede, Lorraine McLean of Turner Valley won calf roping. She also won calf roping at the Canadian Girls' Rodeo Association Championship for four years. Courtesy of Stockmen's Memorial Foundation, SFL 40-06-027.

Women in rodeo became increasingly organized, too. Following the dramatic participation of cowgirls in competition during the second decade of the 1900s, their participation returned to trick riding, running horse races, and barrel racing. However, once again, public opinion shifted. Women's events regained popularity, and cowgirls formed the Canadian Girls' Rodeo Association. In 1962, at High River, Alberta, the association hosted Canada's first All-Girl

Championship Rodeo and Race Meet. Events included barrel racing, bronc riding, calf roping, cow cutting, cow riding, goat tying, and horse races.

As the west was "tamed," views had changed. Safety for both human competitors and animals became a more significant consideration. A few competitions, such as long-horned steer roping, were deemed to violent or too likely to end in injury to man or animal, and they disappeared. Yet, rodeo, horse racing, and their cousin, the wild west show, were destined to be the most popular entertainments on the western Canadian fair circuits.

Wild west shows were brought to the Canadian circuit by Americans. During the first decades of the 20th century, Americans were the majority of the immigrants in some western communities. Steeped in the ideas of entertainment and the myths of the America west, they loved the circuses and wild west shows. By that time, the most successful wild west show in America was the Miller Brothers' 101 Ranch Wild West Show. Its many predecessors, including the Buffalo Bill Wild West Show, fell on hard times, but the 101 Ranch Show continued to impress audiences during the early 1900s. Over a number of years, it toured in western Canada.

To some, the wild west show may have seemed like any other travelling show, a welcome escape from work, school, and reality. Long before the Millers brothers extravaganza appeared, western Canadian fairs booked dog and pony shows, trick riders, and ropers, but the wild west show offered a sense of western history to audiences. Its style of entertainment partnered well with cowboy competitions.

In turn, rodeo became the most common full partner of fairs and exhibitions. Agricultural fairs reflected the personality and industry of their areas. Yet, strangely, rodeo was not only a sport for the ranch land of Alberta and Saskatchewan, it captivated fans all across the west. Major rodeos were held in cities from Victoria to Winnipeg. They even found their way into the hearts of those living in coal mining towns like Coleman, Alberta, or lake-front communities like Kelowna.

That cowboy events and entertainments succeeded all across western Canada meant they somehow reflected the heritage, as well as the "personality," of those who lived in western communities.

By the teens and 20s, western Canadians were launching their own travelling wild west shows and rodeos. The touring companies did achieve surprising successes in eastern Canada and in some U.S. cities, but their most loyal fans were at home.

In Calgary, a passion for rodeo and the mystique of the wild west would determine the direction of the entire show. The Stampede was not The Greatest Show on Earth, of Barnum and Bailey Circus fame. It was The Greatest Outdoor Show on Earth.

The Dusky Demon and Weadick

One of the greatest western performances was by the Dusky Demon, a show name given to Bill Pickett. He appeared in Calgary in 1905. Although he joined the 101 Wild West Show that year, in his early days, he had been booked as an independent act. His performance – which ultimately turned into a full-fledged cowboy competitor event – should have been an outstanding success in the ranching community of early Calgary.

Despite the fame he had already achieved in North America, the response to his act was mixed. He came with another cowboy who would become a big name in Calgary Stampede history – Guy Weadick. As Pickett's new manager, Weadick hadn't yet proven that he could be anything more than a vaudeville roping act. In contrast, Pickett was definitely a rising star. He became known as the first and greatest of the bulldoggers. So, why the surprising reaction in Calgary?

Of mixed Cherokee and black heritage, the Texas-born performer had been a serious cowboy. Unlike Weadick, who claimed to be a working cowboy but whose background held few such jobs, Pickett had worked the range. There, he had invented his unique style of bulldogging.

His technique of dogging a steer involved biting and hanging on with his teeth to the animal's lip until the steer finally dropped and allowed itself to be branded or its health tended. In 1903, while working on a ranch, a long-horned bull had been about to gore his horse. Any talented and brave bulldogger might jump from his running mount to the shoulders of a long horned steer and twist the horns until the man brought down the steer. To bring the reluctant steer down quickly, Pickett bit its upper lip, startling it into submission. His technique worked. At ranch gatherings and rodeos, people wanted to see his amazing "act." He became known by many as the "greatest sweat-and-dirt cowboy that ever lived – bar none."3

In 1905, Pickett wanted a new manager. His manager and announcer had to explain what was happening to audiences when he performed and diffuse the racial prejudice he faced. His first manager had billed him as the Dusky Demon in an attempt to side-step performing contracts and rodeo competitions at fairs and exhibitions where "whites only" were allowed.

Likely, it was clear when Guy Weadick and Pickett met that talk was Weadick's talent. Later in life, he would claim the initials GW on his belt buckle meant "Good with Words." In fact, he was also good at promoting himself, too, and attaching himself to a star like Pickett was a win-win situation. Every world class performer needed a top promoter.

Later stories about Weadick's early life were many. Like others who were good with words and had a theatrical sense, Weadick may have created a somewhat "mythical" past for himself, one that tied him to early ranching in both the USA and western Canada.

He was born in Rochester, New York, in 1886, and he left home while in his mid teens. He did learn to be a good roper, talented enough to perform, and he began in vaudeville during his late teens under the theatrical name Cheyenne Bill.

He maintained that he had first come to Alberta in 1903 or 1904 and worked on the McIntyre Ranch. At the time, he would have been 17 years old. According to another story, he came to the Fort Macleod area in 1904 on a horse buying trip with Montana cowboys, and he attended a Blood Sun Dance Ceremony at Standoff, AB. Staged at the time of the Lethbridge fair, it was considered the largest powwow the area had seen, and the Bloods hosted Peigan and Blackfoot participants. Too, Weadick watched the roping and riding competitions staged by Ray Knight at Cardston. Undoubtedly some of this story is true, but in 1905, Weadick was also on the vaudeville circuit and met Bill Pickett, who hired him as manager and announcer. As a touring act with a company called Creswell and Osborne, they definitely performed in front of the grandstand at the July, 1905 Calgary Exhibition. Ernie Richardson, already general manager for the exhibition, hired the act.

Acknowledging that he was one quarter cowboy and three-quarters showman, Weadick had the words to captivate audiences. For the uninitiated, it was hard to actually see what Pickett was doing at such a distance. With a megaphone, like a circus showman, Weadick announced each move, building excitement around the Dusky Demon's bite'-em style bulldogging.

Some thought the act was outstanding, but an editorial in the *Daily Herald Calgary*, 4 July 1905, suggested it was too violent for others. "That this aroused a feeling of disgust quite generally is to the credit of the Calgary people....when a man is permitted to make an exhibition of this character in the presence of women and children, the finer sensibilities are outraged. The local color can be introduced into these cowboy exhibitions without this sort of thing and authorities should see to it that it is never repeated on the premises over which the city exercises any control."

At the Fort Worth, Texas, Fat Stock Show that year, Pickett and Weadick captured the attention of Zack Miller, a man who changed their lives. The Miller Brothers 101 Real Wild West Show was destined to be one of American's greatest wild west shows. The brothers' dream wasn't simply to stage a theatrical tent show with re-enactments of the big battles in the Indian wars or fleeing stage coaches with robbers racing after them. They wanted to showcase the skills of real cowboys, and they planned actual cowboy competitions. The Miller brothers hired Bill Pickett and his manager to demonstrate bulldogging for their first grand event. That first contract with Miller brothers led to others, changed Pickett's life, and made him world famous.

Weadick remained the announcer for many of Pickett's performances. At about the same time, he met another person who would dramatically affect his life. Florence La Due had a roping act, and the two married. Their vaudeville performances included three bucking ponies, a dog, and their ropes. Calling their act Weadick and LaDue, Wild West Stunts, Roping and Gab, and The Stampede Riders, they worked both the vaudeville circuit and later took contracts with the new Miller brothers' touring show.

Weadick acknowledged being on the vaudeville circuit and working for the Miller brothers' and other wild west shows, but he never suggested just how much he owed to the Miller brothers. In the history of that great American show, Weadick is little more than a footnote, an "also performed." He is credited as an originator of the Calgary Stampede. Some American sources incorrectly credited him for putting up the $100 000 in prize money for that first event.

Had it not been for his association with the famous bulldogger Bill Pickett, the training, employment, and vast network of contacts resulting from working with the Miller Brothers' 101 Show, Weadick might have been a footnote in Calgary's history, too.

The Real Wild West Tours Western Canada

Just as with circuses, wild west shows were contracted for exhibitions and frontier day celebrations. As well, they performed in other communities along the way. To make the most money, the shows made as many stops as possible, and the bigger the community, the better. When the stops didn't coincide with annual events, wild west shows rented horse show buildings or pitched huge tents on exhibition grounds to stage their shows.

Some wild west shows blurred the lines between theatre and vaudeville-style entertainment, demonstrations of cowboy and frontier skills, and cowboy competitions. The Miller Brothers 101 Real Wild West Show did just that.

This ad, published in the Saskatoon Daily Phoenix *on 4 July, 1912, provides rare proof of the tour of Miller Brothers' 101 Ranch Wild West Show in western Canada. Courtesy of Saskatoon Public Library, LH 5423E.*

The show first appeared on the western Canadian fair circuit in 1908. Playing in Winnipeg and Calgary exhibitions that year, the wild west show had found a welcoming environment. Winnipeg had great railway links and was a good sized city. Also, Calgary was staging the Dominion Exhibition that year. For the nationwide exhibition, Calgary fair manager E.L. Richardson and other organizers had a generous budget – thanks to provincial and federal government grants for the special event. They and Winnipeg organizers had the money to bring in the shows that were favorites of big American fairs.

Scheduled as a one day attraction in Calgary and in its first year of touring, already, it was a big catch in terms of travelling shows. At the time, Bill Pickett, Guy Weadick, and Flores [Florence] La Due were with the show.

The Miller Brothers Show grew from the experience of a family that had ranched in both Kansas and Oklahoma, and from the cowboy competitions held on their ranch.

Finally, they decided to take the show on the road, and like other big shows, it actually travelled by rail. Shipping the show was a huge job. There were horses for everyone, some belonging to the Millers, others to the performers. As well, there were tents and tons of gear. On tour, the Millers provided food, transportation, and accommodation, at times on the railway cars and at other times in hotels.

Nineteen hundred and eight seemed a promising year to mount a huge, travelling show. Reality proved otherwise. The first show included many rookies who had not yet perfected their roles and jobs. Nor did the management have enough experience with the challenges of a travelling show. During the season, for 50 days, heavy rains plagued the show. Trains were delayed and a train wreck led to deaths and injuries. In Winnipeg, one of the most talented of the Millers' showmen and managers became deathly ill with typhoid, then running rampant through the city.

Like the Territorial Exhibition in Regina years earlier, the Dominion Exhibition in Calgary began with a spectacular parade, a historical pageant that wound its way through the streets. Showcased were countless traditionally-costumed First Nations people from nearby reserves. As well, the parade included more than 100 cowboys and

Geo Gresaeff was one of the Cossack riders who performed with the 101 Wild West Show while it was in Winnipeg. Courtesy of Stockmen's Memorial Foundation, SFL 110-01-014.

Indians who were travelling with the Miller Brothers Wild West Show. Performances in their tent were featured on only one day, but that fabulous day was not soon forgotten.

Not only did the show visit western Canada in 1908, it played to audiences, including at exhibitions in 1911. At that time, the travelling company included about 1100 people and 600 head of livestock.[4] Even when only a part of the troupe made the western Canadian tour and additional stock had to be contracted from the local area, the show was massive and impressive. Also that year, the show completed a tour of England, Germany, Russia, and France, and the Weadicks were part of it. By the spring of 1912, the Miller Brother Show returned to North America, and despite success, most of the performers were broke. The stage was set for the first Calgary Stampede. In 1912 and again in 1913, the Miller Brothers Wild West Show was in Canada, and stops in various years included Victoria, Vancouver, New Westminster, Calgary, Saskatoon, and Winnipeg.

The 101 Wild West Show offered contracts to many of the best cowboy and cowgirl performers available. Generally, the contracts stated that the performer must present daily shows or demonstrations of their sports while on tour. They were to look the part whenever in the public, so cowboy hats and fancy show outfits were a must. Apart from that, the performers could enter all the local rodeo competitions they wanted. If they paid their own entry fees, they kept

Flores LaDue was a trick rider and fancy roper with the 101 Ranch Wild West Show. She later married Guy Weadick. Courtesy of Glenbow Archives, NA 628-4.

their winnings. If the show owners paid their entry fees, the Millers wanted 50% of the winnings. In fact, early in the century, the Millers' cowboys and cowgirls were considered "professionals" by many ranchers and fairs holding rodeo competitions. As such, they weren't always allowed to compete. However, they were the most significant competitors and winners at both the Calgary 1912 Stampede and the Winnipeg 1913 Stampede.

Weadick was paid for publicity and some management jobs at both events. As someone who also worked for the Miller Brothers Show, he was the natural liaison with the wild west show. Commonly, travelling shows had advance men who did the advertising, wrote press releases, and made local arrangements. Between 1905 and 1912, Weadick toured with the Miller brothers show often enough to learn their winning formula.

Like other travelling shows, the Miller brothers followed many of trends in the business. Eventually, to meet the changing interests of audiences, they included circus acts such as Cossack acrobats. At one time or another, through employees or financial connections, the 101 Ranch Wild West Show had links to Buffalo Bill Cody, Zack Mulhall's Wild West Show and Congress of Rough Riders, Pawnee Bill Lillie, Barnum and Bailey Circus, and others.

One year or another, the Miller brothers had stops from BC to Ontario. In doing so, they brought wild west know-how to western Canada's fair and rodeo scene.

The Millers were certainly not the only wild west show on the road, and early in the century, western Canadians toured with their own wild west companies. One of the first was Milton Dowker, who organized the Canadian Wild West Show in 1900. Others, such as Peter Welsh with his very successful Alberta Stampede Company and Herman Linder with his rodeo company, successfully combined cowboy performance and competition during engagements.

Yet, the Millers had masterminded, financed, and operated a show that left an indelible imprint. Men like Hoot Gibson and Will Rogers had ties to the show, as did the great cowboy artists like Charlie Russell, who would attend Canadian stampedes. Almost a century later, in the form of the Calgary Stampede, western Canada's ability to stage the combined wild west show and stampede was world famous, but not all the men who were responsible for creating the great event received significant recognition.

Calgary 1912 – A Tangled Web

So who really deserved the most credit for the first Calgary Stampede? Did Weadick dream up the Stampede? Was he really the magic man who made the show a reality? Or is the story much more complicated? Was Weadick simply the right man for the job offered to him?

Guy Weadick was never shy about claiming credit for the Calgary Stampede. His big hat and cowboy attire made him ideal. His photogenic image was good publicity. But who were the unsung heroes?

The story becomes a tangled web of who said what and who did what. Medicine Hat's Ad Day should have been in the running for major credit. Calgary Exhibition Manager E.L. Richardson's contribution is too often downplayed. The Big Four have been credited with financing the show, but as big and very successful ranchers, they knew all about cowboy competitions and how to stage them.

Yes, Guy Weadick was one of the players. So was the great Miller Brothers' 101 Ranch Wild West Show. Most of those world champion cowboys and cowgirls at the first Calgary Stampede arrived with the Miller brothers' show. The show not only brought competitors, it was a model for entertainment extravaganzas.

Yes, Weadick was excellent at promotion. He knew about *Billboard* magazine, which noted the routes of travelling shows, including wild west shows. Also the industry magazine carried employment ads, so, it was perfect for getting news out to cowboy showmen and competitors. As a contract act with Miller brothers, Weadick had met the big names in wild west show per-

At least as early as 1907, the Calgary Exhibition featured an Indian village at or near the grounds. This photo appeared in a promotional pamphlet for the 1933 Calgary Stampede. Courtesy of Historical Committee, Calgary Exhibition and Stampede.

formances and American rodeo. He was well aware of the value of wild west show posters and newspaper advertising. He was the right man to announce in the arena and to do advertising.

He performed the same job the following next year at Winnipeg, and he used much the same posters and newspaper advertising features. But if you believed his promotion, both events were the greatest outdoor shows on earth. Certainly, he did deserve payment and credit. Just how much might be questioned.

Although it doesn't have the same flair as the "one big dreamer" theory, more realistically, Calgary's great Stampede grew out of what was already happening in Alberta and the Calgary area. Some said when the idea first surfaced, E.L. Richardson of the Calgary Exhibition opposed the Stampede. Practically speaking, he couldn't put the full weight of the exhibition behind the program. Dates and bookings for exhibition races and entertainment had already been established with the Western Canadian Fair and Racing Circuit, which had long served Calgary in terms of staging a great annual show. Despite the challenging and endless work that he was already doing, Richardson did become treasurer for the 1912 Calgary Stampede, and it was no small thing to be trusted with the huge amounts of money at stake.

Addison Day of Medicine Hat had experience with organizing successful rodeos long before 1912, and his role in helping to launch the Calgary Stampede went way back. In fact, he had connections with the great Miller Brothers 101 Ranch Wild West Show.

This image (original in color) was made into a lantern slide so it could be used in the local theatre to advertise the upcoming stampede. Courtesy of Medicine Hat Museum and Art Gallery.

By 1911, Ad Day was ranching in the Medicine Hat and Swift Current area. He had helped with the 1908 Dominion Exhibition in Calgary, and he knew all about cowboy competition and wild west extravaganzas.

In the late 1800s, Day's family had ranched in the Cherokee Strip area of Texas and Oklahoma, where the Miller brothers' family were early and successful ranchers. Ad Day's brother, Ford, had become hooked on rodeo. He entered competitions and enjoyed the excitement of cowboy performances.

The Day family did not take to the idea of his being a cowboy performer, and he went back to the ranch.

In about 1902, the boys' father, their Uncle Tony, and the rest of the family decided to move to the ranching land of the Swift Current and Medicine Hat area. Ad and Ford came with them.

At their new home on the Canadian prairies, the Days lost no time in getting involved with and organizing rodeos. By about 1903, Ad and local cowboy Ray Knight organized the Knight and Day Rodeo in Raymond, Alberta. Ad's brother Ford still loved competing, especially in roping and barrel racing. In 1904, the Days staged the first Medicine Hat "stampede," with bucking and roping contests, horse races, and harness races. The ranching family had suitable stock, and talented cowboys worked for them, but other cowboys had entered the contests, too. In 1905 and 1906, Indian races and relays were added to the Medicine Hat event.[5] There was no prize money for winners, but the bets on each event meant large sums of money changed hands.

Calgary had been awarded the 1908 Dominion Exhibition, one of the biggest events a community could stage. Grants to host the show were generous, with $50 000 from the federal government, $35 000 from the province, and $25 000 from the city.[6]

For Calgary's Dominion Exhibition, 2500 animals were entered, many of them shipped by rail. Working for the railway, H.C. McMullen was general livestock agent for the CPR, responsible for the shipping of livestock. He knew all the big ranchers, one of whom was Ad Day of Medicine Hat.

The Calgary organizers put on an outstanding show. No one could miss the potential of Calgary as a wild west show city, including Weadick, performing for the Miller brothers.

Maybe Calgary could stage something devoted entirely to frontier day events. Since "frontier days" was one of the themes at the Dominion Exhibition, the idea wasn't much of a stretch, but Weadick was talking to someone receptive to the idea – H.C. McMullen. In earlier times, McMullen had trailed cattle from Montana and ranch-related business had been good to him and to the CPR which employed him as livestock agent. As such, he had been responsible for the transportation needs of the Miller Brothers Show too and they had needed 45 railway cars to move the touring company and its livestock.

Calgary proved it could offer a great show, attract big crowds, and provide an audience interested in both cowboy competitions and wild west show performances. A few years later, not surprisingly, McMullens remembered his 1908 conversation with Weadick.

During the winter of 1911-12, Ad Day and McMullens talked about the increasing popularity of one-day rodeos. The resulting business was good for both of them, but the Days also were true advocates of the sport.

Ad planned that his 1912 event at Medicine Hat would be the first local rodeo to offer prize money. He wanted a big rodeo, a three-day event.[7]

Could a week of rodeo events work in Calgary? they wondered. After all, the city had a population of about 60 000.[8] If a rodeo like those in Pendleton and Cheyenne could be staged in

Both the man behind the visible camera and the one in front of it in this 1926 photo were important to Calgary Stampedes. Photographer W.J. Oliver shot images for postcards. Here, his subject was the flamboyant Guy Weadick. Courtesy of Glenbow Archives, NA 691-46.

Calgary, everyone would win. The added attraction of a travelling wild west show would mean more people attending, and many who would hop on a train to get there. Too, there would be a substantial transportation contract for the wild west show. The Miller brothers travelled with bucking stock and saddle horses, as well as other livestock, but large rodeos meant local stock contracts, too. Day had bucking stock that he could drive or ship to Calgary.

McMullens contacted Weadick. Timing proved perfect. The 101 Show had just returned from its European tour. Willing to do most anything for publicity, in Paris, Weadick rode his horse up the elevator to the top of the Eiffel Tower. He seemed the right type to promote a big show.

In the spring, wild west shows, circuses and midways planned summer touring schedules, and they sent press agents and advance men to meet with organizers in large communities. In March of 1912, Weadick and Tom Mix, who also worked with Miller Brothers, arrived in Calgary. Mix, of French-Canadian and Italian heritage, was another great talker and later became a top western movie star. They met with McMullens. Next, McMullens and Weadick met with Exhibition Manager Richardson and the exhibition's president.

Richardson and the president remained cautious about staging a week-long stampede. They planned to continue with their annual agricultural fair, with its midway and exhibits. Though interested, Richardson could do nothing. The exhibition grounds were booked with community events for the time requested.

However, given enough financial backing, the idea was still a possibility. The wild west show performers didn't work for free. Extra livestock would cost money. Top rodeo competitions should offer good prize money. Advertising was another expense. In fact, the expenses went on and on.

Day was willing to put up $10 000. Here again, H.C. McMullen continued to do his part and talked to the well-known, wealthy ranchers of the Calgary area. Not surprisingly, George Lane of the Bar U Ranch liked the idea. Pat Burns, Archie McLean, and A.E. Cross were also willing to front $25 000 each for the event. Funding was on the condition that the cowboy competitors and visitors got a good deal. There was enough money to offer top prize money, a total of $20 000.

The local ranchers had not become millionaires without knowing how to organize and manage for success. George Lane assumed duties of chairman. Weadick was appointed general manager, most of his work to be in promoting the event and attracting competitors. The other expert they needed was Ad Day. They didn't need his financial backing. They did need his knowledge and experience staging large rodeos. He could provide bucking horses and other livestock, and became arena director for the events.

With the important organizational decisions made and the division of responsibilities becoming clear, by the end of March, Weadick returned to the USA – and to the people he knew so well, the cowboys and cowgirls of the 101 Ranch.

Weadick could promise huge purses for world championship events. He didn't deserve credit for them, but he could promise them, and the backers would pay winners, even if the event lost money. Too, in the days before a governing body for such events, Weadick knew the rules of cowboy competitions. There weren't many. As long as the events were open to anyone in the world, no matter what race, color, or nationality, he could promote them as world championships.

Everything he advertised for the Stampede had been done before by the Miller brothers, other wild west shows, Frontier Days at Cheyenne, the Round-Up at Pendleton, or for past exhibitions at Calgary, Regina, Winnipeg, and other western Canadian communities.

One of those ideas was to invite old timers, a concept that had been reasonably popular since turn of the century. Weadick invited local whiskey trader Fred Kanouse and local ranchers. Another idea was to create replicas or re-enactments of the wild west. The Miller Brothers had looked to the American Cavalry and Indian wars for ideas. In Calgary, the original members of the North-West Mounted Police were invited to attend. Great parades were not new to western Canada, nor was First Nations participation. But Weadick did write letters inviting some of the competitors, performers, and local aboriginal bands to participate in the Stampede and parade.

When things became uncertain, Reverend John McDougal was asked to ensure First Nations participation. Then, just before the Stampede, Weadick and McMullen made a trip to the States, apparently to iron out details with the Miller brothers and recruit more cowboys for events.

The Stampede opened 2 September. Cowboy artists were in attendance. Charlie Russell, another Miller brothers' connection, exhibited work. Ed Borein, who knew Ad Day's family when they had ranched in the Cherokee Strip, brought his work, too.

The second day of the Stampede, it rained. Rain continued to muddy the infield and plague the riders. Despite the weather, the competitions and performances were enthusiastically received.

The Stampede proved a financial success, too. Some made money on it. Initial figures indicated that the event grossed $123 000. Expenses totaled about $103 000, including prize money.

There were many payments to be made, too. Buildings, services, and advertising were not free. The Reverend John McDougall was paid $390 for encouraging and organizing First Nations. Weadick was paid $425 for his publicity and managerial work. Rodeo stock had cost $1500. Competitors won $15 992 in cash, as well as belts and buckles and saddles. Of that, the Canadians claimed $3200 in specifically Canadian championships. They had been an after thought and not part of the advance advertising, but with Americans – many of them on tour with the Miller brothers – winning most competitions and world titles, organizers had quickly added the Canadian titles so locals would be happy. Still, the Big Four were not pleased so little had gone to competitors.

In addition, late bills were submitted for another $5000. That left $15 000 to be disbursed among organizers. Of the profits, 25% was to go to each of Weadick, Day, and McMullen. The last 25% was to be disbursed among the Big Four.[9] The Big Four had promised profits to charity. With so little in the pot, they decided not to take their share but still contribute to the local hospital. Arena Director Day was paid $5000. His jobs were absolutely essential, and he may have disbursed some of it to his pick-up men. He continued to contribute to rodeo history, organizing events from Winnipeg to Montana. Although he and his family sold their Alberta ranch by 1978, in recognition of his contribution to rodeo, Addison P. Day was nominated to the National Cowboy Hall of Fame.

As an organizer, H.C. McMullen had made significant contributions. The CPR had transported the wild west show, livestock, organizers, and performers. Even though the railway might reduce ticket prices, the 40 000 visitors from outside Calgary bought rail tickets. To the Big Four, the CPR and McMullen had done well by the event. He was paid $4000, but Pat Burns urged him to donate part of it to the Calgary hospital.

In the end, Weadick received an additional $3100, an enormous amount of money, given that he had already been paid for his publicity work.[10] Mysteries remain. What had he done that hadn't been done many times before – including in Calgary? How was the Miller Brothers Wild West Show paid? Was it only through ticket sales? And who really deserved the credit?

Again and again, flamboyant Guy Weadick said he dreamed up the Calgary Stampede. Over the years, he did not prove to be its best supporter. In 1923, when the Stampede and exhibition amalgamated, he was hired for the rodeo season as the arena manager. As well, he announced. He liked to drink and talk rodeo, and he was an expert at both. In 1932, the drinking led to trouble. Having tossed back one too many, sure he was not getting all the credit he deserved, and mad at the organization, he decided to broadcast his complaints to the audience. With Weadick making a fool of himself and everyone else, the microphone was grabbed from him.

The organization fired Weadick, who sued the Stampede and exhibition for wrongful dismissal. By March of 1935, the court decided that, despite all Weadick's drinking, he had never been given adequate warning that his job was at risk. Also, the court determined, the socializing could be construed as part of the job and helpful in business dealings. Although the contract was seasonal, he had worked for the exhibition for almost ten years, so he was entitled to six months notice. Weadick was awarded $2700, the equivalent of half his yearly salary.[11]

Katherine Stinson, an American flyer, and E.L. Richardson, General Manager of the Calgary Exhibition and Stampede, created lasting memories for fair and stampede visitors. Courtesy of Glenbow Archives, NA-1451-26.

Also, he sued the exhibition board for $100 000 for using "original ideas and methods, the sole property of Guy Weadick." In addition, he claimed the word "stampede" was his. He wanted the courts to restrain the board from holding a stampede, because it was his show. The exhibition claimed the word had been in common use for years. Also, ideas used during his employment belonged to the organization.[12]

Weadick lost his case, but maintained the myth that he, and he alone, had dreamed up the Calgary Stampede. He continued in the rodeo business and in "selling" his talents. According to *Billboard*, for which he wrote a rodeo column, in August, 1936, Weadick worked for the Yorkton Stampede. Not surprisingly, he got favorable reviews. The same year, the magazine reported Weadick "presented *his* second annual Stampede at Lethbridge Exhibition." Once again, he had credit for an event that already had a very long and successful history. On the 27th of February, 1937, *Billboard* reported that Weadick, "internationally known producer of Western spectacles and championship rodeos and originator and many years guiding hand of Calgary (AB) Stampede" was to direct the state fair in North Dakota.

After his wife died, Weadick returned to the USA. In a good-will gesture, he was invited back to the Calgary Stampede in 1952. Of course, he had contributed to the success of the event, especially between 1923 and the mid-thirties. But his claim to being "originator" and "guiding hand" diminished the contributions of others.

One such forgotten hero was the soft-spoken E.L. Richardson. In 1903, he began working for the Calgary Exhibition Association. In 1911, he was present at the first meeting of fair managers in western Canada. By 1936, he was the only manager in attendance at the first meeting who was still serving as fair manager. At the time, the Western Canada Association of Exhibitions president stated that Richardson was the longest serving fair manager in North America.[13]

While manager, he had both hired and fired Weadick. In 1940, after 37 years and witnessing phenomenal changes, he retired from his position with the Calgary Exhibition and Stampede. He deserved enormous credit, but he didn't ride around the arena on his horse or hold the microphone. He didn't wear a Stetson. He wore glasses and a suit. He looked like the man he really was, an executive who capably managed a huge and complicated business. He went to work every day, didn't overly indulge, and didn't sue the exhibition board.

Undoubtedly, part of the reason Weadick gained so much acclaim was that he could talk the leg off an alligator. Handsome Weadick, wearing his cowboy hat and chaps, looked great in publicity shots, too. It was the image people wanted as the "originator" of the wonderful Calgary Stampede.

Chapter 5

Sporting Competition Anyone?

A Sporting World

At the annual summer events, the competitions were as varied as the country. On the coast, war canoe races thrilled audiences. Where there was lumbering, there were logger contests. Especially in the lake country of central BC and southern Manitoba, countless sparkling lakes meant sports fans cared about canoeing, swimming, diving, and water-skiing contests. The cowboy competitions held at early fairs were so popular they became a unifying theme. In many communities, rodeo was the biggest attraction at the fairgrounds. Over the years, the sporting events became not only a successful component of the festivities, but sometimes they were essential for the survival of the entire event.

JULY 7-12 1947

This photo of winning driver Ron Glass was likely taken in 1946. Glass was from Torrington, AB, and his team was sponsored by John Phelan of Red Deer, AB. Courtesy of Glenbow Archives, Calgary Exhibition & Stampede, M2160 Bk. C151B, f36.

Not every sporting competition was an athletic one. Nor were the events limited to the best athlete in the community or region. Heavy horse pulls and plowing contests required something other than an individual with a fit body and athletic talent. Log rolling competitions required the balance of a gymnast, but some competitions, such as the war canoe races, depended on teamwork. Boxing matches and games such as lacrosse were featured at some fairs, too.

With the exception of later-day chuckwagon races and certain novelty races, the competitions not only attracted crowds, they had very early beginnings. At community sports days, a wide variety of events garnered keen interest, and it was logical to add them to the annual summer gatherings. They guaranteed the attendance of serious sports fans. The families and neighbors who wanted to support one of their own filled seats. Those with limited enthusiasm for sports could choose to spend time at countless exhibits and amusements. The marriage was perfect.

Western Canadian heroes and heroines were created during the sports competitions. Even some of the animal competitors became legends. Still, two forms of competition outshone all others in western Canada. Horse racing and rodeo drew enthusiastic crowds from Victoria to Manitoba. Horse culture was part of daily life both for city and country people at the time of the first fairs. For everyone, horses meant transportation, but they were valued for other reasons, too. A fine horse, whether it could race like the wind, or whirl, buck and descend like a cyclone, was a marvel to behold – and people came in the hundreds and thousands to catch the action at the races or rodeo events.

Sport of Kings and Commoners

Horse races, in every imaginable form, were winners with fair-goers. Throughout the country, people loved the excitement, and some loved the betting action, too.

With countless enthusiasts, from early on, races were held on holidays, at community picnics, and on sports days. Victoria staged its first official thoroughbred race was in 1868, and Vancouver soon followed suit.

Edmonton was a little slower to embrace the races. For Dominion Day in 1884, the most important event of the day was a tug-of-war between a local team and men from Bear Lake [St. Albert]. Of less importance were the horse races, and to the dismay of some, betting led to one person having lost $2. At first, informal bets had been for prized possessions, or a few cents or dollars exchanged hands, but sometimes, the stakes might be shockingly high for the period. In 1894, the top prize in Edmonton was $20 for a one mile [1.6 km] stallion trot.

By early in the 1900s, horse races had become an important part of many fairs, and provinces had their own special derbies in which competing horses had to be from the province. In 1905, the first Alberta Derby in Calgary had a field of five horses. The winner was a well-known eight-year-old named The Bishop, who was owned by a local man and had run in many races.

In fact, the races became so important the Western Canada Fair and Racing Circuit [WCFRC] was organized to oversee not only fairs but races. By 1913, pari-mutuel betting had become popular. When New York State made gambling illegal, pari-mutuel equipment became readily available at bargain basement prices.

Edmonton Exhibition Manager W.J. Stark was off to New York. He bought 10 machines for $900. On his return trip, he was able to off-set costs by renting them to Regina for a week at a price of $200. By August of 1913, employees operating the pari-mutuel machines for the Edmonton Exhibition were better paid than any other workers on the grounds, and they were busy. That year, the pari-mutuels returned 95 percent of the wagers to bettors, but the exhibition still made a profit of $6781.15.[1]

Eventually, members of the western Canada circuit felt some pressure to join the Canadian Trotting Association, centred in Toronto. It was a force in organizing and regulating races, but in the west, the regional and American associations were the major players. The western Canadian association was Johnny-on-the-spot, and members felt certain it could better handle all the business.

"Where we get one horse from east of Winnipeg, we get ten from south of the line," said E.L. Richardson of Calgary in a 27 August, 1914, letter to W.J. Stark, in Edmonton.[2]

Most races were mixed, including both running races and harness races. They were sponsored by various groups, some members of the organization, some more loosely associated with the WCFRC. One race might be intended primarily for local horses while others drew some of the best horses, jockeys, and drivers on the continent. Also, races were organized by local turf clubs or driving clubs, but there was usually a strong relationship between these clubs, the local fair associations, and local agricultural societies.

Turf and driving clubs used the same grounds, grandstand, gates, and race track as the fair association. When the race track needed attention, the turf club might put up funds to pay workers while the fair association provided wagons and teams. Often the annual advertising materials included dates for both races and fairs. Sometimes even the people organizing the events were the same. The touring circuit for jockeys and horses was scheduled to accommodate everyone, and sometimes the races were held a number of times in the same community between spring and fall.

In 1914, for the WCFRC, the total purse was $355 000. Much more than fair entertainment, the races impacted purses, pockets, and bottom lines, especially at the larger exhibitions, where pari-mutuel machines handled bets. Even with the First World War, the 1915 season was not entirely cancelled. Exhibition grounds were ideal for military training facilities, but communities often negotiated with militia and armed forces departments to ensure their access to the grounds for the annual fairs and races.

During the war, some associations scheduled fewer days for fairs, and some fairs scheduled fewer races or opted for local jockeys and horses. With the business of the WCFRC curtailed but not discontinued, financial negotiations were more crucial. By February of 1915, circuit managers were negotiating with Francis A. O'Toole for handling some pari-mutuel machines. Winnipeg had opted out of the races, and instead of guaranteeing the 32 days of the previous season, the association could offer only 25 days. Even that was uncertain. Brandon and Calgary were definite. Edmonton wanted races for both the exhibition and spring meet, but Regina hadn't fully committed. Saskatoon was considering withdrawing and resurrecting its less formal Races and Sports Day. The tour might be 21 or fewer days!

Downtime while on the circuit was a hardship. Writing from New York, O'Toole complained about the problems for himself and his assistant, Mr. Crofts, in a letter to Ernie Richardson, secretary for the association.

"We practically would be working for the Railroad and Hotels which you know are expensive in the Northwest," he said. The two men had got along well before, but O'Toole had his price. "One hundred and thirty-five dollars per day, but the total days must be at least twenty one."

In early April, they came to a settlement but O'Toole had not been the only one to be concerned. According to Chas Trimble, also an American, who had negotiated with the circuit, paying the hotel bills and transportation would be at least $250, but he was willing to compromise on his fee and even take a 25% cut from the previous year.

For the circuit members, there were many expected expenses, specifically related to the races. Gates and starters cost money. At the time, a leather saddle cost $8 to $15. Stockmen and runners wanted $12 per racing day. A head cashier expected $10 per day; other cashiers wanted $6 to $8 each; the ticket seller expected $8; and the clickers wanted $3 per day.

But there was money in the races, too.

In March, the race committee for the WCFRC settled on a total available purse of $7900 for harness race events and $6100 for running events. The Saskatoon Industrial Exhibition went ahead with five races for each day of their event. The purses ranged from usually $150 to $500, but $700 was at stake for the 1½ mile Saskatoon Derby. Generally, winners received 70%, second 20%, and third 10% in each race, though local autonomy could dictate differently.

Finally, details were in place and the races were on. The war continued to affect the races as attractions at fairs. Americans continued to bring horses, act as starters, and handle the pari-mutuel betting. With the end of the war, the cost of services went up, but by 1920, the summer racing circuit was as strong as ever. Class A Circuit consisted of Calgary, Edmonton, Saskatoon, Brandon, and Regina. Class B Circuit now included Red Deer, Camrose, Lloydminster, North Battleford, Prince Albert, Yorkton, Swift Current, Weyburn, and Medicine Hat.

Over the years, some great Canadian jockeys were raised in the ranch lands of western Canada and got their start at fairs in small towns. Two such jockeys were George Woolf and Johnny Longden.

Nicknamed the Ice Man, Woolf had parents who might have encouraged him to be a great rodeo competitor or circus performer. Woolf's parents had settled in Cardston, AB, in 1903.

Horse races have been a popular spectator sport at western Canadian fairs and rodeos for well over a century. These races were staged in 1912 at Queen's Park in Penticton, BC. Courtesy of Penticton Museum, 2666 B.

Before that, his father had ridden in rodeos in Utah and driven a stage in Montana. His mother had performed as a trick rider in circuses. George was born in 1909, and his talented family knew almost everything there was to know about riding horses. By the time George was seven, he was racing on bush tracks, even riding his father's horses in races at Cardston and Fort Macleod.

His two brothers gravitated to rodeo, but George loved racing horses.

In 1926, Woolf first rode in a Calgary race, and in 1928, during his first year of "recognized" competition, he won 106 of 556 races.[3] That year, he rode more horses and won more races than in any other year, but those on the American circuit of later years would be the most important in his career.

Woolf became one of the most successful and affluent jockeys in the business. In 1938, he rode the famous winner Seabiscuit to victory in the Pimlico Special, a match race between Seabiscuit and War Admiral, the great North American horse who had never been beaten. The ride guaranteed Woolf's spot in the annals of racing history.

The Iceman's most successful years were 1942-1944. In 1942, he won 23 stakes with purses for the owners totaling $341 680. In 1944, his 14 wins netted $338 135 for owners.[4] Woolf rode horses to many other wins over the years, including all the major American races. A diabetic, he took a fall from a horse during the 1946 Santa Anna race and died at age 36, but for years to come, he was still considered the greatest jockey ever to come from western Canada.

Johnny Longden was another great jockey who got his start at fairs in southern Alberta. He was born in England in 1907, but his Mormon parents moved to Taber, AB. At 13, he quit school and started working in the mines. After an accident in the mine in which he could have been hurt and lost his sight, Longden left the job. At 4 feet 10 inches [147 cm], weighing only 100 pounds [45.3 kg] but very strong, he was a natural as a jockey.

Longden rode at local fairs, competing in quarter-horse races, relays, and Roman riding races. His first jockey contract in Calgary was eventually sold to Harry Young, who held the contract but had no horses. When Young couldn't get horses for Longden to ride, the early years became a matter of survival. He raced in the USA and other western Canadian cities, but his record was not glorious.

His contract was sold and resold. Finally, he graduated to riding thoroughbreds for E.A. "Sleepy" Armstrong. Soon he was on his way to the major American circuits and phenomenal fame. During the 1940s and 1950s, he rode horses that garnered Horse of the Year and Top Money Maker awards in the US. In 1943 and 1945, Longden was the North American champion for both number of wins and money won. In 1947 and 1948, he also won more races than any other jockey.

Some of his most memorable rides were in British Columbia and Longden chose to break one of his records at Vancouver's Exhibition Park. On a horse called Prince Scorpion, 16 August 1965, he became the first jockey to record 6000 wins.

In 1966, Longden retired. Although his last race was in California, it was on a British Columbia bred horse named Royal George. The race would mean the 6026th win for Longden. Years later, in the 1970s, Bill Shoemaker broke his record. Still, the jockey who spent his early life in Taber and first raced at small Alberta fairs remained among North America's greatest.

During four years of competing in Canada and the USA, Royal George won 21 of 45 races. In terms of money won, the race horse would place second to Northern Dancer, the great winner of later years, but the Canadian bred horse was also one of western Canada's greats.

Tom Three Persons, Cyclone, and a Whirlwind of Prejudice

Some winners did not get the treatment they deserved. One of the great heroes of the rodeo arena was Tom Three Persons. Unfortunately, in rodeo, as elsewhere, prejudice could raise its ugly head. It didn't matter how good he was as a contestant, he was Indian, and that made him susceptible to stereotyping.

The indigenous people had their share of excellent riders, and many competed in rodeo. They also succeeded in horse races – both in the races open to anyone and those open only to First Nations men or women. Sometimes, though not always, the newspapers reported their names. By 1912, Tom Three Persons was a world champion bucking bronc rider, but along with his fame came defamation and libel.

Tom was born in 1888; his mother was from the Blood tribe near Fort Macleod. From his teen to early adult years, working both with his own cattle and during roundups on the reserve, Tom turned into a great rider. He was friendly, generous, well-liked, loved challenge, and feared nothing. Good looking, he attracted women, but trouble lurked in matters of love, and he did have a dark side.

In his numerous marriages and relationships with women, he was verbally and physically abusive. He gambled. Though proof was often scanty, rumors circulated about thefts. Alcohol was another nemesis. The vices were evident in his youth. By middle age, he had serious problems, even though he had become wealthy.

Tom first competed in an official cowboy competition in 1908 at the Lethbridge Fair. The field of contestants was small, and bucking was the only rodeo event. Twenty-year-old Tom came in second. Later that year, he competed in Montana, and in 1909, he took the prize money for the bucking event at Lethbridge. His reputation as an outstanding contestant grew.

The libel suffered by Native cowboy and rodeo champion Tom Three Persons became a personal and life-long tragedy. The lie was repeated so many times by so many people, he could never escape the damage to his reputation. Courtesy of Glenbow Archives, NA 1137-1.

Interested in travelling wild west shows, rancher Ad Day of Medicine Hat decided to take four top cowboys to the 1911 Winnipeg Exhibition. He had heard of Tom's talent and wrote the Indian agent, who supported the venture. By the time the group left Winnipeg, Tom was an avid rodeo competitor. Ad liked Tom, who stayed at the Day ranch for a while, breaking horses and working on the round-up. With Tom's connections to Ad and with support from the Indian agent, Tom entered bareback and saddle bronc riding at the 1912 Calgary Stampede.

The star of the bucking stock was owned by Bertha Blanchett, who arrived in Calgary with the Miller Brothers' Wild West Show. A fine horse with a star on his face, Cyclone had never been ridden. First making a name for himself at Big Bear, California, in 1910, he had been nicknamed "The Terror."

Saddling him was almost as difficult as riding him. Without proper chutes, bucking stock was saddled by a group of cowboys, some on foot, while others butted their saddle horses tight against the broncs to hold them still. Cyclone reared so high, the job was impossible. Cowboys had to throw him down and hold him there while others somehow saddled him.

During the Stampede, Cyclone lived up to his nickname. Tom watched while Cyclone threw his 128th rider. The next rider to draw him was local Canadian cowboy Clem Gardner. Again, Cyclone reared so high he seemed destined to throw himself on his back. Then he pitched forward. Five times, he reared to throw the cowboy. Finally, Clem lost his balance, and Tom watched as Clem hit the dirt.

Tom, four other Canadians, and eight Americans were in the finals for the saddle bronc. Three Persons drew Cyclone.

For the finals, the rain subsided, but the infield was sloppy. Painstakingly Cyclone was saddled, but once he was up, he pulled away. Wanting to throw the saddle, he bucked his way around

Between 1927 and 1936, the Canada Kid (Lee Ferris) thrilled crowds. His star performances were in steer riding, steer decorating, bareback, and saddle bronc. He was Canadian All Around Cowboy in 1928 and 1929. Courtesy of Stockmen's Memorial Foundation, CHRA 052-Vol.2.

the infield. Finally, he was recaptured. Had the bucking taken the edge off Cyclone? Or was the horse angry? Was Tom in for even greater trouble? Tom had watched the earlier attempts to break the bronc. Did he know enough to beat the horse?

"Tom, don't loosen up when Cyclone rears up."

Years later, A.P. Day, Jr., had remembered his father's advice to Tom. "Give him plenty of slack on your halter rope and hit him down the hind leg with your quirt."[5]

Day, Jr. was ten or eleven when he heard those words and watched the famous ride.

Finally, Tom was in the saddle. Cyclone reared. Tom left the rein loose but he did not loosen up in the saddle and allow himself to sit back when the horse reared. Instead, he leaned forward. When Cyclone pitched forward, Tom was ready, and he didn't hurl over the bronc's head.

As if confirming his name, Cyclone twisted relentlessly. He reared and leaped on all fours. Tom sat firm. Cyclone reared again. It was no use. As the horse's owner Bertha Blanchett watched, she and the crowd realized Cyclone had been beaten. Tom had won against the top American riders and on the toughest horse of all. The crowd was on its feet, applauding and roaring approval.

Tom Three Persons of the Blood reserve was saddle bronc champion of the world. As well as fame, he had won $1000 in prize money, a new saddle, and gold championship belt buckle. Since he was the only Canadian to claim world honors at the event, Pat Burns added $500 to his prize money.[6]

The win was followed by heartbreak. Tom was a winner and a Canadian Indian. The local newspapers reported his glorious achievement. One, the *Albertan*, went further. The paper reported that, after a bout of drunkenness, Tom had been freed from jail to compete in the Stampede.

"I was more sick than drunk," the paper supposedly quoted Tom.[7]

This time, he had not been guilty of drunkenness. Before the Stampede, he had been guilty of nothing. The reports were lies.

Only following his win had his actions been unconscionable. First, he did a fine thing, buying his wife a new silk dress to celebrate.

But ugly things happen. Someone pushed Tom's wife while near an outdoor toilet. The dress was dirtied. Tom was furious, and he beat her for allowing it to happen. They didn't attend the lavish celebrations. Perhaps they hadn't been invited.[8] Perhaps the incident with his wife had dampened spirits and changed plans.

When the people of Fort Macleod learned of the news story about Tom's drunken jailhouse episode and learned from the Mounties that it was not true, they were enraged their local hero had suffered the attack. They threatened to sue the newspaper and writer on Tom's behalf. Finally, the newspaper published an apology, but it was too late. The "story" had become widely known and was repeated again and again.

In the following years, Tom had numerous rodeo injuries. He competed and won contests but not another world championship. His problems with alcohol did land him in jail. But, a good cowboy, he became wealthy with his ranching and cattle operation.

To some, Tom remained a great friend, fine mentor, and helpful neighbor. First Nations people honored him repeatedly after his victory. He was a hero in both white and Native cultures – despite what the press had done to taint his image.

Cowgirl Champs: Calgary

"Whoopp-e-e," not "Yahoo," was the cry in Calgary in 1912. What was really worth a "Whoopp-e-e" was the competition amongst the cowgirls! Not all of them were born or had homes in Oklahoma, but almost all were connected with the Miller Brothers 101 Ranch Wild West Show from Oklahoma, which staged the evening performance in the horse show building. Despite most of the cowgirls knowing each other very well, they were intensely competitive in the arena for both the 1912 Calgary Stampede and the 1913 Winnipeg Stampede.

Having the women compete, as well as perform in the evening show, was a huge draw. By then, many 101 girls were big names in cowgirl circles. At rodeos in Cheyenne, Pendleton, and Los Angeles, they had been performers, competitors, and great crowd pleasers. Prior to 1912, both Calgary and Winnipeg audiences had seen some of the famous cowgirls, and organizers and financiers were willing to put up hefty purses to entice them to compete in the rodeo arena of the two Canadian cities.

A.P. DAY

In both Calgary and Winnipeg, four women's events were planned: fancy and trick riding, relay race, fancy roping, and bucking horse riding. Because they were open to women from anywhere, the events were advertised as world championships. As at many other rodeos, to encourage them, the women weren't required to pay the entry fees levied against cowboys. The only exception was the bucking bronc competition, where the prize was $1000, the

As arena director, Ad Day was responsible for the infield, track, competitors, stock, and safety. Courtesy of Archives of Manitoba, Winnipeg Stampede, 1913, 28.

same as for the bronc riding cowboys and double the amount of any other category except cowboy steer roping.

Of course, the cowboys and cowgirls had to submit entry forms, but very few local girls entered the 1912 Calgary competitions. Where three cash prizes were to be awarded in a category, at least five entries were usually required. However, with so few cowgirls competing, three or four became acceptable in a competition.

When early registrations remained light, Manager Guy Weadick, already in Calgary, wrote Fanny Sperry, offering special encouragement. "I'm sure you can win some big money," he said, adding that it would be a world championship.

After its Calgary stop, the Wild West Show was to continue its tour, but since it was September and near the end of the touring season, the show and competitors had some flexibility regarding time.

So, most of the 101 cowgirls finally entered the contests. Flores [Florence] La Due, married to Weadick, was a fancy roper and she definitely planned to compete. Prairie Rose Henderson was an impressive rider with the wild west show, and as early as 1904, she had been riding broncs at Cheyenne. Too, Dolly Mullins, married to the assistant arena director for Calgary, was a great trick rider. Other 101 performers to compete or perform at the event were Bertha Blancett, Goldie St. Clair, Hazel Walker, Tillie Baldwin, Annie Shaffer, and Blanche McGaughey, but they didn't all compete in each event.

The best known of the women performers and competitors was Lucille Mulhall. Audiences across the continent were spell-bound as they watched her rope and throw long-horned steers. As a child, she had begun performing with her father's wild west show, moved to the Miller Brothers' Show, and was not only talented with a horse and a rope, but a seasoned performer. In many instances, she came out a winner against male competitors and won money, whether prize money or wagers. In 1904, she had garnered fame by roping and tying three steers in just over two minutes. For doing so, she won $10 000.

In Calgary, the cowgirls received the warmest of welcomes, and from the start, the competition among them was intense. Mulhall was La Due's toughest competition in fancy or trick roping. But La Due had been dazzling and had even roped and tied a man in little more than an instant. She won the title of wold champion for Cowgirl Fancy Roping. As well as the title, her win netted $300 and a belt and buckle. For Cowgirl Contest Best Outfit Open to the World, Saddle, Bridle, Costume and Horse, La Due won a city lot valued at $200. A Calgary cowgirl to win in the same category was Elberta McMullen, organizer H. McMullen's daughter, and the $100 diamond ring seems to have placed her second to La Due, or have been one of the Canadian titles.

Dolly Mullins wond $300, a belt and buckle, and title for Fancy and Trick Riding. For the Cowgirl Relay Race, only saddle horses were allowed, not professional racing horses, and the competitors had to ride a mount a distance, dismount, and continue racing on the next horse. Bertha Blancett won the title and purse of $500.

Lucille Mulhall had the skills to compete not only against women, but against cowboys. At many rodeos, the competition rules didn't mention women, so bending them was possible. Then Mulhall could compete against the men, and she did. Despite her long divided skirt, which seemed a disadvantage, she offered exhibition performances of steer roping at Calgary. On two days, her times were so good she could have beaten the cowboys. She was such a huge hit, organizers awarded her the title, Cowgirl Steer Roping Champion of the World.

The big story was the women's bronc riding event, and the first prize money was $1000. In the 1912 competition, five women entered: Hazel Walker, Annie Shaffer, Bertha Kilpernick Blancett, Fanny Sperry Steele, and Goldie St. Clair. All were linked to the 101.

Bertha Blancett (Blanchett) was a talented steer roper and multi-talented cowgirl. She had competed at numerous rodeos, including at Cheyenne, where she performed exhibition bronc riding in 1904. At Pendleton in 1911, the rodeo featured its first cowgirl bronc riding competition as an official event. In it, she had an easy win for the world championship title. She rode slick, meaning that, like the men, she didn't have her stirrups hobbled under the horse's belly. The style of riding was more difficult, but women were awarded extra points for doing so. In 1912, she won the world championship at Pendleton, too. The same year, for the world championship in Calgary, she had more trouble with Fanny Sperry Steele and Goldie St. Clair.

Fanny Sperry (Steele) was a big-name cowgirl who sometimes worked for the Miller brothers. At the time, she competed under her maiden name, Sperry, and considered Mitchell, Montana, as home. Between 1905 and 1908, Fanny competed in relay races, many with three other Montana women, and made a great income at it. As well, she could bust a bronc.

Goldie St. Clair, also with the 101 and actually from the Cherokee strip in Oklahoma, was another outstanding talent. Unlike Sperry, she rode hobble in bronc riding. A flamboyant rider, she had won the women's bronc riding world championships at the Jamestown World's Fair in 1907. Like Flores La Due, who eventually made her home near High River, AB, Goldie would settle at Brooks, AB, with her husband – but that came later in life.

Stories about the show-down between the women abound, some of them more fanciful, but because some rides were exhibition performances at the horse show building, the finals were on a weekend, cowboy competitions were more thoroughly reported than the women's, and newspapers weren't published on the Sunday, exact information about the cowgirls' battles with the broncs remains a mystery.

However, each day the women rode and crowds were enthusiastic, despite rainy weather and a few lacklustre performances by horses. Some of the most exciting moments were not in the outdoor arena but during the evening shows. In fact, on the last Friday evening performance, 8 September, McGaughey rode Wildcat. The horse plunged against the board fence. He plunged against it again, jamming the cowgirl's leg, and as she tried to get free, she was thrown. Then when she staggered to her feet, the audience cheered wildly.

During the bronc riding competition, Hazel Walker also had her troubles. Riding Buttons, she took the worst spill of the contest. Neither did Annie Shaffer have outstanding rides. That

Acclaimed at early American rodeos and on the wild west show circuit, these three women competed and performed at the 1912 Calgary Stampede. Blanche McGaughey is at left, Bertha Blanchett is centre, and Dollie Mullins is on the right. Courtesy of Historical Committee, Calgary Exhibition and Stampede.

left Fanny, Goldie, and Bertha as prime contenders. The weather was so terrible the Stampede had to be extended for two days, but that only built suspense when the battle raged on amongst the women.

For one of her final rides, St. Clair drew Red Wing. Although her husband didn't want her to ride the killer horse, she intended to do so. A number of days before the Stampede, in the horse show building, some cowboys had been trying out the broncs. One afternoon, when bucked from a horse and kicked, a cowboy named Joe La Mar died. Most accounts, including newspapers, said the horse was Red Wing, through years later, Johnny Mullins, assistant arena director, maintained the killer horse was McLane Sorrel.

Other cowgirls rode before Goldie. The horses bucked but did not give outstanding performances. Then, the audience was roused when Hazel Walker had trouble with a horse called Hellcat. It stumbled, fell to its knees, and her foot caught under her mount. She had to be pulled free. Some said she fainted into the arms of a cowboy; others that she remounted and rode the horse.

Next came the announcement that Goldie St. Clair would ride Red Wing. The crowd gasped.

Coming out of the chute, Red Wing plunged, twisted, pitched, heaved like a demon. Riding hobbled, her arm thrashed, but somehow, St. Clair stayed in the saddle.

The crowd went wild.

The next day, the competition was close, and Sperry came in third, behind St. Clair and Blancett.

The following rainy day, soaked to the bone, Fanny drew a bronc who gave her a wildcat ride, but she did well. Blancett stayed in the saddle, but her bronc was not spectacular. Drawing a "ladies" horse, St. Clair had a weak ride.

Leading up to the finals, Blancett, St. Clair, and Sperry were neck and neck for points.

The day of the finals the sky was blue. Weadick rode into the ring. All proceeds from the evening show would go to the wife and children of the cowboy killed by Red Wing, he announced.

Then the finals got underway. The men's competitions were thrilling. For the women competitors, the crowd was even louder.

This time, at least according to some accounts, Sperry had drawn Red Wing! With a good ride and the extra points for slick riding, she could beat Blancett and St. Clair. Blancett, who drew a horse called Two Bars, had a spectacular ride. Not only that, she rode slick. The crowd roared approval. Next was St. Clair on a bronc called Dish Rag. The horse gave a brutal perform-

ance. St. Clair managed to stay on its back – but she was riding hobbled. Still, the crowd applauded wildly.

Sperry was next. The best had been saved until the last, the announcer claimed.

Red Wing performed like the outlaw he was. Fanny competed like the greatest of contestants. Not for an instant did she lose her balance or control as the killer horse plunged and twisted. Finally, the hazer pulled her free.[10]

Fanny Sperry Steele won the World Champion Lady Bucking Horse Rider title in both the Calgary 1912 and Winnipeg 1913 stampedes. As well as competing, she performed with the 101 Ranch Wild West Show. Courtesy of Archives of Manitoba, Winnipeg Stampede 1913, 9.

Almost instantaneously, to the roars of the crowd, the announcer proclaimed Sperry Cowgirl Bronc Riding Champion of the World. Not only was she the cowgirl champ, she claimed the $1000 first prize money, and prize belt, buckle, and saddle.[11]

Most certainly, she won the championship. Other memories of competition details faded over the years and stories changed. Who really did ride the outlaw and when? Some said St. Clair's final ride had been on Red Wing.

Johnny Mullins, assistant arena director, didn't remember the event quite as others had. A man of integrity, in later years, he was made a member of the Cowboy Hall of Fame.

St. Clair had never ridden Red Wing in competition, Mullins maintained. Her ride on the killer horse was during the exhibition performance to benefit the La Mar family. It had been at the horse show building, where most performances were part of the 101 Miller Brothers Wild West Show.[12]

What is certain is that Sperry won, though some claimed St. Clair should have had the title.

Winning Horses, Winning Young Riders

Each year, cowboys and cowgirls established reputations as the best in the west and often in the world. They seemed born to the saddle and born to the life. The horses and bulls that couldn't be ridden gained reputations, too. Some saddle horses were naturals for calf-roping or cattle penning competitions. Some horses seemed born to be jumpers and others to be bucking broncs.

Peter Welsh toured with the best of the best. Intuitively, he spotted winners, and he drew them into his business. A Scottish immigrant, he had a livery stable at Calgary. Soon after settling, he had begun buying horses, which the CPR resold to settlers. As a judge of horses, few could compare. Too, he knew riding talent when he saw it.

Constantly around horses, his sons became outstanding riders, and Welsh recognized their abilities. Despite being only children and teenagers, Josie, Lawrence (known as Louis), Alfie, and "Tiny" were among the best riders in the country

To many fans of great horses and great cowboys, the time between about 1919 and late 1940s was a golden period. During the twenties, Welsh, his sons, his horses, and his rodeo company became known throughout Canada and in parts of the USA. Initially, Welsh had entered horses, ridden by his sons, in the show jump competitions. Their first serious competitions were on the horse show circuit and in jumping competitions staged at community fairs, some of which had wild west show tents or performers.

Welsh decided to gather the best cowboys and best stock for a travelling rodeo, one that would truly impress audiences. By 1925, Welsh had his own travelling rodeo, the Alberta Stampede Company.

Despite their youth, his boys both rode competitively and helped stage events. It seemed that there was almost nothing Josie couldn't do when it came to riding and horses. For the company, along with newspaper man and publicist Fred Kennedy, he ran much of the day-to-day work of the rodeos. When he wasn't helping stage events, Josie thrilled crowds with his abilities, one of which was performing a standing Roman ride over jumps.

The other cowboys that Welsh, Sr., contracted for his tours had enormous talent, too. In the years to come, they proved their talent time and time again, and some became rodeo champions. To run a travelling rodeo meant contracting many cowboys. The competition was real, and they worked hard to win day money and the final event, with its $1500 purse. By contract, they made exhibition rides, and usually, they could add even more to their wallets with additional jobs or rides.

These friendly looking cowboys, Pete Knight and Pete LeGrandeur, were serious competitors and champions. Each had dozens of wins in the rodeo arena. Courtesy of Historical Committee, Calgary Exhibition and Stampede.

The winning cowboys – men such as Pete Knight, the Canada Kid, the La Grandeur brothers, Slim and Leo Watrin, Frank Sharp, Peter Vandermeer, Joe Fisher, and Dick Cosgrave, who would later become one of the great chuckwagon drivers of all time – were with Welsh during his glory years from late 1924 to 1927. Also with him was talented roper Jim Carry and wife Stastia Carry, who had made a name for herself in great American circuses and who was as comfortable riding a horse as an elephant.

In 1927, Welsh's travelling rodeo faced financial ruin. His show was over, but many of the cowboys he had recruited went on to impress the world. So did the horses in his string – or at least some continued to perform as the winners they were. One of those all-time greats was Midnight. Others included Five to Midnight, Tumbleweed, Grave Digger, Bassano, Bay Dynamite, and the Gold Dust Twins. Welsh had his show jumpers, too, including Madamoiselle, Calgary Lad, Kickapoo, and Barra Lad.

Whether animal or human, the competitors with the Alberta Stampede Company had more than the physical qualities needed to capture titles. Heart, perseverance, and daring made them winners.

The innovative Welsh brought show jumping into his rodeos, and he had the horse talent to do it. His best proved to be a big bay called Barra Lad. The horse's best performance came when the Welshes were just getting into the rodeo business.

The most important show of all was in BC at the New Westminster Provincial Exhibition on 12 September 1925. The Welshes, and especially rider young[13] Louis, were sure that Barra Lad could beat the world record achieved by a horse named Great Heart from Chicago. Its record was just under 8 feet 1 inch [24.53 m]. For the September event, about 6000 people gathered at the horse show arena.

The bar was raised to 8 feet 1½ inches. Louis guided Barra Lad toward the bar to mentally measure what loomed above them and must be done.

The boy and his mount rode to the far corner of the arena. The judges re-measured the bar's height. One dropped the flag, ready to begin.

The young rider bent low and urged his horse forward. Barra Lad charged toward the jump. The crowd held its collective breath. His front legs cleared the bar. As his back legs followed, the barrier seemed destined to come down on the rider and horse.

Barra Lad's back legs cleared the bar, but as everyone watched, the horse came down so hard his head seemed to hit the dirt. To the audience, Barra Lad had landed on his head, but in fact his front legs had crumpled under him.

"BARA LAD"
Louis Welsh up, age 15
Holder of Pacific Coast Record
7' 4½", 1924. Made at New Westminster
B.C. and Loose Pole Record at Regina.
Sask. 1925.

Challenges any high jumping
horse in the world.

Photo... OLIVER

Barra Lad is the usual spelling of this famous horse's name. Louis' birth date indicates he was age ten, however, the postcard commemorates the success of horse and rider. Courtesy of Glenbow Archives, NA 3478-1.

Louis managed to stay in the saddle. Finally, the horse stood under its own power. Two veterinarians checked the animal. Its pulse was fast, but Barra Lad appeared to be fine.

The audience roared! They moved like a mob towards the show ring. An Alberta horse had won the world record! Next was the moment of glory. Placing a horse show wreath around his neck, officials acknowledged the great, new champion. Louis and Barra Lad paraded in the arena, and then the police made way for them through the crowd so the horse and rider could return to the stable.

There, Barra Lad was not himself. Three vets looked for an injury. They found nothing. Internal hemorrhage was their best guess.

Barra Lad lay in the stable runway, and Louis sat by the horse. The hours dragged on. Barra Lad did not improve. Louis cried.

Eventually, the Welshs' gear and other horses had to be taken from their stalls. Those with jobs stepped around the champion. Scheduled to jump at a Washington state fair, the horses had to be loaded on the train for transport. They, too, stepped around the show jumper.

Barra Lad's stable mate, Madamoiselle, whinnied repeatedly to him, but there was no answer. Eventually, she was led around the daring and great-hearted horse.

He became weaker and weaker, and five hours after his greatest performance, Barra Lad died.

Welsh and his boys were deeply moved. They had lost one of their greatest horses, a world title holder. His final resting place was at the New Westminster fairgrounds. Still the family did not give up the dream of presenting the best competitors to the world.

In the past, Welsh had watched carefully during the Calgary Stampede. He had rated all the best horses, and he set out to buy them. One was Midnight, who belonged to Jim McNab.

A coal black horse born in 1916, the gelding had been sired by a Percheron/Morgan cross, and his mother was a thoroughbred. Foaled at the Cottonwood Ranch near Fort MacLeod, AB, when McNab was still serving overseas in the First World War, Midnight had a complex personality. In fact, he was destined for the rodeo hall of fame as one of the best bucking horses in the world.

From the beginning, the horse loved to buck, and no one rode him until Jim returned from the war. Then, the determined and capable rider stayed in the saddle until Midnight finally decided he would concede to his owner.

Jim wanted him for a saddle horse, and for two years, the horse worked the range. Still, the black beauty would allow no one to ride him except Jim. When the owner or his daughter were leading Midnight by with halter, he was as gentle as the best of saddle horses, and a few lumps of sugar made him happy.

Although the horse's temperament was just too unpredictable for a good cattle horse, McNab loved him. By 1920, he decided to enter Midnight as a bucking horse in some local rodeos. Increasingly, the horse proved himself as a bronc. The more cowboys he pitched, the

Calgary Stampede B132
Joe Fisher on Midnight.

Midnight thrilled audiences with his relentless bucking. In this photo, Joe Fisher from Millarville, AB, attempted to ride the famous horse. Courtesy of Stockmen's Memorial Foundation, CHRA 020-Vol. 1.

more cowboys lined up to prove themselves and pressed McNab to enter Midnight at the Calgary Stampede. Finally, McNab caved to the pressure.

Midnight seemed excited, nervous, and not the least happy during his first three days at Calgary. Still, when the gate opened, resolutely, he bucked off every competitor.

After Welsh had watched the bronc throw all his riders at the Stampede, the savvy horseman went to the McNab ranch. He wanted Midnight and was ready to pay any price. Jim had received many offers for the horse, but had no intention of selling him. Eventually, the offer just seemed too good.

Welsh paid $500 for Midnight, the most ever paid for a bucking horse at the time. As well, he took two other bucking horses for $150 each. In total, before taking his rodeo company on the road, Welsh bought 30 of the best bucking horses available, but the star of the string was Midnight.

He was a fierce competitor, yet he had a reputation for being fair. He never tried to kick or step on a fallen rider. Sometimes, after bucking off a cowboy, Midnight did nuzzle the fallen rider before trotting out of the arena, as if he took pleasure rubbing in his victory, but he was never nasty.

During the years that followed, McNab had opportunities to ride Midnight, but the horse never again allowed it, as if the betrayal could not be forgiven.

In the meantime, Midnight became more and more famous.

America's great riders wanted their chance to conquer the world-class bronc too. When Welsh took Midnight to Toronto for the Alberta Stampede Company's rodeo in 1926, Bobby Askins of Montana made his attempt. As they came out of the chute, Askin startled Midnight by spurring him high behind the ears. The great horse stopped, minced, and the crowd had the daring to laugh. Then the battle was on. Midnight pitched, leaped, dropped his head, bucked, and pitched until the talented rider was on the ground. Even without the rider, Midnight continued to show the audience he was worthy of his reputation and their laughter had been undeserved.

Pete Knight was another super hero who had to tangle with Midnight during the tour. Knight had grown up on a farm near Crossfield, AB. By 1923, he was winning the bronc riding competitions at rodeos. Welsh had recognized his potential and signed him up to travel with the company.

When the 1926 tour reached Montreal, one of the best-remembered competitions in rodeo history took place. Pete Knight had drawn Midnight. The horse jumped and pitched. Later, Knight remembered it as the wildest ride he had ever had, but somehow he stayed in the saddle.

Although Knight had been victorious, Midnight remained an outstanding bucking horse, though his career had also turned him into an outlaw.

Long after the Alberta Stampede Company had called it quits, Pete Knight was sticking to his saddle and impressing rodeo audiences everywhere. He was Canadian Saddle Bronc Champion in 1927 and in 1930, and he won countless awards and trophies. Competing against the best broncs in North America, Pete Knight became recognized as one of the all-time greats.

Like Barra Lad, tragedy ended his career. The rodeo was in Hayward, California in May of 1937. Pete drew a horse called Duster.

"He was a good horse, but Pete had ridden him previously," Pete's wife Babe said years later to *Albertan* newspaper and rodeo reporter Fred Kennedy.[14]

At the chutes, Pete mounted his horse. The gate opened, and the bucking horse and champion were in the infield. Duster bucked, and this time, he bucked Pete from his back. Then, while the champion rider was on the ground, Duster kicked at him. The horse's hoof landed against Pete's chest.

Finally, Pete stood up. To the crowd's applause, he slowly made his way back to the chutes. There, he collapsed. The ambulance rushed him to the hospital where Babe learned his condition. Pete had a compound fracture of his rib.

"...the jagged edge had pierced his spleen," recalled Babe.

Within hours, the champion and hero to thousands of rodeo fans was dead.

The glory years of the Alberta Stampede Company passed quickly, but the company had provided an excellent training ground for Knight and others. Welsh had owned some of the best horses and had worked with the great riders of the day. They were men and animals with talent, heart, determination, and daring, and they created passionate fans for their sports.

Exhibitions and fairs celebrated local communities and the best they had to offer in both old and new technologies, in history, and plans for the future. Also on display was the community's ability to house and feed huge crowds of people, handle mishaps, deal with strangers, and attend to medical or other concerns. The communities continued to be on display throughout the annual local event, but many took their exhibits to fairs in other communities, too. Entering competitions, displaying successes, and advertising their communities, western Canadians shipped produce, livestock, grain samples, natural resource samples, and displays to national and international exhibitions.

Chapter 6

Communities On Display

Usually, at large fairs, organizing exhibitors and display space was handled by committees. This 1920s exhibit by the Chilliwack Agricultural Association of BC would have required hours of work. Courtesy of Chilliwack Museum and Historical Society P7460.

A wide range of contests showcased the best in the field. New and established communities readied displays suggesting bountiful harvests and superior livestock. Talented exhibitors – with baked goods, flowers, handicrafts, and art – added final touches before competitions began. The winning trophies, medals, and ribbons were symbols displayed with pride, not only by individuals but by communities.

Interested and sometimes skeptical crowds watched the judges, and people judged for themselves whether the competitions' outcomes had been fair or biased. Problems with judges seemed perennial. Judges wouldn't turn up at the scheduled time for judging. They complained that they weren't given adequate time or space to do the job properly. Entries in categories were sometimes considered inappropriate by judges, and as a result, excellent entries lost while "scrubs" took the day. Increasingly, categories and rules were clarified. Judges were required to have expertise and even experience in the area that they were judging. Too, detailing specific characteristics to be considered in judging helped bring consistency.

Commonly, small towns sent representatives to fairs in other communities as a way of promoting the town and area to those interested in settling or setting up businesses. This display was featured at the Dominion Exhibition in Calgary, 1908. Courtesy of Stettler & District Museum & Archives.

Winners from local and regional fair competitions were proud enough of their successes to take them on the road. Western Canadian livestock, grain, fruit, and other produce could compete with the best in the world. Soon, producers were shipping their stock and grain to fairs around the world. Big name fairs of interest to western Canadian farmers included Chicago Fat Stock Show, the Chicago International Grain and Hay Show, Royal Horticultural Society Shows, and world fairs in various cities.

For communities, the advantage of participating went beyond winning. Sometimes, the intent was to attract new settlers. In 1910, grains and grasses were part of a display sent from Edmonton to Chicago for the ten-day stock show. The western Canadian community had a 36 foot [11 metre] exhibit space to showcase the city and farming. Like other community representatives at such fairs, the Edmonton exhibitors had distributed 10,000 postcards, which could be mailed to request further information from the board of trade.

F.T. Fisher of the board of trade attended and reported to the *Edmonton Bulletin*. "As a result of our exhibit, and conversation with visitors, quite a number of farmers have made up their minds to visit the Edmonton diestrict (sic) next year, who otherwise would never have done so."[1]

Most fairs involved boosterism, and provincial exhibitions were another outstanding way of advertising the community. Sometimes travelling great distances, visitors arrived and learned – first hand – what the area had to offer. Local businesses, from hotels and restaurants to clothing retailers, wanted the new customers.

Brandon – A Two-fold Success

"Who will best present the agriculture, industry, and success of the province?" was the question.

Of course, communities in each province answered, "We will!"

After that, the argument – as presented in the local newspapers – often became a matter of bragging and mud slinging.

Winning a designation of "provincial exhibition" meant grants and other perks. Competition for such status was intense. Usually, the capital of the province vied with one or two other communities. For various reasons, each maintained that it was better suited to hosting the big event.

Often the competing communities had slightly different visions about what made the best fair. The community that staged the exhibition might brag of the number of visitors, how well they were handled, how few problematic incidents, how progressive the displays, how thrilling the midways and concessions. In contrast, its competitor found faults.

In Manitoba, in 1891, Brandon and Winnipeg were chief competitors for the provincial agricultural exhibition. That year, for the first time, Winnipeg's Provincial Exhibition combined both agricultural and industrial priorities. Before the fair had ended, a journalist for the *Brandon*

Prior to the extensive use of motorized vehicles and machinery, competitions and displays related to horses interested most fair goers. These fine animals were entered in the livestock competitions during the fair at Brandon, MB, in 1917. Courtesy of Archives of Manitoba, Brandon-Fair 1917 1.

Mail dared to write, "It is a pity Winnipeg has not adjourned its mongrel exhibition of fireworks and dogs."[2]

The criticism went even further. When Brandonites returned from the Winnipeg fair, "Without exception, they reported having the most disagreeable experience since coming to the country."[3]

In Winnipeg, the same fair was considered an unprecedented success. The city had attempted a first agricultural fair in 1871. It had been canceled, but successful fairs soon followed. With status as capital city and becoming the hub for the railway, Winnipeg felt entitled, but it was not the agricultural centre for the province.

Established in 1881, Brandon was the agricultural hub. It, too, floundered with its first fair in 1882. Advertising prizes of $200, the fair was scheduled for October. Given a population of only 700 in the town, rainy weather, and the progress of fall farm work, the turnout was poor.

By 1883, with donations and grants totaling $4500, organizers built a huge fair building, which they called the Crystal Palace, after its British namesake. Once again scheduling the fair for October, planners had not accommodated farmers. Still, Brandon had her eye on provincial exhibition status for the following year. It didn't happen.

In fact, Winnipeg had proven it could host successful exhibitions and had been granted the provincial exhibition for 1884 and 1885.

The editor of the *Brandon Sun* was not impressed with Winnipeg's 1885 fair.

"...a greater failure has not been known in the province," he wrote of the Winnipeg fair, adding, "the sooner the town wiseacres there learn that it is impossible to make brick without straw, or make a successful agricultural exhibition where the exhibits have to be carried hundreds of miles, the sooner will a provincial exhibition prove a success."[4]

Brandon was closer to the majority of Manitoba's farmers, but as capital city, Winnipeg had the political clout. It was a common enough struggle, one that went on between Calgary and Edmonton; Regina and Saskatoon; New Westminster, Vancouver, and Victoria.

Despite everything that Winnipeg offered, hosting a top agricultural fair had not been easy, especially given the local interest in industrial concerns too.

At the same time, Brandon was discovering the formula for a successful fair. One important move was shifting the date from October to July to compete against Winnipeg in 1889. Early organizers had wanted agriculture showcased, but to attract visitors, they had to become open to the interests of a more urban audience. In 1904, Brandon wanted the Dominion Exhibition, which would have meant a federal grant of $50 000 to help stage the event. The agricultural community lost to Winnipeg.

At the interprovincial fair held at Brandon in 1912, during judging, each animal was tended by its owner or caretaker. Other farmers gathered around the pens to watch. They evaluated the animals – and the competence of the judges – for themselves. Courtesy of McKee Archives, Brandon University, Alf Fowler Collection 6-1999.

Still, Brandon did not abandon its agricultural priorities. Instead, by 1906, the community determined to have two major fairs. A separate group of organizers began working on a winter fair with the sole objective was advancing and promoting agriculture.

The summer fair would pay more attention to nonagricultural concerns. Admittedly, Winnipeg was good in those areas. Reluctantly, Brandon organizers followed the capital city's example. They put more effort, energy, and money into the things most summer fair-goers wanted: sporting competitions, midway, shows, and concessions. Horse races had been very popular in Winnipeg; they were consistent with agricultural themes; the local Turf Club was co-operative; and the races soon drew audiences to Brandon, too. Attendance went up, and so did visitor enthusiasm.

In 1906, Brandon held its first winter fair. Concerned with showing and improving stock, as well as advancing grain farming, it did showcase community success by featuring a Poultry Show, Seed Grain Fair, and the first Provincial Spring Stallion Show. Also, it proved a convenient time and location for the annual meetings of such farm-related groups as the Grain Growers' Association, Canadian Seed Growers' Association, Sheep and Swine Stock Breeders' Association, Cattle Breeders' Association, and Horse Breeders' Association.

It was the beginning of one of the most important winter agricultural fairs in western Canada. The fairs featured countless educational lectures and agricultural competitions. A short musical was usually the only entertainment that might interrupt the business and learning of the fair days.

With it becoming increasingly clear to organizers that the purpose and audience for each fair was different, instead of competing against each other, the winter and summer fair associations in the city co-operated. Brandon hosted two exhibitions: a summer fair and a winter fair.

It was a city determined to become the centre for the best in Manitoba's agricultural fairs and be granted provincial exhibition status. And eventually, all that happened.

Small Town Greets the World

Lethbridge, AB, had only 8500 people in 1912, but the community knew it was world-class – at least in two fields. The land was arid, but by the end of the first decade in the twentieth century, farmers were producing outstanding grain. Too, organizers could compete with the best when it came to hosting farmers and farm-related interest groups.

Lethbridge's history was rooted in other commodities. Before the North West Mounted Police intervened in their trade in 1874, American whiskey traders had built a small post called Fort Whoop-Up. Then coal mining brought others to the area. Finally, ranchers and farmers moved in, and by October, 1897, the agricultural society held the community's first fair.

For the event, Lethbridge followed in the tradition of other western Canadian exhibitions with displays and competitions for livestock, grains, homemaking skills, and gardening as the focal point. However, there were also other competitions that were more unusual. One prize was for the best lump of bituminous coal weighing over 500 pounds [227 kg]. Another rewarded the best pair of horseshoes. Prizes were as high as $10.

Unlike most early fairs in smaller communities, Lethbridge organizers printed a whopping 20-page program. In it was information about the wild steer roping and bronc riding competitions. Too, the first Lethbridge and District Exhibition featured horse and foot races. Other sporting events included soccer and baseball.

Over more than a decade, local volunteers refined their organizing skills and dreamed of even bigger and more successful events. With the introduction of irrigation into the area by Alexander Galt and Son's companies and with the advances in farming supported by the Lethbridge Dominion Experimental Station, farm interests had burgeoned in the region. The coal industry had required good transportation links. Early railways made travel less difficult than in some areas, and local farmers were able to participate in the larger international farming community.

Already in 1909, Lethbridge was represented at the World's Dry-Farming Congress. City council had its eye on hosting the event, and to make the community a more desirable choice, council began acquiring land for a new and larger exhibition grounds.

Machinery displays were important in conveying technology of the past and future. Most exhibitions had displays relating to the science and technology of agriculture and everyday life. Courtesy of Glenbow Archives, NA 5354-6.

Again, in 1910, representatives attended the Congress, this time in Spokane. Not only did Lethbridge set up a display booth, farmers from the area and province won competitions, so many that Alberta was nicknamed the Sweepstake Province.

In 1911, the event was held in Colorado Springs, Colorado. Successful in the bid for the 1912 World Dry-Farming Congress, the southern Alberta city made preparations in earnest. During the event, Lethbridge would also host the second International Congress of Farm Women and the International Congress of Agricultural Colleges.

To host the world's fair of farming, the agricultural society was incorporated as the Lethbridge Exhibition Board. That meant the men who had shouldered the financial risks for the earlier fairs would not be individually liable for debts.

The world was coming to the community's doorstep, and the annual summer fair in August provided a perfect trial run. It had taken 88 days to build a new pavilion, a huge mosque-like structure, on the grounds. There were new offices, display buildings, race track, ten barns, sheep sheds, and other facilities to meet the needs of delegates and visitors. The grandstand at the first fair had a seating capacity of 600. The new building could seat 5000. Streets had been paved; concrete sidewalks were constructed; sewage and water systems were improved; commercial buildings had been transformed into dormitories; tents in which to feed visitors were erected. Even a streetcar system had been built to the grounds, then about 2 miles [3 kilometres] from town.

By the opening of the October 21-26 Dry Land Farming Congress, everything was in readiness – except the police. Unfair hiring practices for the new chief and his assistant had angered local officers, and 14 walked off the job. Since the CPR had arranged special excursion trains to Lethbridge, not only delegates and locals, but huge crowds of other visitors were expected. The call for help went out. City police from both Edmonton and Calgary, as well as Mounties, were soon on the job, watching for the petty criminals who were always drawn to events with a carnival-like atmosphere.

Arriving from 15 countries, the 2500 delegates, more than five times as many as at Colorado Springs, came from as far away as China, Italy, and Persia. They brought contest entries of watermelons, potatoes, other root vegetables, grains, and grasses. As well as the delegates, 2500 additional visitors arrived.

The festivities began with a huge parade. At the grand opening, flags flew. There were tributes and pledges to world brotherhood, but for most, the priorities were the science of agriculture and the enjoyment of fair amusements.

Entertainment thrills had not been neglected. Miss Carver and her horse plunged from a platform at the top of a 33 foot [10-metre] tower into a huge water tank. Another daredevil raced down a high, steep ramp and plunged into still another water tank. In one tent, cyclists raced around a track. Show girls, bands, and folk dancing also drew enthusiasts. Few visitors worried that the hot air balloons floating above them were at risk from strong winds. Instead, farming techniques were the talk of the town, and impressive machinery exhibits arrived.

Rumley was the big name in tractors, and one had been brought from La Porte, Indiana, as a major prize at the fair.

"The tractor [will] soon replace the horse in the heavy work on the farm," insisted a Rumley representative. Replace 15 horses! Cost less than keeping horses! Support greater farm production and therefore increase incomes!

Not likely! was the response of many farmers.

At fairs, even how the grain samples were bundled was important, partly to make judging as easy as possible, but also to create attractive displays. Courtesy of Archives of Manitoba, Agriculture-Exhibitions 42 (1917).

Still, one farmer walked away with nothing but goodwill towards Rumley even though he never used a tractor for farming. Henry Holmes and his family of five lived in a two room shack, where they farmed northwest of Raymond, AB. Getting his grain to nearby Lethbridge for the world grain competitions was easy, but that meant little if a farmer didn't have good grain samples to enter. Marquis, a hard red spring wheat, had been developed at the Lethbridge Experimental Farm and was being locally grown by 1909. It suited southern Alberta conditions, and Holmes had a particularly good patch in his field. Not wanting his sample to bleach, after cutting it, he covered the stooks and later threshed by hand.

The family helped, including his twelve-year-old son Godfrey. They picked through the kernels, selecting only hard, uniform ones for the competition, and when the sample was ready, Holmes drove to Lethbridge with it.

The main door of the display building was locked. With no one to accept the entry, he walked to a side door and left his sample among the others. By then, a new arrival hurried Holmes out of the building.

Returning to his farm, Holmes was shocked when, days later, a Mountie appeared on the farm. Was he in trouble for entering the locked building? No. The Mountie brought good news. Holmes had won the title of World Wheat King.

The prize thrilled his family, too, and they were invited to see Henry honored by the Congress. It was son Godfrey's first train trip and his chance to see the fair. When Henry arrived in Lethbridge, there were photos and hoop-la. Best of all, he was the new owner of a Rumley Oil-Pull gasoline tractor, a prize valued at $2500-3000. After the excitement was over, Holmes sold the Rumley rather than using it himself.

"The money he got put the family on its feet," recalled Godfrey.[5]

The tractor could have pulled six or seven ploughs. Instead, Holmes farmed using 16 horses. Every farm family needed a decent house and a barn, and those became Holmes' priority.

The Dry-Farming Congress hosted by Lethbridge was a phenomenal success in term of numbers. Delegate attendance was high, and Saskatchewan took the lead with 125 delegates, but there were also more exhibits than ever.

During the first four days of the event, 20 000 passed through the gates.[6] Of those, 13 000 were paid admissions. At the end of the event, about 5000 passengers boarded the six CPR special trains leaving Lethbridge.

As with so many world-class fairs, despite phenomenal attendance, the expenditures on infrastructure had been so high the Lethbridge Exhibition Board was saddled with three million in debts that plagued them until the Second World War. Ironically, some of the principles of dry-farming proved to worsen soil conditions. Among the principles advocated for farmers had been planting deep, keeping surface soil loose and fine, and using summer fallow to control weeds and ensure moisture retention. In the end, they contributed to the wind erosion during the drought of the 1930s.

Still, hosting the Congress meant spreading the news about the farming possibilities in southern Alberta, publicizing the quality of prairie grains, and connecting local farmers with farming technology and science from around the world. Always high on the agenda of other agricultural fairs, these were priorities for the successful Seed Fairs later hosted by Lethbridge and other communities, too.

A City, A Fair and Press Coverage on Display

Press coverage usually meant boosterism. The press was expected to advertise events and show the community's enthusiasm and accomplishments. Local papers did just that. The *Manitoba Free Press*, later named the *Winnipeg Free Press,* focused on competition, entrants, and winners. It told readers about organizational efforts and offered as much space as fair boards might want for advertising. Yet the *Free Press*, more than almost any paper in the country, gave the full story of exhibitions and stampedes. It retold moments of glory, and it gave the gory details of injuries. It told of crime on the grounds, gave details of shows, and made predictions.

In 1912, Winnipeg staged its annual Industrial Exhibition, and the press gave column after column to the Duke of Connaught, who officially opened the exhibition, and to his daughter, the Duchess of Connaught. The paper headlines claimed the "Reception to Royal Party an Event Unparalleled in Winnipeg's History." "Practically Whole Population Cheers Gallant Duke." In fact, a "Surging Sea of Humanity Filled Winnipeg Streets," to see the governor general. Sometimes prose became even more flowery. The Duke was greeted by "A royal western welcome, whole hearted and as free as the prairie breeze that kept the threatening clouds at bay throughout the day...," but the superlatives were expected by readers.[7]

The Winnipeg newspaper gave a bird's eye view of the action. "... the exhibition grounds presented a lively and decidedly industrial appearance yesterday afternoon. The distant rumble of many voices in the grandstand as the horses came on the home stretch could be heard mingling and almost drowning out the marital [sic] music of the different military bands."[8]

Also, it gave full coverage to George Mestach's attempted flight and crash on opening day, as well as to Jimmy Ward's successful and impressive flights, which followed. For children's day, it predicted that 25 000 school children would visit the fair.[9] It told of the boy scout tournament and scoutmaster races. The press announced that, on Wednesday, a new four minute street car service to the grounds had been opened, but it was only in service in the afternoons to handle the largest of the crowds. Inspections of the new manufacturer's building, lunch counters, and improved midway were worthy of comment.

Traditional exhibits and competitions received the coverage they deserved. Not only did cattle, heavy horse, and show jumping competitions garner attention, poultry prize winners were covered. Farmers who had brought sheep – whether Leicester, Shropshire, or Hampshire – saw their names in the paper. The cocker spaniel who was grand champion in the dog show received praise. Motorcycle race competition results were announced, too. Through the paper, the mayor invited every automobile owner in Winnipeg to bring his decorated vehicle and join the automobile parade on the evening of 17 July.

According to the paper, the Besses of the Barn band entertained. One of the most famous in the world, it was from Lancashire, England, and was on a return tour after six years absence. Despite its name, the band brought the music of Rossini and Wagner.

The midway and shows received attention, too. Robinson's Elephant act, one of the best acts to visit the exhibition, had been booked for the entire week. Sea lions were present, too. The bucking mule, among the vaudeville acts, deserved a few lines of type, but the *Manitoba Free Press* also made one of the few mentions of the Negro laborers who worked with numerous midways.

"Two negroes [sic] were sent to convey the mule from the stable to the platform. It was pouring rain and the mule was loathe to leave its cosy quarters. After much dragging and pulling, they at length succeeded in getting him out but he was no sooner in the open air than a wild desire for freedom seemed to possess him. Mr. Mule leaped and jumped until the negroes, afraid for their lives, were forced to let him go. Then a wild chase in and around the barns commenced. At length, the negroes as well as several jockeys succeeded in catching [him.]"[10]

In fact, the *Manitoba Free Press* covered, in detail, very serious situations related to fairs, and it did not shy away from accidents or crime and police activity on the grounds. The community paper was willing to tell all. There was little – if anything – it was not prepared to put on display, to reveal to its reading public, so people could judge for themselves what was good and bad about the fairs and community services.

For 1912, the problems were as diverse as in later years. There were the standard warnings, such as the problem with loose planks on the boardwalks at the grounds. Someone was bound to end up hurt.

On Friday, 12 July, two policemen became lost on the grounds. They were new fellows hired for the exhibition. When they didn't turn up for their meal tickets, another policeman went searching and finally found them in a distant and quiet area of the grounds.

A frightening circumstance occurred during a show where a "coloured gentleman," waited for people to throw balls at him for a cigar prize. Suddenly, "the negro uttered a terrified scream, jerked his head....and fell sprawling to the ground, kicking lustily and showing his white teeth."

People rushed to the scene. He had "merely received a severe shock." Above his head was the wiring for an electric light. To the side was wire netting. Improperly insulated, the wire had touched the wire netting. When the concession worker touched the netting, he "received the full current. The man was not seriously injured."[11]

Police were kept busy. "Exhibition week in Winnipeg is a week prolific of crime," the *Free Press* reported.[12] With the fair opening on Wednesday, the police docket for Thursday already listed 101 cases. They included suspects from city streets and the grounds, those picked up by uniformed officers and by plain clothes detectives, some of whom had been brought in from the US.

Later, the paper reported that there were no major crimes or thefts in the first days, "due in a great degree to the clever work of plain clothes men who ... since the exhibition opened have arrested 50 suspicious looking characters, 'con' men and crooks before they have had a chance to acquire any Winnipeg money."[13]

The docket was filled with men, and many were simply remanded and told to "improve the standard morals in Winnipeg by leaving within 24 hours."

Disorderly conduct, pick-pocketing, assault, drunkenness, and vagrancy were the usual charges, but some men were hauled in without clear cause. Picked up at the grounds "on suspicion," one man had $200 in his pocket.

"You must get out within 24 hours or you will be sent down, " declared the judge.

Of another defendant, the detective said, "This is another exhibition crook. He is anxious to get out."

"All right," said the judge. "Get out."

According to the paper, "Only one of the bunch of crooks gathered in by the police Wednesday, is alleged to have any definite record."[14]

Monday, 15 July, was also a busy day for police. The "red wagon" hurried back and forth between the grounds and police cells. The race track was the centre of the action. At about 4:00 p.m., three plain clothes detectives entered the paddock by the grandstand.

"The ring was crowded with bettors and the bookies were doing a flourishing business." The detectives were intent on five men who were standing with "bundles of long green in their hands."

Somehow the suspects knew the police were after them. They made a dash to escape, "but the sleuths had their men marked."[15]

They were caught and taken to the police station, where they were searched. One carried an employee's ticket to the grounds but he wasn't an employee. All had large sums of money on them. They were from south of the border. American police had been on their trails and had made the arrests.

By Tuesday of the following week, there was a scandal. There had been large crowds. Gate receipts didn't add up to what the treasurer expected. He had ticket takers watched. At least two had accepted tickets, gave them to another accomplice, and had them resold over and over again before dividing the extra take. Finally, police caught one man red-handed. He had 30 previously sold tickets concealed on him. Three gatemen were arrested, and a serious interrogation ensued. No one confessed, but their statements were incriminating.

"Three and possibly more ticket collectors employed at the exhibition grounds have, it is believed, been systematically robbing the Exhibition association of large sums of money since the Exhibition opened."[16]

A further investigation was to follow, but in the meantime, the three were kept in police cells.

Another report told of a near disaster. A gas stove in a tent food booth, where wieners and steaks were cooked, sat close to the wood structure. The wood caught fire. Fortunately, a quick-thinking employee threw a pail of lemonade on the flames and extinguished the fire.

Saturday, 20 July, in the grand stand, a cry of "Fire" created havoc. There was a stampede of people, worried they were in peril, and others wanting to see what was happening. The fire brigade was called, but by then the fire was out. A man, lighting a cigar, had thrown his match. It had lit the paper below his feet, but the fire was eventually put out by the people nearby.

The 1912 Winnipeg Exhibition was successful, despite a bout of bad weather that reduced crowds and wind that tore at midway tents. That it was reported with a degree of honesty and thoroughness few newspapers or their supporting communities were willing to risk was also worthy of tributes.

Fruit Growers of Okanagan

Geography made the Okanagan Valley in central of BC into lake country, but settlement transformed it into ranch country, Canada's fruit belt, and its vacation wonderland. All four were to play central roles in the development of summer festivals in the area. Water sports and horse races had been part of the Kelowna's fall fairs since the end of the 1800s. The huge lakes had a profound effect on lifestyle, and water sports were the stuff of serious competition and fun. Cowboy competitions and gymkhanas were a deeply-rooted part of local tradition, too. By 1912, Kelowna held a gymkhana, sponsored by the polo club and held on the club grounds, but other races and cowboy competitions preceded the main event. By then, orchards were gaining ground, and competing and displaying fruit at fairs and shows nationally and internationally garnered the area a world-wide reputation.

In terms of agriculture, the Okanagan sun belt was perfect for the development of fruit and produce kings, and many interested farmers entered competitions and displayed the fine agricultural produce of the area. Success at fairs outside the local community came very early. Some competitions were officially part of traditional fairs; some, such as apple shows, were more limited in scope.

In 1900, the BC Fruit Growers' Association placed third at the International Exposition in France, but earlier international wins had been scored. One such achiever was James Gartrell, who first settled in Penticton and then moved to Summerland. By 1887, he had cleared land of his own and planted apple trees, shipped from Ontario and the state of Washington. Also, he planted peach trees – from peach stones. He was involved with early irrigation projects, and by 1897, he took fruit to the Spokane Fruit Fair. Not only did he win competitions, he displayed the potential of the area as fruit growing land to Americans.

The provincially sponsored fruit exhibits were winners, too, claiming gold medals at the 1904 Royal Horticultural Society Show. From then on, the province and individuals continued to claim top prizes for their entries in international competitions.[17]

Transporting the fruit to the shows so it would arrive in perfect condition was not easy. In 1910, Gartrell had shipped fruit by rail to the Vancouver Exhibition. From there, the shipment was to go to London, England. By then, it was late fall. The fruit had to be shipped across Canada to Halifax when suddenly the temperatures dropped. With danger of the apples freezing, the individual accompanying the shipment had to check temperatures constantly and attend charcoal burners, keeping the railway cars warm enough to prevent damage to the produce. Finally, the apples were loaded on a ship, and the cargo arrived in England. Despite the conditions, the exhibit won awards. Some of the apples became a gift to the Queen, and others were sold at Covent Gardens.

At this early Spokane Apple Show, Kelowna area orchardists won over $4600 in prizes, winning first in all but one class. Here, Messrs. De Hart and Gibbs, expert packers in the Okanagan, are photographed beside Kelowna's booth at the fair. Courtesy Kelowna Museum Archives.

Another Okanagan resident, Francis DeHart of Kelowna, exhibited cherries at the Dominion Exhibition in Calgary in 1908. An American exhibitor convinced him to take apples to the National Apple Show at Spokane that same year. He and J. Gibb of Kelowna entered an apple exhibit of 43 boxes to the show.

According to the *Spokane Review*, DeHart's exhibit was outstanding. He had an artistic flair. The apples had been "arranged in terraces with fancy quarter boxes filled with different varieties against a pale green and white background. Vases with carnations, bottles with cider and apple wine occupy spaces among the apple boxes causing the fruit to stand out...."[18]

Wins with the exhibit totaled $5000 in prize money. News of their success preceded them home. When the men stepped off the S.S. Okanagan, they were greeted by a large crowd, eager to congratulate the local heroes.

DeHart continued to win at shows and claimed three gold medals at the Canadian National Apple Exhibition at Vancouver in 1910. Often, he selected produce for provincial exhibits and competition entries, and he was responsible for designing the displays. For the provincial entries to the exhibition at Wembley, England, in 1924, DeHart was once again placed in charge.

Although he was most closely associated with the growing of fruit and peonies, DeHart entered hard Red Spring wheat in the World's Grain Show and Exhibition at Regina in 1933, and he walked away with four prizes. He and others like him brought world attention to the agricultural products of their communities. They were successful growers, but they also knew how to display their products. It took a certain degree of courage to place locally grown fruits, vegetables, and grains in international competitions. Still, proud of what was possible in their communities, they committed time, energy, and money to making sure the world knew just how good western Canada was in agriculture.

Homemakers as Winners

Although partners with their husbands on farms and in business, pioneer women were seldom named on competition entries of grain, produce, and inventions. Both farm and town women did enter competitions such as those for the best saddle horse, or horse and buggy, and from the early days, some won in those competitions against men.

After the 1940s, more women did enter other farm-related competitions under their own

names. As early as the 1920s, girls in 4H or farm clubs were enthusiastic competitors. Young, unmarried women still living on their parents' farms entered their own fine horse or milk cows. On farms, care of poultry was often handled by women, and gardens were part of their traditional domain. Eventually, more and more entered the related contests, and most took an interest in farm, floral, and garden exhibits. However, the two areas where almost all entrants were women related to handiwork and cooking.

Undoubtedly, some women paid their own contest fees while others would have had their fees paid out of the joint family

Some aspects of judging, such as weighing and measuring produce, were straightforward. These huge potatoes were submitted to judges at the Edmonton Exhibition in about 1911. Courtesy of Glenbow Archives, NA-1328-62710.

income or what was commonly considered their husband's income. Even at the early fairs, prize money in those categories was reasonable for the time, but not as much as for the competitions in which men were the primary contest entrants. Despite the numbers of women who entered the contests and the sometimes massive numbers of individual items entered, the winners received far less attention and press than the winners in the traditionally male-oriented contests.

In 1923, prizes for handiwork such as embroidered pillow slips or scarves were good. The award for a crocheted camisole or yard of lace was often about $1, but some competitions offered as much as $2.

Some women won prizes year after year at local and regional fairs. Their names might be listed in the local newspaper, but seldom – if ever – was their "career," biography, or skill in traditional women's work given any significant space in newspaper columns.

However, western Canadian newspapers did cover competitions related to household arts. Charles L. Willis owned the *Stettler Independent*, and he wrote most of the articles. On a regular basis, he covered the local fair and listed winners in the paper. One such story, published after

These fine handicrafts were on display at the Saskatoon Industrial Exhibition in 1931. The booth was sponsored and operated by the Ukrainian Women's Association of Canada. Courtesy of Glenbow Archives, ND 13-93.

the August, 1930, fair and presumably written by Willis, names all the winners for horses, cattle, sheep, and hogs. Last is the news report for traditional women's work.

"No mere man can afford to give a description of the Ladies' Work...." the newspaperman wrote. With a tongue-in-cheek style, he continues, "He is quite incapable for the job.... For example, what does he know about pillow slips except as a place to lay his head on. His ignorance of embroidery work, of crochet work, or of tatting particularly is colossal. All he knows is that the work looks good and is good, while in the case of the cooking department it also tastes good."

The viewpoint was fairly standard for the time frame. In fact, so was the humorous tone.

"Unfortunately, from one standpoint, most of the prize winners were married," he wrote. "This is satisfactory as far as it goes but gives no opportunity to build up the community by paving the way for future weddings. The single girls have overlooked a golden opportunity in not exhibiting more of their fancy work and cooking at the Exhibition. There should be special prizes for their class at the next Fair."[19]

Female winners weren't named in the front page story that year, but reporting was more detailed for the 1931 fair. Horses and cattle received a two-column treatment on the front page, and women's competitions were worthy of slightly more than a column on the first page!

"We note that there is a class for lady's plain house dress. The class is well within the comprehension for the average reader among the men." Again, the somewhat deprecating sense of humor prevails, but the newspaperman does indicate what he feels is one of the most useful classes of competition.

"No. 233 includes the best articles made from flour sacks, dyed or not dyed. This country will never go back to when the ladies can take a flour sack and make out of it an overcoat or a suit which is worth considerably more than a sack of wheat or even more than a sack of flour."[20]

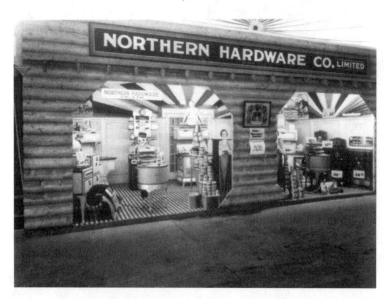

At the 1934 Edmonton Exhibition, visitors could view the latest in stoves, radios, and washing machines. Courtesy of Glenbow Archives, ND 3-6784.

Given the impact of the Depression, the flour sack competition was a practical category, but the journalist's conclusion and prediction proved optimistic. With the deepening economic situation and the drought, more and more women did find themselves making clothes out of flour sacks and old sheets or lining overcoats with old blankets. In many families, those few warm clothes became enormously valuable.

In the same article, Mrs. F.S. McQuarrie was credited with wins in 11 unnamed categories. Many more of the male winners were listed on the front page, but at least a complete prize list for women was elsewhere in the paper, not a common practice for newspapers at the time.

In all, the accomplishments of a number of female winners were credited. Mrs. Lyle was clearly a great cook; Mrs. Nelson had won for her wild flower collection but, in competition with men, she also won a first for her saddle horse.

Stettler was little different than communities throughout western Canada at the time. Winners in the Ladies' Department competition were acknowledged, but, in terms of importance, doilies, quilts, pillow cases, knitted socks, jams, and jellies never quite received the acclaim of a prize bull or stallion.

Transporting Livestock to the Fair

Winners from the summer fairs were keen to collect more ribbons and medals as well as enhance their reputations. By early winter, the hectic fall work ended, and for many, there was time to go on the road with their prize winners. Farmers wanted to compete with the best in the nation, and many set off for the most important winter competition in Canada. The big event was the Royal Agriculture Winter Fair in Toronto launched November 22-29, 1922.

Apart from the weather, the biggest obstacle for farmers from across the nation when it came to meeting and competing was transportation. The railways provided everyone with the best access to the Toronto fair, but the far-flung farmers of the east and west coats faced a heavy financial burden to ship livestock. For decades, the CPR had transported livestock and visitors to regional fairs. Almost always, special passenger excursion trains were scheduled. The ticket price was made reasonable, but with all the extra passengers, the business remained lucrative. Too, CPR lands were often the first considered by fair organizations when they intended to purchase space for fairgrounds. Needing land next to the tracks so the farmers could ship livestock to the exhibitions, they were willing to pay the price. Again, when fair organizers wanted bigger and better fairgrounds, they turned to the railway companies.

The CPR did offer some service for free. Nevertheless, with the added transportation needs of competitors, machinery, dealers, large scale exhibitors, fair-goers, as well as midway and show companies, fairs made a solid contribution to the railway's bottom line.

For shipping exhibition livestock, the CPR and CNR introduced a tariff system. Many farmers exhibited their stock or entered animals throughout the summer on the fair circuit in their own region. The railways charged the shipper full price to the first destination, half price from there to the next point, and again half price to the next destination. From the last stop home, shipping was free.

Although the tariff system gave farmers a break, the November fair in Toronto did not fit into the regional circuits. Few would have been able to afford sending their stock directly from home to the proposed national fair. To support the event, the federal government stepped in and agreed to pay 75% of freight costs to the Royal Winter Fairs. By November each year, tourist traffic had lessened. To farmers and the railways, the subsidized contracts for the Toronto fairs were a win-win.

In addition, for the CPR, the fair meant advertising and an opportunity to display its own livestock. With the intent of providing livestock to new settlers, the railway had its own farms in western Canada. The farms raised quality breeding stock, and the Royal Winter Fair was a fine place to show the animals. Even better, for prizewinning livestock, the market was always excellent.

Both eastern and western farmers looked forward to the event and competition. Alberta sent three railway cars of livestock and exhibits to the first national winter fair. By 1961, 23 railway cars left the province for the Royal.[21] Over the years, Canadian farmers from all provinces sent cattle, swine, sheep, poultry, and horses to be judged. A selection process for animals was established by livestock boards in each province. Usually the boards confirmed two or more animals – that had already been winners at regional fairs – to be entered in each competition category, but policies varied.

Increasingly, provincial governments provided additional support for the event. Agriculture Canada maintained transportation subsidies, but provinces added further subsidies for the many other costs incurred. Livestock cars had to be decked to handle the stock and their human caretakers. Feed, bedding, and water was costly. Provincial staff had to attend meetings, advertise competitions, collect nominations, arrange transportation, and oversee the exhibits. Too, prize money was important, and provinces contributed to prizes for some competitions.

Over the years, exhibition boards made contributions in kind to support exhibitors for the Royal. In Alberta, the Edmonton Exhibition allowed its grounds and CNR siding to be used for livestock freight cars. Alberta Agriculture maintained barns there, where cattle and swine waited to be boarded on trains. The Calgary Exhibition and Stampede offered similar assistance, providing a barn for a workshop and storing materials, and a water truck for filling barrels. Lumber for decking was stored at the Olds Agricultural College, and the college provided a truck and three men to help. In other provinces, similar assistance supported exhibitors.

Travelling to the Royal could be challenging for stock owners. In the early days, the trip was a harrowing and long one for the staff overseeing the entries, and for owners who accompanied their livestock. First, exhibitors outfitted or decked their own railcar at their nearest station. Stock handlers bunked in the railcars with their animals. Once en route, proper care of the animals required that they be unloaded every 72 hours. Exhibitors unloaded their stock; rested, fed, and watered them; and then reloaded the animals. Between stops, in each car, owners stacked feed and filled a huge water tank. Eventually, cars were fitted with a mini stove for cooking, but heating and lighting the cars was a different matter. It just didn't happen.

In 1935, Doug Buchanan made the trip with livestock from Coaldale, Alberta, to the Royal. When the train left Coaldale, it was -20° F [-29° C]. A grain car had been fitted with two decks. The lower had livestock pens. The upper one held exhibit materials and feed, with just enough space left over for a few men to sleep. For light, they had a lantern. Except at the stopping points, their meals were usually sandwiches. Before the time of warm sleeping bags, for bedding Buchanan and his two fellow travellers had a few blankets. According to Buchanan, throughout the journey, the men nearly froze to death. The frigid temperatures were unrelenting until the train reached the Great Lakes, but low temperatures were not the only problem for travelling exhibitors.

By 1947, colonist cars were added for the travel comfort of staff and exhibitors, but most owners spent their time in the stock cars. Dairy cattle had to be milked and other animals fed and tended. Usually about 50 to 60 exhibitors and their helpers were aboard the trains, and many still slept in the stock cars in order to care for their animals. Within certain distances from towns and cities, stockmen could not clean their livestock pens, so the smell added unpleasantness to the ambience of their lodgings.

On occasion, smell was the least of the problems. In 1954, Lawrence Rye was overseer for an Edmonton area contingent on its way to the Royal. He and two other men decked exhibit cars in the usual manner. On loading the University of Alberta exhibit car, four men had struggled to lift the 500 pound [227 kg] box that held harness for a six-horse hitch. The heavy box was stored on the top deck at one side of the car, and fortunately, the deck held the weight. Cattle were loaded and tied beneath the deck. All seemed well, but the trip brought real trouble for livestock, exhibitors, and the overseer.

Travelling east via the main line of the CNR en route to Saskatoon and then south, the exhibition livestock cars were at the rear of the train, behind a tanker car. One car held steers and a few Holstein cows from the U. of A. farm.

In another car, Bill Russell cared for horses, including a large Percheron stallion. Like other stockmen, he planned to sleep in the car. In a swine car, Ken Greenway had his sleeping bag on the top deck bunk, which was almost directly above the 60 gallon [273 L] water tank. Still other stockmen rode and slept in a coach car.

The beginning of the trip was uneventful. By dark, Greenway settled into his sleeping bag, only his head protruding from the zippered cocoon. Russell slept between the two rows of horses in his car.

Suddenly, in the middle of the night, near Biggar, SK, chaos erupted everywhere. There was a loud banging. The force of an impact threw everything that was loose into the air. In stock cars, feed and bedding created such a thick dust there seemed almost no air to breathe.

The sleeping Greenway was launched from his bunk. In Russell's car, the sudden stop had thrown the stallion against his stall and his restraints broke. The horse landed in the aisle. He stood directly over Russell, front hooves on one side of the stockman, back hooves on the other side. In the U. of A. car, the deck with the heavy harness broke. In the coaches, travellers were tossed around.

Immediately, the train crew responded. First, they set out flares to warn trains that might be following. Then they began going through one car after another to see if anyone was badly hurt.

The cause of the accident had been the release of the coupling between a tanker car and the exhibit cars at the end of the train. Realizing there was a problem, the engineer had applied the train brakes. The train stopped. It didn't derail, but the loose cars slammed into the cars ahead of them. The jolt had been very severe.

The passengers in the coaches suffered bumps and bruises, but no one was seriously hurt. Greenway had landed head first in the pen of swine. In doing so, he had missed landing head first in the water barrel, where, pinned in his sleeping bag, he might have drowned.

Jarred awake, Russell found himself in a position where he could easily be kicked by the startled horse. The nervous stallion standing over Russell was well-trained, and the stockman was good with horses. He talked to the stallion, calmed the animal, and managed to safely extricate himself from under its belly.

In the university stock car, the situation was more serious. With the weight of the harness box, the top deck had broken, and it fell on the backs of the animals. Two Holsteins had been tied at each end of the row of steers under the deck. They stood up under the brunt of the weight. With difficulty, the men lifted the heavy burden from the Holsteins' backs and propped up the deck. In fact, though their backs were scraped, the cattle were OK and had saved the steers from any injury. That no other decks collapsed and caused further injury was a tribute to the men who had built them.

Eventually, damage was addressed as well as possible, and the train made its way to Saskatoon for repairs to the cars. Finally, the train reached Toronto, and Alberta livestock competed with the best in the country. That year, a Daysland farm captured the title for Senior Champion and Grand Champion Hereford bull. A Shorthorn steer from the University of Alberta herd became a champion, but livestock from all across western Canada had an excellent showing, and many animals won competitions.

In the years that followed, competition categories expanded, as did the number of competitors. The national fair proved a great opportunity for showing the region's best livestock. Like other fairs, the Royal Agricultural Winter Fair was an occasion for like-minded people to meet and learn from each other about how best to improve their herds.

Chapter 7

Insider Stories from the Midway

Fantasies, Fears, Thrills, and Prizes

The midway was the most exciting place for a child to be in summer. With their pennies, nickels or dimes, they bought tickets for the tilt-a-whirl, Ferris wheel, Lindy Loop, Spitfire, Moon Rocket and carousel. Happy to line up so they could whirl, twirl, dive, and fly, many held on to the mechanical wonders with a death grip.

Midways brought a carnival atmosphere and carnival-style entertainments. Some had rides, side shows, games of chance, food and beverage concessions. Others might only hold a contract for rides and food concessions. A few carried big name stage acts, but just as often, circuses or theatrical performers were hired for more extravagant shows.

The steed on this merry-go-round at the Edmonton Exhibition in the 1930s seemed to belong in the days of knights and castles. Glenbow Archives, NA-3-5267.

Over the years, three of the largest and most successful midways were Conklin All-Canadian Shows, Royal American Shows, and West Coast Shows in Western Canada. But there were a number of other midway companies, of varying sizes, touring across Canada during the fair season, often wintering in warmer climes.

Whether the company was large or small, in order to succeed financially, the touring schedule was often grueling. First the companies bid for engagements. Some contracts were signed independently between small communities and small midways. In other cases, fair associations contracted an entire circuit with a specific midway. Financially, the associations could negotiate better deals, bigger midways, and better talent for their money. Each fair might net less profit, but stops were guaranteed by the more lucrative large communities.

The ideal was to have as many stops as possible with a minimum number of days off. Midways preferred "live" engagements, which meant they were part of a fair or other important community event. Numbers were always higher than "still" engagements when they were the only gig in town.

The companies and people working the midways were outsiders. Few in the communities where they stopped realized the issues for owners and employees. Much was unique about "the life," and carnies even had their own vocabulary. A "joint" was a concession booth built with hinges so it was collapsible. Such temporary buildings were easily erected, pulled down and stored for travel. Some carnies were on the look-out for "marks," especially if the carnie was running a gambling joint. Some loved the work, travelling the countryside, and meeting people. Some hated it, but often, it was the only job they could get. They had their own rules, ones for life on the road and ones about proper treatment of customers, but not every carnie lived by rules.

For most, carnival work was a demanding way to make a meagre income. A few made excellent money. Still fewer dreamed of owning their own carnival company and made that dream into a reality. But every carnie had a story or many stories to tell.

Getting a Fair Break

Patty Conklin made Conklin All-Canadian Shows one of the big names in North American midways. From 1921 to 1932, the Conklins called Vancouver, BC, home. Yet, western Canada failed to keep them. The business was moved to Hamilton and then to Brantford, ON. There were big markets and more markets in the east, but perhaps Ontario was more open to the possibility that Canadian interests could achieve a truly world-class midway. The Conklins did that, despite being hit with the Depression and Second World War.

Patty Conklin wanted the western Canadian A Circuit, but despite having a unprecedented background in the travelling midway and concessions business, Conklin All-Canadian had a tough time winning an initial contract.

Patty Conklin had a big smile, a sense of humor, a vision regarding his industry, and a phenomenal business acumen. Courtesy of Conklin Shows.

The story of Patty Conklin began in 1892 when Joe Renker was born in Brooklyn. The boy who eventually became Patty Conklin had a difficult early life. Problems at home were so bad he left when he was about 10. For a while, he lived with a foster family, but soon he was out on his own. To survive, he sold peanuts, newspapers, and herrings. Then, finding work at Coney Island, he became a side show talker. By the time he was about 20, he had worked the gambling joints on midways in Oklahoma and Texas.

When he joined Clark and Conklin Shows, the world suddenly changed for him. The owners of the show, J.W. Conklin and his wife, saw something in Joe, something that led them to embrace him as part of the family. Frank Conklin, about ten years Joe's junior, became like a brother to him. In fact, the sense of family was so strong, Joe took on their name. He became J.W. "Patty" Conklin, Jr.

In 1920, J.W. died, and the next year, Frank, Patty, and his adopted mother decided to take their chances in Canada. Patty was 29 when the family decided to seek a subcontract in Manitoba. Mrs. Conklin had extensive friends in the world of travelling carnivals. One was C.A. Wortham, whose show was making its first tour of western Canada. So, the Conklins headed to Winnipeg with their boxcar of concessions. They hit a banner year for shows in the city and nearby St. Boniface. For the fair and Dominion Day, Wortham was at Happyland; the Greater Sheesley Show was on North Main Street; A.G. Barnes Circus was in town; and Lavoie's International Amusement and another show were there. Despite the number of shows, business was great for all.

The Conklins hired on with Lavoie International Amusement Company and finished the season. It was not the top show, but it had a new "Joyland" with a merry-go-round, whip, and Ferris wheel, and it was on its way up. The Conklins added their six concessions including dolls, a wheel, a race track joint, and Patty's own ball and bucket game, which he was already advertising in *Billboard* magazine.

> *My buckets are positively the original. Price, $100. This price includes eight-ounce canvas cover, solid red base balls and frame to set bucket up on, ready to operate. Concession men who are live wires, take advantage of this wonderful offer. You can use anything, from a ten-cent doll to a Beacon blanket for flash. I am the sole manufacturer of the original Conklin one-ball bucket. Price, complete, ready to go to work, $100. Please don't write, asking questions. Send $25. Bucket will be shipped for the balance C.O.D. $75.*[1]

At the end of the Lavoie tour, the Conklins decided to follow the show to its winter quarters in Vancouver. Luck was with them. The show added an extra week to the tour with a stop at Kelowna, but winter was a time for upgrading and expanding the show. The Conklins expanded their concessions and, occasionally, they opened when local charities wanted to sponsor a special event.

The owners of concessions could contract booths with various shows, packing their touring schedule as full as possible. In 1922, Conklin operated concessions with Snapp Brothers, which stopped at distant communities such as Yorkton, SK. It was also scheduled for the important Provincial Exhibition at New Westminster, BC. As well, Conklin concessions went out with Levitt-Brown-Huggins Shows, and they were used at the Vancouver Exhibition.

The family had begun to make a name for itself in Canada. By 1923, with Patty and his brother working the management end of their business, they had 15 concessions and 25 employees. Blairmore, AB, wasn't too small to book concessions, nor Vancouver too big. For the family, work – endless work – was a plus.

They had bad weather during two solid months of bookings, most of them repeats from the previous year. In one of his frequent updates to the *Billboard*, Conklin wrote "We have successfully made as many as five spots in one week without losing a day – altho it requires some special train moves to do it."[2]

By 1924, Patty saw a new opportunity. He had met Speed Garrett, who had a small show out of Seattle. The Conklins bought half the show. Conklin and Garrett All-Canadian Shows was on the road or busy at the warehouse, at the downtown offices in the Castle Hotel, or on Cambrie Street for winter charity shows sponsored by service clubs.

Fair competition was keen, but finally, in 1925, there was excitement in the air. As well as playing BC dates, the company won shows, rides, and concessions for the Western Canada Fairs' Association Class B Circuit. During the seven-week tour, the midway hit 14 fairs without losing a day, with WCFA stops across Manitoba, Saskatchewan, and Alberta. In other towns not staging fairs, there was excitement, too. For the first time in 10 years, Drumheller, AB, held a carnival featuring Conklin and Garrett Shows.

With 25 concessions and five riding devices such as a Ferris wheel, merry-go-round and seaplanes, the show traveled in 10 railway cars. Sideshows included a snake show, jungleland, motordrome, circus side show, athletic show, bughouse, and mystery show.

Problems plagued the Conklins, too. In 1927, Speed Garrett was stricken with T.B. and quickly became an invalid. Frank Conklin caught the devastating disease, too, and was hospitalized in a Los Angeles sanitarium. Subject to bronchial problems, during the 1928 season, Mrs. Conklin was again sick while they were at Winnipeg. In 1929, the company's press representative died while they were in North Battleford, SK.

As well, other events and decisions were beyond control. The exhibition association in Vancouver decided to build its own permanent carnival area, which affected winter bookings. In 1929, the stock market crashed, and in 1930, Conklin and Garrett lost the B Circuit contract to Royal American Shows. Still, Patty signed with 35 smaller communities from May to October.

In 1930, going out on a limb, the Conklins bought out Garrett. Patty owned half the show and Frank the other half, but Frank remained in hospital for two more years. Patty became fully responsible for the business and re-named it Conklin All-Canadian Shows. With the Conklins on their own, winning and losing contracts was tense business. Patty wanted the larger audiences, longer stops, and fewer down times of the Class A Circuit, but for years, it eluded him.

In the meantime, the Conklins did not become provincial in their attitudes, commitments, hiring, marketing, or other business-dealings. In the off season, family members travelled, most often to places like New York, Chicago, and Los Angeles. Patty had joined the Pacific Coast Showmen's Association, and in 1931, he became its youngest president.

He certainly had his own problems. In 1932, he decided to tour as far east as the Maritimes. The show lost money but managed to avoid bankruptcy. Still, the East seemed to hold more opportunity than the West, and finally, the family moved its winter quarters to Hamilton, ON.

In the industry, others had recognized Patty's organizational talents, energy, and ability to make things happen. He lobbied the Canadian railways about the cost of carnival transportation, and he won significant concessions during the 30s. In 1935, the Showman's League of America, around since Bill Cody initiated it in 1913, elected Patty Conklin as president. The next year, he was re-elected as the only president since Cody to serve two terms for the Showman's League.

In his positions, he stayed friendly with competitors and encouraged them to work together within the showmen associations for the good of all. He promoted a fund for retired showmen and supported a cemetery fund for them. He spear-headed show productions and banquets to raise money for charities. After all, charity was good business, but association members had a responsibility to community, too.

Despite the move east, the Conklins had not abandoned the idea of touring the A Circuit in western Canada. Winning was a different story. In 1936, Patty bid for concessions only – not the midway – at the Western Canada Association of Exhibitions, which governed the big fairs. Again, the competition was stiff. Hocks, Goodman Bazaars Ltd., in business for 35 years, had operated the concessions on the circuit for the past four years. Another competitor was C.J. Sedlmayr, representing Royal American Shows. R.R. Castle represented United Shows of America, and Max Linderman spoke for World of Mirth from New York.

Royal American offered new canvas, new panel fronts, colored lighting and neon tubing for 1936. It had the longest touring season in outdoor show business. As a result, it could get the best operators, Sedlmayr bragged. His concessions were big time. Royal American had all the games available and had won two-year contracts for fairs in Florida and Atlanta, Georgia. But "Canada was the only territory covered by his organizations where his concessions did not work," he complained.[3]

What proportion of merchandise would be bought in Canada? asked an association representative. As much as possible, but some novelties weren't available in Canada.

Patty Conklin made his pitch after several others. He and his brother had wanted the fairs for some years. They were Canadian. The only merchandise not bought in Canada was some Japanese chinaware and English pottery. They employed Canadians; he had 27 merchandising concessions. People always won merchandise, so there was no gambling. The company would accept any ruling or direction from the chairman of concessions at each location. Conklins could provide all the right banking assurances and credentials. The Depression had taken a toll, but Conklin was growing again. He didn't have enough equipment for midways in the A Circuit, but the company was prepared to go in that direction to "ensure their retaining the business for a long time."

Some association members saw a problem in offering concessions to one bidder and the midway to another. In the end, Sedlmayr of Royal American won both.

Still determined to have a shot at the A Circuit and the big time, Conklin All-Canadian Shows expanded its midway. Patty worked hard at improving the business for everyone. Rather than holding a grudge, he acknowledged success and accomplishment when it was due.

In August of 1936, about six months after losing his bid for concessions to Royal American Shows, he made a two-day visit to his competition's fair location in Cincinnati. Representing the SLA, he was promoting new memberships. Of Royal American's midway, he had nothing but praise.

It is by far the most gigantic piece of show equipment that I have ever seen in my entire show career. The lighting effects are so beautiful that they are really astounding, and their attractions are superior to most anything that I have had the pleasure of seeing....While visiting this show I was treated royally by the management and the entire staff.[4]

As a testament to his own show, in 1937, Conklins won its bid for the biggest annual out-door exhibition in Canada. The Canadian National Exhibition [CNE] in Toronto was the plum contract. Also, during the years of the Second World War, when fairgrounds were used for train-ing troops, and there were labor and transportation shortages for the industry, Patty seemed to know the government's policies and rules regarding fairs and midways better than anyone. Still, knowledge, energy, perseverance, brains, and success had not won him the Class A Circuit in western Canada.

In 1940, "looking to the future," Patty made yet another bid for the circuit. He lost. In 1941, "again looking to the future," he made still another bid. The circuit just wouldn't go with Conklin, despite Patty's having making huge profits for the CNE, and eventually shattering records when grosses from the rides and shows were compared to other exhibitions around the world.

His breaking into the A Circuit was unbelievably, perhaps unduly, difficult, but in 1944, Conklin won a contract. With of the war effort, government became rigid in its transportation, employment, and importation policies, and Canadian companies were preferred for contracts. However, after the war, Conklin's major competitor Royal American once again gained a stran-glehold on the circuit, one that lasted from the 1950s into the mid-1970s.

By 1975, management had passed to Patty's son Jim. When a huge scandal about Royal American Shows, fraud, and the manager of the Edmonton Exhibition broke, Royal American was prohibited from working in Canada. Finally, Conklin Shows won the A Circuit, but Patty Conklin had died in 1970. The show he had worked so hard to build had prevailed over his old "friend" and competitor, but he had missed witnessing his own success.

Fun, Games, and Endless Work

Launching their own midway when they hadn't grown up in the carnival business seemed like a high risk choice, but Lou and Ethel Garratt were among the few western Canadians with fair, rodeo, or midway-related businesses. Between about 1949 and 1966, Garratt Shows, which was in no way related to Conklin and Garrett Shows, toured the small-town circuit in south and central Alberta and Saskatchewan. Some years, the midway travelled into BC, too. At first, their only child, Oney, then a young adult, helped. Occasionally, so did their son-in-law, Doug Martin.

Lou Garratt was born in 1901 at Brandon, MB, and he grew up on a farm near Medicine Hat. Ethel Olsen Garratt was born in South Dakota, but the newly married couple settled on the outskirts of Medicine Hat. Young Lou worked as a brakeman on the railway, and Ethel was a nurse. Their midway business grew out of the fact that they were great marksmen.

Like many prairie people who grew up in the 1920s and earlier, the two could handle rifles. They belonged to the Medicine Hat Rifle and Revolver Club, were good at target shooting, and enjoyed the sport. When the Second World War broke out, interest in guns and target shooting skyrocketed, even on the home front. Marksmanship competitions, such as those offered through the local gun club, were increasingly important. Sharpshooter Ethel was so proficient

The young boys at this shooting game were attending the September 1912 Calgary Stampede. They were likely cadets. Even in the late 1950s, some games used real guns and bullets. Courtesy of Glenbow Archives, NA 370-15.

she won the Grand Aggregate Championship for Southern Alberta – competing against male sharpshooters, including some from the city police, air force training camp, prisoner of war camp, and army bases at Suffield and Maple Creek.

Given their own talents and the presence of the air force base, the Garratts opened a shooting gallery for target practice in Medicine Hat. When an army base opened in Fort Macleod, they opened another, and Ethel ran the businesses, which did well.

Decision time came in the mid-1940s. With the war ending and soldiers returning, the CPR introduced a new rule. Its employees could not have another job or business. When in town, one of the owners of Gayland Shows had been impressed by the Garratt operation. He wanted Lou to take the shooting gallery on the road as a subcontractor with the Gayland midway. The Garratts took the offer. Lou quit his job, shut down the shooting gallery, and went on the summer tours.

Since the gallery used real guns and ammunition, the Garratts had to ensure safety. The guns were mounted and chained in large hollow, metal tubes that were aimed toward the target cards. The cards, with fives or eights printed on them, had been purchased from Amusement Wholesale. Behind them was material to absorb the bullets and prevent ricocheting. Clients were in no danger, but winning was difficult. The marksmen had to shoot out the entire number on a card and that meant perfect aim and shots.

For the next four to five years, travelling with Gayland, Lou set up his shooting gallery in the arcade game trailer, which also housed slot and pinball machines. Lou learned the summer tour business while Ethel remained in Medicine Hat and went back to nursing.

Daughter Oney was born in Medicine Hat, and when she was nineteen years old and just married, Ethel decided to go on the road. So, that year, Ethel and Lou operated the shooting gallery, while Oney and husband Doug Martin had the candy apples and candy floss for Gayland.

Lou Garratt (second from left) sits with his male employees on top of one of the truck-mounted trailers built by Lou for transporting the midway, concessions, employees, and belongings. Norman Cook (Sharein) is 5th from the right. Courtesy of Oney Martin.

The show was a good-sized midway. Owners Tiny Nicoles and Ab Greenway knew their business and were successful, but the show had strippers and a reputation for "skin games" or "shell game," which were the gambling joints found objectionable in some communities.

"Very large Teddy bears were displayed, a novelty item at the time. They...could not be purchased in any store, and they would have been purchased from the Amusement Wholesale,"[5] remembered Oney. The stuffed animals or other prizes attracted customers. "They would end up just cleaning some poor innocent guy out of his pay cheque."[6]

But the Garratts saw other possible approaches in the business. Before the next season, the family had decided to launch their own midway, Garratt Shows. From their home base, Lou began buying rides and concession booths. He hired workers and set out with his first show. The midway played its hometown and was soon touring small towns.

That first year, Ethel operated the shooting gallery. Also known as Blondie, some years, she had the ice cream stand, but her greatest success came with Blondie's Burger Bar. At home, Ethel had considered herself a terrible cook. On the road, her hamburger stand and chip concession was always a popular spot. Not only were midway patrons served burgers, the trailer was where meals were prepared for the staff, too. As a nurse, Ethel tended cuts and bruises of midway patrons and workers. Then, there was the necessary office work, which was handled in a house trailer when the show was on the road.

Periodically, Oney and Doug operated the candy floss stand, and one year, Doug did all the bookings for the show. Usually, Oney worked only when the midway was busy because it was part of a "live" show, such as a stampede, fair, or other community event. At her stand, she stood from 10:00 a.m. until 10:00 p.m. making floss and selling it for ten cents a cone.

Lou was in charge of operations and workers, and other Medicine Hat people joined the tour, too. One fellow took over the arcade. A couple whose restaurant offered fine dining during the off season, operated the ice cream stand in the summer. Sometimes a couple from Taber brought along ponies for the kiddies to ride. "Had there been a vote for most valuable employee – Vaugh Cotton would have won it every time. Vaugh had only one arm – but could do the work of two men," Oney recalled.[7]

Preparation always began long before touring season. For income from October to May, Ethel continued nursing. At their modest home and acreage, work for the next year's show was underway. The Garratts acquired new equipment, mostly purchased from manufacturers in the USA, but sometimes from other operators.

During the winter, Lou hired a local man named Ashley Butterwick to do all the painting and repainting of the rides, wooden components of concessions, and trucks. In the meantime, Lou repaired rides and designed some of his own games.

Before RVs and mobile homes became popular and readily available, Lou was a transportation pioneer. Large midways generally transported people and equipment from one big city or town to another by railway. Then, locals with wagons or trucks were hired to haul the cargo to the grounds. The first small midways had travelled in horse-drawn covered wagons. Later, trailers were pulled by cars or trucks, but Lou used his design and handyman skills to build trailer boxes that fit on large truck beds. One such re-designed vehicle became the company's office. Others carried equipment and concessions. The model that Lou built for his wife as her summer home while on the road was unique at the time. It had everything she could need, and today, it would be licensed as a motor home, but Lou had trouble getting license and registration, as the vehicles didn't fit in the truck nor car categories.

Each spring, every piece of equipment was carefully checked. During tours, government inspectors might appear, but safety was the owner's responsibility. Usually, the only direction from an inspector might be that a wire needed to be buried on fair grounds.

Inevitably, important decisions loomed. What kind of business did they want? The Garratts chose to carry games of chance, but the police could and did shut down offensive games, and Lou didn't want the risk or trouble.

"My dad worked closely with the RCMP...Gayland could have trouble and did have. Maybe that is why my dad took a softer approach."

They decided gambling games such as crown and anchor, 7 over and under, and the slot known as the one armed bandit would be operated only when sponsored by local service clubs. So Lou negotiated deals with the Elks, Kiwanis, Kinsmen, and Rotarians. Volunteers ran the games.

The photo was midway humor, but for Gayland Shows, Whiskey and Rum (the owners' two dogs) were part of life on the road. Unfortunately, the behavior of some fair-goers and workers after drinking presented problems. Courtesy of Oney Martin.

Garratts provided a cash float, usually about $100 in their aprons, and at closing, the money was counted. $100 was put back in the apron, and the club and Garratts split the balance.

"The odd time, to a club's embarrassment, there wouldn't even be $100 in the apron at the end of a busy night – which would mean the club had a dishonest member," remembered Oney. "They would feel real bad....it didn't happen often, but it did happen."

The midway lights remained on and the music played until every one left. Only then was the midway shut down – no matter how late the hour.

The liquor laws were very strict at the time. Only those over 21 could legally drink. Bars closed down for supper time, and no liquor was served on Sunday. Still, alcohol could mean trouble for the midway.

"[Some] had been drinking at bars until closing...then they would go down to check out the midway...In some of those towns with a population of three or four thousand, the only excitement they had was ball tournaments. The midway coming to town was a cause for celebration!"

"Those last people would be the ones that were gambling, too....probably...drinking and seeking the additional thrill of gambling," remembered Oney.

"Often, the customers would come on the lot drunk and be cruising for a fight, whether justified or not. Sometimes there would be trouble – sometimes not."

In contrast, Gayland "...had two strong men that were partners and able to deal with that. Dad just didn't want that trouble even though he dealt with it well when it did happen."

"Why we weren't robbed on any given night, I don't know...we never had the problem...never had the problem. Never even thought about it, but Dad would be able the odd time to go to a bank and they would transfer the funds to Medicine Hat. He had to keep a lot of money on hand just for change. Concessionaires had to have a purse to start."[8]

Although money was never stolen, other things were. Problems were part of the business, and as often as not, they were employee-related.

"Tired and cranky employees sometimes don't get along. Sometimes the police would come looking for someone – and take away one of our hard-working people. Sometimes an employee would just leave in the middle of the night before a big move or tear down. Equipment breakdown was the other half of the equation," noted Oney.

Before the touring season, show trailers sat empty on the Garratt acreage, but sometimes, Lou and Ethel housed a few employees over the winter.

Early in the spring, former employees and would-be employees just turned up at the Garratt home. By the May 24th weekend and the first show of the season, at nearby Taber, Alberta, the extra rooms and trailers were bursting with workers.

"What caused people to go? What was in it for them?...It had sort of a call to it," remembered Doug. "Once you went out, you'd complain, complain, but you missed it....the camaraderie...There may be 50 on the show, but you hit some little town, and some of these little places just distrusted anybody from outside of town."

"Figured we were all crooks," added Oney.

Doug continued, "They almost came as a mob, and that would cause problems. So [shows] had their little secret code...You would call out a certain word. Larger shows at the time used the code 'HEY RUBE,' to alert everybody in the show there was trouble."

"You wouldn't even need to do that....You should absolutely have no trouble with the candy floss, but every now and then a drunk would come up, and start giving you a bad time. Over what? The candy floss was too small or too big or the wrong color, and he would stand there and berate you. When the candy floss machine is throwing out candy floss – there is not time for anything else as it needs your constant attention. And when I would get a chance to look up – there would be staff standing all around – just to make sure I was going to be able to handle the situation."

Travelling with the shows, women as well as men became quite capable of handling troublesome patrons.

"My mother could handle it pretty well. She wouldn't take much," said Oney.

The midway "family" did spill into the family of marriage and birth, so much so that Joe Renker had become a Conklin. Similarly, the Garratts became especially close to one of their young workers.

Some years, Ethel Garratt operated the ice cream stand, always a popular concession when the weather was hot and dry. Courtesy of Oney Martin.

Forty years later, having moved to Australia, Norman Sharein, known as Norman Cook when he had worked for the Garratts, returned to visit Oney and Doug. He was welcome to stay at their home. After all, he was "family," and he, too, had stories.

Born in Nelson, BC, he lived with his single mother until about 1953, when he was 17. In July of 1953, he went to the Benalto Stampede. Garratt Shows was there and Norman wanted a job. He started working on a kiddy ride and finished out the season.

Of most Garratt employees, Norman remembered, "they were so thankful to have a job... they wouldn't do anything on the show to endanger [that]...anything big, like steal the generator and sell it."

Oney added, "There's an expression 'knock down.' [The concessionaires] are going to knock down a little bit because they are going to eat out of their apron, and you expect that, so you don't cause a big fuss over it. If there was a lot missing, that was different."[9]

Norman made a great employee in the shooting gallery. He could always find a little bit of the red number left on the card after the patron's three shots. In fact, he was more diligent than his boss about it. One time in Cold Lake, AB, where there were many good riflemen associated with the army base, Norman left the gallery in the hands of his boss. He could hardly believe it when he came back to find that Lou had given away the big $50 prize.

"I would have fired him," laughed Norman.

The first year Norman worked for the Garratts, he learned the harsh facts of life for some people. One night on the grounds, a man wanted a bootlegger and offered his daughter as prize or payment for a bottle of whiskey. Norman refused.

"Being young and naive ...I was really upset...To think that a man would do that ...! It's something that stuck with me all these years...It was a shocker and I couldn't get over it."[10]

Other aspects of carnie life were great.

"I loved travelling, going to a different place all the time...To me it was an exciting job."

Sleep deprivation was one of the greatest problems for Norman and everyone else. Milo and Brooks, AB, were regular stops. Both had big summer stampedes. The problem was that one event was the day following the other event, and every year, Garratt Shows worked both towns. The distance wasn't great, but workers had to pack everything just as carefully. It took four hours to knock down the show. The night was spent travelling, and it took another four hours to set up the next day. The goal was to be ready by the mid-morning when community events started. Sleep was not on the agenda there or for some other locations, too. Norman was young, so he slept in concession tents, in the trucks, under them, or where ever he could find space.

Lack of bathing and toilet facilities were other problems.

"Some [toilets] were in a terrible state....Finding a place to bathe...Some of those guys got pretty high. There was one fellow, his feet would have knocked the flies off a garbage can."

Older hotels in small towns had full bathrooms at the end of the hall. For one dollar, people could use the bathrooms to clean up. Carnies took advantage of the option, but lack of time made it difficult to bath as often as they wanted.

According to Norman, most workers didn't really need strong people skills. A few of the barkers were the con man type, but mostly, employees had to be "willing to work any hour of the day...or night. You can't be a union person," he claimed. "You have to be just a good worker... because everyone has to pitch in."

Those who didn't, didn't last long.

"Lou had this authority about him. I think he would just go up and say 'Get lost.'...He would have been a good policeman."

But problems with patrons could become serious, too. Especially when they were drunk.

"I remember one, maybe two people, on that shooting gallery. They were so cross when I said there was some red left on the card, the one guy, he yanked the gun loose from the chain. The chain didn't give, but he really yanked it. I think he would have shot me."

In 1955, he left the show a little early. Lou had hired someone to manage the concessions. The new manager wanted Norman to set up his joint first thing, but Norman was good at it, and he was fast, so he liked helping the others put up the rides. The relationship didn't work out.

The Ferris wheel owned by Garratt Shows was purchased from a factory in Chicago. Oney Martin believes it was a refurbished model. Courtesy of Oney Martin.

"This guy took all the joy out of working there," Norman remembered, and his judge of character was not wrong. The couple had stayed at the Garratt's.

"They stole a gun that Dad had, a pistol. And Mom had quite a collection of antique coins. They stole that, as well as a car Dad had lent them," recalled Oney.

Other problems were devastating for the entire show and affected the bottom line.

"With show business, the great enemy is weather. You struggle to get someplace. You get settled. The people come, and all of a sudden, the sky opens up and it rains for three days. Then you get to tear down in the mud and move on," recalled Oney.

During one of the worst weather disasters for Garratt Shows, Oney was along. Near Sylvan Lake, "The skies opened up and it poured...."

Roads flooded.

"We were going then...I think to...Stettler or Wetaskiwin....When we came to this place, there was a farmer on a tractor sitting on a hill, and every truck that came, he would wait until they got real stuck. Then he would go down, hook them up, pull them out, charge them $50 and then watch them go into the next puddle and do the same thing again. Talk about a bandit!"

Running a midway – whether large or small – meant work and lots of it. Large midways had more rides and concessions, but they also had more workers. There were elements of adventure, but few outsiders understood the hardships and amount of physical and organizational work. For Ethel and Lou, the midway was a good business but not a huge money maker – mostly because they chose to only run the gambling joints when partnered with service clubs. Still, there were other intrinsic rewards.

Over the years, Garratt Shows never became nearly as large as Gayland, but they had the family show they wanted. Midways, like other businesses, have a beginning and end. Sometimes, the end was a sad one. Ethel was struck with two different cancers.

"Dad panicked. Somebody came along and wanted to buy it, and he sold it. Mind you, the guy never paid for it. He...ran it into the ground for a couple of years. And it became nothing. Dad repossessed some of the equipment...but never really got the money out of it."

In the Blood

Hazel Hall Elves started as a carnival artist, but like other carnies, she learned to do whatever needed to be done. Most carnival art involved painting the fronts and banners that drew crowds to side shows. In the carnie world, being the show artist was prestigious, but Hazel soon learned the work was intermittent and collecting her pay from the independent joint and side show operators was an art in itself. To make a living, she worked dozens of different games on the midway. She even developed her own dart game, but it wasn't a money maker. She worked and lived in a world of jargon and colorful cuss words and of people known as geeks and freaks, crooks and kooks, marks and gunkies.

Hazel was born into a carnie family. From her infancy in the 1920s, she had been on the road with her mom and dad. During his 45 years in the business, Frank Hall had a strong man act, a trapeze act, magic act, and snake act. He operated joints, designed games, built rides such as a motorcycle motordrome, repaired rides or whatever else needed repairing, and managed Kiddyland. Frank worked a number of midways traveling throughout British Columbia and the Canadian prairies. From time to time, his employers took their shows across Canada, too, but the Hall home was in the lower mainland of BC.

There, Vancouver, New Westminster, Burnaby, and Coquitlam offered winter contracts to midway companies. So, the Hall family didn't suffer from the seasonal unemployment of most midway workers. Though not happy about it, most summers, Hazel's mother raised her children in midway tents and small-town hotels, and the children played in the sawdust and dirt of the exhibition grounds.

Harold, Hazel's older brother, was only four when he became part of Frank's trapeze act. Soon, Harold and a second brother had their own act, billed as the Boy Wrestling Wonders. Also, when Frank had a strong man act, he stretched out on a bed of nails, and the boys walked on his chest. Still later, they became part of his magic act.

As a girl, Hazel was not expected to start work as early in life as her brothers. In fact, she was protected from some of the harsher realities, but all the while, she learned every trick in the trade. Her father loved carnival life, and he respected his fellow workers, including the "freaks," the strippers, and the men who could "reel in a mark" and make a good living at their jobs – but do it honestly.

"Don't ever let me catch you looking down on anyone....Them people have it tough enough, so don't make it any tougher for them by hurting their feelings," Frank directed his daughter.[11]

Hazel was fascinated by carnival life, but eventually, her mother stopped following the circuit. Then, in the 1940s, to her mother's disappointment, 15-year-old Hazel decided to join her father on the road. At the time, the company that employed Frank had stops in Ontario and Quebec, and Hazel caught the train for Ontario.

Young, daring, and on her own, Hazel made friends with soldiers on the train. When the train was side-tracked for days, she drank and had a fine time – until the next day when a dismal hang-over meant regrets. The train was late. Her father was worried, but her life as a carnie worker began.

Although hired as the show artist, she didn't get paid. Instead, she was expected to subcontract her services and had to negotiate with the independent operators. Following her father's advice, no matter how much haggling was involved, she was insistent about her prices. Still, during her first year and in subsequent years, she could not make enough money as an artist to cover her expenses and make the season worthwhile. Facing that reality, she opted to run one or another of the joints and soon learned that Kids' Day was the most difficult day on the lot. Parents let

For decades, Kewpie dolls could be purchased or won on midways. Popular with girls, most were inexpensive and attached to thin bamboo canes. Some were available as decorations on lamps and other items. Courtesy of Glenbow Archives, ND-3-1373 (a).

loose their children, who ran wild, became insolent brats, and even stole prizes. But the other ups and downs of being an artist were equally frustrating.

One slick operator, who her mother had called a "gentleman gangster" and who was always dressed to kill, asked her to paint banners for his new girlie show. Hazel wanted $100. They settled on $80 plus paint and plywood. Hazel's father had warned her about operators who reneged on bills, so she demanded prepayment of half, the rest when she was finished.

Good at painting realistic human figures, Hazel put them on a black background to emphasize their shapeliness and make the art unlike the run-of-the-mill carnival work. She felt proud when she delivered her work and received her final payment.

The next year, when she saw her banners, she didn't immediately recognize them. The gentleman gangster hadn't liked the background, so someone painted orange and yellow over it. Worse yet, he had black borders painted around each female figure.

The women's breasts were nothing like the realistic ones that Hazel had worked so hard to perfect. Repainted in off-white, they were ugly and flat, hanging there like two white balls.

"How ghastly," she complained, refusing to ever paint for him again.

He replied, "I'll never ask you again."

While he was in Quebec, the law required the bare breasts be covered.

"At least you could have taped cloth over them....that way you wouldn't have completely ruined them."

The gentleman gangster laughed. "I did at first, but some goofy frog lifted up the cover for a peek and a priest turned me in for showing pornography."[12]

Hazel couldn't help but laugh, too.

One year, a handsome operator pressed her to learn the dance steps and go on stage with the girlie show. It would be easy; she would be great; and she would make good money. Hazel watched the strip show.

"No," she answered. It was not a matter of morality. She had no hesitancy about painting bare-breasted women for the shows. It wasn't right for her, she claimed. She was just too tall and awkward.

Hazel was not eager to follow the wild crowd amongst the carnies, but even if she had wanted to, it would have been very difficult. Her father was a fierce protector who laid down the law about who she could associate with and who she was to avoid.

For her friends, he preferred big girls, just off the farm. "Corn-fed," he called them. They were to be good girls and honest girls who had joined the tour simply because they needed a job. Often, Hazel had nothing in common with them, and just as often, they were really looking for high risk adventures.

When she had first joined the tour, Frank didn't want Hazel hanging out with the strippers, but eventually, he decided the nice ones might keep her out of trouble. Instead, they were as likely to get her into trouble as save her from it. Still, when she wanted to get a hotel room so she could have a bath and a decent night's sleep, at least she had friends who would split the cost with her.

As for finding her own boyfriend, the problem was totally different for Hazel than for other girls her age. Rules of the show dictated that carnival workers were not to date locals. As far as Frank was concerned, even other carnies weren't suitable for his daughter. Only the son of a good friend seemed an acceptable escort.

Hazel and the young man sometimes went for meals together, and they had lots in common, but they were allowed little real freedom. Once when they went to a movie in town, they were late in returning. By the time they arrived back at the lot, Frank and his friend had midway workers scouring the entire community.

Eventually, like other girls, Hazel met a special someone. Would marriage and children mean the end of life as a carnie?

No, the connection remained. She, her husband, and children visited midways where her father was working. At first, it was just for fun. Then, when she and her husband separated, Hazel went back to the employment she knew so well. With her own young son and two daughters, Hazel was again tagging along on a summer tour with her father.

Despite the hardships, Hazel was hooked on the carnival lifestyle. Like her father, it was in her blood. She trained countless kids and young adults to help her run some of the joints, and she developed her own talents at pawning off junk jewelry and inexpensive prizes as if they were really worthy of the player's effort, talents, and money.

Her son, too, was a natural carnie. From the time he was seven, he loved helping at the joints. By 14, he had proven that he was a great talker with a keen eye and good sense when it came to judging fair visitors and fellow carnies. In contrast, Hazel's daughters, Toni and Rolli, were not so enthusiastic. They helped if required, and their help was needed the year Frank intended to retire from the business.

Things had not gone well over a few years, but Hazel's brother staked Frank the cost of reptiles he needed for a snake show. Someone lent him a tent, and to help, Hazel painted exotic banners.

Frank hired a young woman, who he named Zoma the Wild Girl, to sit in the pit with the snakes. She proved a dud. Worse yet, saying she was lonely, she nagged him to let a friend sit with her. After five days, Zoma quit, but both girls wanted payment. Frank refused to pay the extra girl, and the two came back with a labor relations worker.

Reluctantly, Frank agreed to a settlement.

The show had to go on. Hazel's job was selling tickets, so she couldn't become the snake girl, even though she and the whole family knew the expected patter.

Hazel phoned her girls, who loved their grandfather and would do anything for him.

"But sit in the snake pit. Mother, how could you? Can't you find anybody?"[13]

Finally, for their grandfather, both sat in the pit for the price of one.

Not only did they sit there, the girls educated the audience about the different snakes – and did a fine job of it. Their mother and grandfather were proud.

One day, from where he was out front, Frank heard a scream. Toni ran from the tent yelling. Rolli had been bitten.

Always a performer, Frank turned the mic over to Hazel.

"Keep 'em coming," he said and rushed into the tent.

"It's OK folks, don't leave. We have anti snake bite ointment and she'll be alright."

Making a performance of it, he sucked the spot where drops of blood were on his granddaughter's finger.

"Twenty years ago, folks, this girl would have died within twenty-four hours but thanks to modern science, she will be able to go about her usual duties within an hour," he had added.

Again, he made a performance of settling Rolli into a chair.

"After a little rest she will again be able to explain the secrets of reptilian rituals, the secrets of which through superstition and ignorance have never before been revealed. Come back tomorrow folks and bring your friends for another fine lecture by this brave intelligent girl."

In the meantime, it was Toni's turn to sit in the snake pit and lecture the crowd.

In fact, the snake bite had not been a poisonous one. Rolli had been in no real danger. The bite was just one more experience to add to the countless stories of three generations who grew up travelling the midway circuit of western Canada.

Murphy's Law Wreaks Havoc

Chapter 8

So, What Could Go Wrong?

What couldn't go wrong in preparation for a fair? Most problems had to do with sunburn and sick stomachs. Scratches, bruises, and minor injuries were common, but other injuries to animal and human competitors were sometimes serious, and very few were fatal. Other day-to-day problems concerned lost children, lost wallets, and lost tempers. Drunkenness and petty crime often escalated during the fair.

Much more distressing were fires. Some rampaged through exhibition buildings. The race horse barns burned at Edmonton in 1942, and

When Fred McCall's plane crashed on the top of the merry-go-round at Calgary, the incident was reported in some newspapers as "The World's Most Unique Air Accident." Courtesy of Glenbow Archives, NA-1451-27.

fires destroyed the Regina grandstand and the Aquatic Club at Kelowna before the 1969 regatta. In that instance, only the building burned, but there could be no replacing loss of life – whether human or livestock. Buildings could be replaced, and increasingly, they were insured, but often construction costs exceeded insurance payout.

There were other significant problems, too. Weather and freak storms wreaked havoc. In terms of weather, planners expected the unexpected. Temperatures and skies might be perfect, or it might rain for days on end, obliterating attendance. A deluge could create a sloppy track for racing events, a muddy infield for rodeo, or cancellation of water sports at regattas. Hail the size of golf balls might rain down on midway crowds. For those communities that had their major celebration early in the spring or late in the fall, snow and freezing temperatures were always a possibility north of the 49th. Crowds could be cold – even if they had blankets – or they sweltered in t-shirts or shorts. Just in case, larger communities contracted strong indoor or under-the-big-top acts, but there was little else they could do.

Sometimes it was technology or the combination of new technologies and the age-old problem of bad weather that led to trouble. One of the purposes of the community events was to showcase new technology. Sometimes quirks in the "new machines" created risks for the fair-going public. The dirigibles and airplanes that were such a hit at fairs were subject to mechanical problems, or grounded, or destroyed by weather and fire.

As early as 1896, the man-made world failed fun seekers at the most important festival of the year. Victoria Day was a major celebration in BC's capital city of Victoria. Each year, May 24 had all the excitement of any other community fair. There were races, a military re-enactment, bands, rides for the children, and loads of food and fun. Eighteen-ninety-six was no different from other years – or so it seemed when the day began. Thousands of people were going to Macaulay Point where the events were held. While a crowded streetcar was crossing the Point Ellice Bridge, the structure collapsed. With 124 passengers on board, twice as many as usual, the streetcar fell into the water below. Despite heroic efforts to save them, 58 men, women, and children died.

Global economics and international politics were beyond control, too. Early communities might be small and even isolated, but they could not escape the impact of nature and the world community. The thirties emptied the pocketbooks of fair organizations, visitors, and locals. As a result, many community events were cancelled. Yet a fair, rodeo, or regatta could brighten a few hours, a day, or a few days for people burdened with the terrible conditions of the Depression.

"Is there any way to keep the event going? Give the kids a few days of fun? Lighten people's spirits?" organizers wondered, and some found surprising solutions to the dilemma.

The economics of the 1930s played a devastating role for many community festivals, but compared to the drought-stricken, dust bowl of the prairies, the Okanagan was better able to continue its festivals. Food was very available and mild winters meant the cost of living was somewhat more manageable. As a result, more outsiders were attracted to the region. This meant Okanagan fairs and festivals were less seriously affected by the economic downturn. As well, the

War canoe races remained popular and competitive. Increasingly, women's teams entered the races. This team competed at the Penticton Regatta in 1936. Penticton Museum and Archives, 37-2854.

playground of the west had so much to offer in terms of inexpensive fun. For many, May Day was an important, traditional celebration focusing on children. Water sports, rodeo, and children's events could be managed fairly inexpensively, so many Okanagan communities did not cancel their festivities.

War was another world event that dramatically affected community associations responsible for planning the gatherings and good times of summer. They wanted to save money for the war effort. Did that mean they had to cancel the regatta, fair, or rodeo?

Some problems were unusual but logical given the industry and geography of the area. In 1952, Weyburn, Saskatchewan, held its annual fair, but no cloven-hoofed animals were allowed due to foot and mouth disease.

"A fair without animals is like a kite without a tail," wrote the fair's secretary, Roy Schultz. "It just doesn't go anywhere."[1] In the farm and ranch country of the Canadian prairies, his words rang true.

Organizers did their best to right the wrongs, weigh risks, plan options, and hire good people. They joined with other communities to solve problems. They weathered all storms and returned to the drawing board each year with unending optimism and resilience.

Weathering the Weather

No community escaped one weather problem or another during the annual fairs, rodeos, or regattas.

Full-blown cyclones were not normal prairie weather, but on May 28, 1904, Brandon was hit. The fair building was flattened. Strangely enough, locals didn't consider the event an absolute hardship. The wood was useful kindling, and the community was ready for a bigger and more modern facility. Time was of the essence to finish the new building before the fair. The

$15 000 in construction costs was significant, but not to be deterred, the community went to work. All except the finishing touches were completed by fair time, and fair-goers had a fine, new, domed building.

Ironically, during the drought on the prairies in the Dirty Thirties, lack of rain wasn't always the problem. In 1937, the Moose Jaw Exhibition was hit with heavy rains. Scheduled for a four-day run, ending June 26, the exhibition began with dust and heat. Then came the thunderstorms. The next two days brought continued bad weather, and on one day, the racing and grandstand show had to be cancelled.

That summer, the Royal Canadian Shows midway was at Saskatoon in central Saskatchewan. Monday, 19 July, all hell broke loose. A storm swept in with gale-force winds. Throughout the grounds, crowds raced for shelter. The monkey show was in the path of the storm. Nearby were four huge light standards. If any of it came down, lives would be endangered by the iron standards, heavy iron stakes and tubing. Patrons, workers, and animals were quickly evacuated from the tent. Minutes later, the tent was flattened and the light standards had been bent in two by the wind.[2]

The combinations of weather-related problems seemed endless. Winnipeg was in a flood plain. Even in the early decades of the 1900s, the city was devastated by floods, including during exhibition dates. During the second decade, not only was the water overflowing the banks of the river problematic, so was the sanitation problem that accompanied it. On one visit of the Miller Brothers 101 Wild West Show, performers, as well as locals, were struck by typhoid.

The summer of 1939, the Winnipeg Exhibition and the city experienced wind, hail, and torrential rain. Sparks Circus provided the shows and entertainment, and Conklin Shows had the midway. The storm struck on Tuesday night around 8:00 in the evening, which meant the crowds weren't as heavy as they would have been on a Friday or Saturday night.

Winds hit with a vengeance; hail pummeled the ground – and everything else. Display banners resembled the tattered memory of a past event. Down they came. Down too came tents. Neon lights and signs blew several feet. Even the Ferris wheel was dislodged, and the metal of some attractions became twisted.

Canvas men and blacksmiths worked all night cleaning up. Amazingly, the next day, most of the shows and rides were operating. By Thursday, life on the grounds was back to normal, but the cost of the damage had been heavy. Damage to the Conklin midway had amounted to about $10 000, and Sparks Circus had similar repair bills.[3]

Especially in later years, many shows and fair boards purchased insurance, but the amount of insurance was often inadequate, and of course, there were problems related to weather for which no insurance was available. Heat was one of them.

In July, 1941, during the Exhibition, Edmonton suffered a heat wave. The torrid temperatures meant some visitors stayed home. Compared with the 1940 figures, the gate was down by about 11 000 people, but not all was lost. Young people still frequented the midway, and in the cool of the evening, fair-goers filled the grandstand on four nights for the Barnes-Carruthers show.[4]

Chinook City's Dominion Exhibition, 1908

Calgarians had painstakingly planned for every contingency during the July 1-July 9 Dominion Exhibition of 1908. Usually in early July, sunny Alberta lived up to her reputation, but ambulances, firemen, and hospitals were ready – just in case. Still, workers assumed their actual job was to be boosters, go on parade, decorate fire wagons and civic floats, show off fine horses and wave proudly to the enthusiastic men, women, and children who would line the streets.

Backed by $60 000 from the federal, provincial, and local governments, the bustling, young city was confident. Like a small world's fair, the Dominion Exhibition showcased the latest and greatest. Detractors had claimed Calgary wasn't large enough to play host. Locals were adamant they could overcome the handicap of size, and they determined to stage the biggest and best ever show.

Many had been born or raised in the United States and still had family and friends south of the border. So Calgary planned to celebrate Canada's next-door neighbor, too. American show-men were booked. Advertising was directed at ordinary Americans, and for July 4th, an Independence Day parade was scheduled. The Canadian Pacific Railway agreed to run a special excursion train between Spokane and Calgary. Six cars of revelers would detrain early enough to enjoy the special parade and the salute to America.

Closer to home, from dry and windy communities like Lethbridge and from tranquil, park-land towns such as Innisfail, people travelled on other rail routes and by stage coaches, wagons, and buggies. Some arrived during the two days of event preparation, others in time for the July 1 Dominion Day parade and opening ceremonies. Extending a hearty welcome, Calgary was ready for a good time.

One of the most awe-inspiring demonstrations was an airship designed by an American pro-fessor, C. J. Strobel, from Toledo, Ohio. During the most important race of its kind, in October 1907, at St. Louis, Missouri, Strobel's airship not only proved a winner, it broke airship speed records. Booked for the Calgary event, Strobel's airship would be in a category of its own.

Days before the exhibition opened, the American airship pilot, Captain Jack Dallas, and his wife pitched their tent just east of the race track. Later, the unassembled airship arrived by train. Brett Hall, one of the men entrusted with its care, had raised his own tent, as well as one for the airship. Located behind the new grandstand, the tent sheltered the huge balloon, which stretched for 60 feet [18 m] long when deflated. As well, the maintenance tent housed the hydrogen source or "plant" used to fill the dirigible, the cans of gasoline for the engine, and the men's tools and gear.

Soon, flight fans gathered in and around the airship tent. Captain Dallas' reputation for dar-ing had been well reported. At Kalamazoo, he had piloted his flying machine to an altitude of 2000 feet [610 m], and to the astonishment of crowds, he had circled a 40-story skyscraper.

Daring went hand-in-hand with risk, and crashing was always a possibility, but Dallas was undeterred. Valves controlled the hydrogen and ballast, so generally, the airship ascended or descended according to his will. But the hydrogen that carried him skyward was highly combustible, and if anything failed when he was flying, he had a long way to fall. So, despite the cost, each year, Dallas built new flying machines.

Almost identical to the doomed Calgary dirigible, this one made two flights daily at the 1909 fair in New Westminster, with aeronaut Harry Ginter. Courtesy of New Westminster Public Library, 2359.

Weeks before his arrival in Calgary, the high winds around Utah's salt lake had brought catastrophe. A storm dashed the dirigible towards the lake, and struggle as he might, Dallas was powerless. When he dipped into the lake, waves broke the propeller. For hours, he fought to get his ship airborne again. Finally, with his dirigible 20 feet [6 m] above ground, he lost consciousness and fell. The airship was wrecked. Not seriously injured, Dallas had prepared another dirigible for the Calgary contract.

His initial flight followed the evening performance on Dominion Day. Shortly after 8:00 p.m., crowds waited for Strobel's huge balloon-like structure to ascend. Six hundred yards [549 m] of Japanese silk formed the outer shell, and 8000 cubic feet [743.2 cubic m] of hydrogen gas had been pumped into the bag. Beneath it was the pilot's seat. Triangular and sled-like, the 45 foot [14 meter] frame of Oregon spruce was covered with a French linen net. At one end was a propeller, powered by a four-cylinder gasoline engine. At the other was a large rudder.[5]

Slowly, the amazing ship rose into the sky. Crowds were mesmerized; some watchers gasped; others pointed. The Captain's movements were spell-binding. Not only did he use the rudder for steering, he navigated direction by shifting the weight of his body. Performing high above them, the aeronaut moved from side to side, end to end, and the great inflated bag drifted and turned, unaffected by Calgary breezes. To some who watched the floating ship, it was more than an a masterpiece of American engineering. It was a symbol vividly declaring that mankind's dominion included the air.

By the time the exhibition grounds closed that evening, attendance had already surpassed the citizenry living in the ambitious, ranching community. More than 23 000 people had paid the 25 cent gate admission. They had enjoyed the exhibition's entertainments and demonstrations, caught glimpses of the future, been impressed by advanced brick-making technology, and listened to a new-style player piano that completely outshone its predecessors.

There seemed no end to exhibits and entertainments, and the following day, Alberta Day, hundreds more ambled around the grounds, gulped lunches, and drank soft drinks available at booths. They were lured into tents by barkers and bought the snake oil from convincing characters. On the 3rd of July, Farmers' Day, despite the intrusion of a shower that cooled the air, the huge balloon made three scheduled flights. During each, it was not the distance or speed that the dirigible travelled, but the looming ship's phenomenal maneuverability that impressed the sky gazers.

For the 4th of July and American Day celebrations, a huge banner across the parade route blazoned, "Welcome to our American friends." Unfortunately, sunny Alberta awoke in a temperamental mood. Showers delayed the parade. Worse yet, the CPR excursion train had not arrived when, finally, organizers decided the show must go on. Still, the morning parade was as big or even better than the Dominion Day parade.

The airship made a successful morning flight, and then Captain Dallas and his dirigible returned to the maintenance tent for refueling. By early afternoon, 10 000 people roamed the grounds. When the American excursionists finally arrived just before two o'clock, Calgary's weather was again living up to its reputation for moodiness. Locals reassured that five minutes could change everything.

The storm front hit from the northwest. Sudden, violent, its winds tore across the grounds. Everywhere, bits of paper and debris were tossed in the air like playthings. Banners and flags were quickly ripped to shreds.

In an instant, near the grandstand, chaos broke loose. Tents were flattened or lifted in the wind. Booths and bleachers were ready prey. Tearing the wooden roof from one booth, the wind hurled it across the fence at the bleachers. Abruptly aware that they were in its path, shocked spectators covered their heads. One inch [2.54 cm] boards broke apart. Huge splinters of wood gashed arms and faces of men and women. The worst of the flying weapons driven toward them were solid two by fours.

In the bleachers sat an older man who had made the trip from Innisfail that morning. The full force of flying timber knocked him to the ground and gashed open his head. When rescuers picked him up, he was conscious and calm. He came to see the fair, he said, but with one leg and his back broken, he didn't survive.

Havoc reigned in the grandstand, too. Fearful spectators wanted out before the building collapsed, but the calmer heads prevailed, took charge, and urged sitting tight.

Merciless winds swirled behind the grandstand, and it seemed fortunate that Dallas had his balloon docked in its tent. Although the partially-filled airship was an overwhelming presence in the tent, neither the dirigible captain nor his assistant dreamed the airship might escape the ropes that secured it in place.

But, as winds tore at the tent, the huge airbag brushed again and again against the constraining ropes. Then, the gale struck at the canvas walls so hard it displaced a tent pole. The pole fell, piercing the huge balloon. The silk and linen covering ripped. Hydrogen hissed through the rent in the cloth. The heat generated by the friction of the ropes against the airship's bag warmed the inflammable air.

Suddenly, the highly combustible gas transformed the balloon into a bomb. The sound of the explosion rocketed throughout the fairgrounds. Flames burst through the top of the tent and leaped 50 feet [15 m] into the air.[6]

Firemen did not arrive in time to prevent the balloon, hydrogen plant, gear and tent from being destroyed. But the flames were quelled before they spread to the grandstand, remaining booths and tattered tents.

Captain Dallas and Bert Hall escaped with their lives. They were rushed to the hospital, and Dallas had serious burns to his face and hands. Hall's burns were much worse. One arm was burned so badly little flesh remained. His recovery would be slow and painful.

Before evening on that 4th of July, the storm dissipated. Resolute Calgarians, organizers, and performers returned to the primary business of exhibitions – providing leisure and pleasure. The salute to America concluded with the spectacular fireworks, and the next day, once again, the trained animal acts, Japanese trapeze artists, and the comedy of mock bullfights entertained crowds.

By the end of the exhibition, Captain Dallas was released from hospital. He would not attend the upcoming Brandon fair, but he planned to build another dirigible.

The Calgary accident was by no means the only hot air balloon accident during fair time. The accident at the 1913 Dominion Exhibition in Brandon had a bizarre twist.

A hot air balloon was a featured attraction. When the inflated balloon was no longer anchored, men held the ropes to keep it from drifting away before the balloonist was ready. One of the men on the ropes was J.W. Marks, a local professor.

Eventually, the call came to release the ropes. Everyone released their hold – everyone but Marks. Looped around his arm, the rope had tightened. He struggled to get his arm loose. He was caught. The crowd watched as the balloon lifted off, dragging and lifting Marks with it.

Seeing him dangling from the rope far below the balloon basket, crowds gasped and a few women fainted. The wind carried him up 600-700 feet [183-213 m], and the balloon drifted several blocks.[7]

With Marks still tangled in the rope, finally, the balloon set down. Marks was uninjured, but the unplanned event was one of the most thrilling and frightening scenes visitors to the Brandon fair would experience.

Fly Boys and Fly Girls Tackle the Wind

The vagaries of the new technologies and western Canadian weather meant risks – the greater the technological spectacle, the greater the possibility of problems.

Ever-popular were the airplane flights, and again and again, fair organizers made local and regional history when they booked flyers. The national and international flight stars were a huge draw, creating fans and enthusiasts across the country. At first, almost all the flight performers were from the USA. Eventually, local flyers, many of them pilots who had returned from the First World War, became enormously popular, too.

Lethbridge seemed an unlikely place for flying when flight technology and training were still relatively young. The community could boast some of the highest winds on the prairies, not an advantage when it came to spectacular flight demonstrations. Still, those who had lived in Canada's windy city and attended the fair weren't about to let a few breezes stop them.

On the positive side, the southern Alberta community was big sky country. There was little chance of rain, and most summer days, the clear blue skies seemed to stretch forever – perfect for watching one of the flying machines. Too, it was short grass country. So the centre of the race track was a suitable open space for landing a plane. As a result, the entire show could be staged in front of the grandstand.

When it came to booking flight stars, Lethbridge organizers were aware of the experiences of both Edmonton and Calgary. By 1911, balloon and dirigible flights had appeared in those cities, but there had never been a truly successful airshow in Alberta. Early that year, Edmonton had a plane in its skies, but the weather was nasty. Later, at the exhibition in Calgary, another flight was scheduled. Howard La Van, assistant to J. Strobel who had appeared at the Calgary exhibition with his dirigible in 1908, piloted a Curtis-type pusher plane called The Golden Flyer, which he ended up crashing.

Lethbridge organizers wanted the best for their fair, too. They determined to have the famous bird-man Eugene Ely maneuver one of the big machines above visitors, and they offered $2000. Ely was busy elsewhere in August when the Lethbridge fair usually opened, but in July,

Exhibition flights took place at summer events throughout the west. In Lethbridge, AB, on 11 July, 1914, Eugene Ely flew this Glenn Curtis biplane above fair-goers. Courtesy of Sir Alexander Galt Museum and Archives.

he would be in the north western states. So organizers simply changed their fair date to 14 July. Ely was booked and scheduled to fly a Glenn Curtis biplane in the skies above fair-goers.

The flight was such big news, the local newspaper published a full page ad about the Great Aviation Exhibition.

"Eugene Ely world famous Anglo-American Aviator and hero of several world-wide sensation creating flights with his Curtis Aeroplane," announced the *Lethbridge Herald* on 11 July, 1911. With the true booster spirit and optimism of the west, it continued, "Aviation is the most modern and fascinating of the Sciences and the Aeroplane the most ingenious and wonderful contrivance ever designed by man's mind or fashioned by man's hand."[8]

Two days later, the plane arrived by rail from Oregon. With it came a representative from the Curtis manufacturing company of New York, and he arranged for the plane to be taken from the railway station to the grounds by truck.

The next day, the day of his flight, Ely arrived by train from Spokane, Washington.

Enthusiasts traveled to Lethbridge from as far away as the Crowsnest Pass to the west and Medicine Hat to the east. For the event, most downtown businesses had closed. The regional railway and irrigation company had run special trains to the exhibition park at Henderson Lake. Of course, nothing came cheaply. Enthusiasts paid $1 for the train ticket. Then, tickets to the event were 75 cents, but long before flight time, crowds had gathered.

Ely's take-off for the first of three 15-minute flights was planned for 1:30. Powered by an eight cylinder engine, the plane and pilot were to perform an ocean dip and a spiral dive. At 2:48 in the afternoon, the plane took to the sky.

The pilot soon learned that Lethbridge air was "full of holes." Still, he maneuvered his plane high above the fairground for seven minutes. The audience was thrilled.

Ely took off again at about 3:30. This time, he stayed up for a breath-taking 13 minutes, and his plane circled the crowds. The flight was awe-inspiring, but air conditions led to the cancellation of the third flight.

The story was the same elsewhere on the prairies. As far away as Winnipeg, top flyers had their problems dealing with winds. In 1912, the fair featured a French airman named George Mestach. A top flier, after arriving in the USA the previous year, he had flown exhibition and air mail flights.

The second pilot that the fair planned to showcase was Jimmy Ward with his biplane. Short in stature, Ward had a reputation as an intrepid little aviator, but he had trouble getting his plane in the air that morning. Once aloft, he was buffeted by cross winds, but he landed safely. Concerned about his fellow pilot, Ward told Mestach that it was not a good day for flying.

Clearly, Mestach intended to ignore the warning, so for safety's sake, Ward headed along their make-shift runway to move boxes that he feared might be in the way. Meanwhile, the more famous aviator was testing and readying his engine. Then, Ward heard Mestach's plane, turned, sensed something was wrong, and tore across the field.

Mestach had started out and then lost control. The plane crashed against the inside rail of the race track, and when Ward got to him, he was shocked but not seriously injured. However, his plane was badly damaged, so damaged, it had to be shipped back to Chicago for repairs. The famed flyer was out of action.

George Mestach's Borel monoplane crashed at the Winnipeg Exhibition on 10 July, 1912. Courtesy of Archives of Manitoba, Foote 893, N2493.

In the meantime, Ward remained cautious concerning the flying conditions. He was scheduled for an evening flight, but he didn't attempt it. When he finally did take to the air, he had one of the roughest flights he had experienced, but another day, he had four successful flights. Not only did he fly around the fairground, he circled the entire city. The loud hum of his engine attracted "tens of thousands of eager eyes all over the city....spectators craned their necks for a better sight of the bird man...."9 who climbed to over 4000 feet [1292 metres]. Above the city and fair grounds, he did dips and dives and spirals. And he became a hero, not just during the exhibition, but for years to come in the memories of those who saw him.

Another flight hero was Katherine Stinson, who gave flight performances at many western Canadian exhibitions. A tiny woman with an innocent, feminine appearance, she was sometimes nicknamed The Flying Schoolgirl, but she looked less like a schoolgirl in her flight goggles, leather helmet, and belted flight coat. Having received her pilot's license in 1912 at the age of 21, the young woman became a hit at state fairs. Demonstrating loop the loop, and night sky writing, she earned a whopping $4000 for one afternoon performance.

Then came the war, and she taught flying to Canadian pilots whose home base was Gimli, MB. In 1916, the Edmonton Exhibition contracted her to drop mock bombs from her plane and demonstrate dog fight flying techniques. Stinson set out to do just that, but first time out, she crash landed. Not hurt, she continued to perform, thrilling spectators for her afternoon and evening shows during the following three days. In 1917, she returned to the exhibition, but she was plagued with problems. Although she had two planes shipped to Calgary, the engines of both were damaged during shipping, so there was no flying the first few days of the fair. Finally, on the third day, she made two flights, one in the afternoon, when she circled and looped in the sky and then made a perfect landing in front of the grandstand. The 9:00 p.m. performance was even better.

"With the plane electrically illuminated, and the vision of the machine whirling high in the air, spangled with lights, [it] was a vision which few who were present will ever forget," claimed the *Morning Albertan*.[10]

The next year, again determined to make up for the problems of the previous year, Stinson returned. Arriving on the first day of the 1918 exhibition, Stinson made daily flights, some less eventful than others, and during one of her landings, the plane's wheels bumped the top of a car. More excitement was to come.

On 9 July, at the grounds, she boarded her plane and was handed a sack of 259 letters to be delivered to Edmonton. She would be making the first airmail flight in the province. Stinson had no problems taking off. But her engine balked. She had to land about 6.8 miles [11 km] from the exhibition grounds. Walking until she found a phone, she called for help from her mechanic, who fixed the problem.

Then, rather than have the delay added to her flying time and go into the fair's history books, she returned to the exhibition grounds. The delay had taken about five hours. Given the long hours of daylight, Katherine determined to make the historic flight that evening. This time, she reached Edmonton in two hours and five minutes. A talented, brave, and daring flyer, she continued to thrill audiences with flights in both Alberta and Saskatchewan.

Another flamboyant and popular pilot at fairs was Fred McCall. On 5 July, 1919, at the Victory Stampede in Calgary, he chose to crash his Curtis biplane on top of the merry-go-round rather than risk the lives of drivers on the race track, where auto races were in progress. McCall had been an expert patrol and fighter pilot during the First World War and had won the Military Cross. During the first days of the 1919 Stampede, he had thrilled audiences with aerial stunts, and he offered rides to passengers. His usual fare was three cents a pound, but some lucky enthusiasts paid only a cent a pound. Aboard the fated flight were the two sons of E.L. Richardson, exhibition manager. Take-off appeared normal, but at about 200 feet [61 m] above the ground, the plane stalled. Then it careened into a telephone pole before crashing on the midway.

Fortunately, no one was hurt. The engine wasn't damaged, but the propeller blades and the shell of the plane were smashed. McCall could not use the plane for flight during the upcoming Edmonton Exhibition, but fair goers are a curious lot. He put the wreck on display and charged Edmontonians 50 cents apiece to view the wreck. Thousands paid the price.

Empty Pockets at Saskatoon

The Great Depression hit fairgrounds as well as individuals. Many of the annual summer celebrations had become extravagant affairs during the twenties. Attendance was strong, and there were numerous midway companies and shows from which to choose. Organizers could call the shots and get anything they wanted, and at times, show and midway owners felt they competed in a dog-eat-dog world.

When the world-wide economic downturn was coupled with drought on the prairies, some fairs, rodeos, and regattas folded. Other communities ran bare-bones style fairs, and still others "invented" ways of keeping their annual celebrations alive.

Moral support for the events had never failed. Even governments believed people would get through the trying times more easily if there was an occasional escape from hard times. Of course, with bread lines and riots, frivolous expenditures could never be condoned, but the value of fairs remained clear to officials. Too, ordinary people were willing to spend some money to escape the hardship, if only for a few hours. They just didn't have much money to spend.

For the midway and show companies, labor was plentiful and cheap. A few of the established Canadian companies that didn't need to buy extra equipment or spend too much on transportation actually increased profits. New import duties favored Canadian operators. Still, some companies barely survived or didn't survive because many communities put a freeze on festivities.

With its economic base so tied to farming, Saskatchewan was hit particularly hard. At Regina, in 1928, adults had paid 50 cents for admission to the fairgrounds. In 1934, with the Depression, the price of admission tickets was cut in half.

Saskatoon's first fair was in 1886, and locals were determined to prove wrong Palliser's proclamation that the area was unfit for cultivation. Fair visitors paid no admission fees, but there were 200 agricultural entries and a total of $100 in prizes for the competitions and trotting races. When the fair became even more successful, it was moved to City Park. By 1907 and 1908, deficits were huge, but the society survived. For 1911, gate receipts were low due to bad weather and the staging of the Calgary fair on the same date. Still, the fair grew. In 1912, renamed the Saskatoon Industrial Exhibition, the fair was bigger and better. With 3600 exhibition entries and an aviator as an attraction, the sky seemed the limit. Women's exhibits were expanded. Even a farm boys' camp was added.[11]

By 1922, Sid Johns had become secretary-manager for the association, and he steered the organization in the trying times that lay ahead. A "dean of showmen," he possessed optimism, ideas, and the wherewithal to make them work.

The troubles of the 1929 fair were not particularly unusual, more a simple reminder that things could go wrong. The air shows were a problem. A hydrogen balloon was to make an ascent, but the hydrogen didn't arrive from Chicago. A parachute "race" was scheduled with one jumper from the American army and the other from the marines. A storm brewed, but the Waco plane they were to jump from took off. With the bad weather giving the pilot problems, he decided to make another fly over in front of the grandstand. Already, one of the jumpers was on the wing. In the turbulence, the jumper finally let go and parachuted to the ground. Meanwhile, the plane had gone into a downward spiral, but the pilot made his forced landing successfully.[12]

That kind of excitement was all in a day at the fair. Then the thirties brought a very different challenge. For the 1931 Saskatoon fair, no one knew how bad things would get, and that year Secretary Manager Johns had spearheaded the re-designing of the grounds.

"Even though the conditions are far from what we hoped for, the exhibition offers such a very wonderful show and marvelous attractions at such a nominal cost, we are confident of the success for 1931," Johns had predicted. "[People] won't do without their exhibition, their week of reunion, entertainment and instruction, no matter what conditions may prevail."[13]

The organizers expected 100 000 people, and $50 000 in prizes were up for grabs. The fair went on as scheduled, but attendance was disastrous, almost 40 000 less than expected. By the next year, economic and crop conditions were even worse. Many families couldn't afford food and housing. Women were making clothes out of flour sacks. Trains travelled through the community with as many as 200 unemployed men riding the rails each trip. In the midst of that, did it make any sense to hold a fair?

Proud of their fair's long history, organizers were determined to continue staging the event. They made their daring decision. There would be no admission charge to get into the fair grounds, not just free to kids, or to pioneers on Frontier Day, but to everyone! Also, children under 14 would get free seats in the grandstand for the evening performance if they were with their parents.

"The eyes of the North American continent and all Canada would be focused on Saskatoon during fair week, watching with the keenest interest the result of the experiment," Sid Johns announced to the press.[14]

No midway owner would bring his company for free, but they did agree to charge only a nickel for most rides and shows. The idea was a success.

As in other communities, the annual fair was not the only event handled by the exhibition association. Swine and poultry shows, as well as a winter fair, were also featured during the year.

Despite the range of activities hosted and sponsored, in 1931, the Saskatoon Industrial Exhibition Association had a deficit of $20 391.62 for the year. The total deficit for 1932 was only $7117.85. Certainly, reducing budgeted expenditures had been part of keeping down the deficit.[15] But the free summer fair had played its part, too. During fair week, 152 011 fair-goers visited the grounds, which was 89 187 more that the previous year. Not only were there more people, but about 1000 more automobiles than the previous year had entered the autopark, at a time when many thought travel was just too expensive.

To keep expenses down, prize money wasn't as attractive as previously, but competition entries were as numerous. One of the livestock judges insisted there were four times as many farmers around the livestock judging ring when compared to other prairie fairs.

In fact, the summer fair itself racked up a profit. The daring organizers had made $12 011.14, and they did it while offering free admission. Not only did the fair association benefit, but local businesses, such as hotels, department stores, restaurants, and even jewelry stores, reported that business was up from 1931. With the Depression, they had reduced prices, so their actual income wasn't necessarily up, but they had done much better than expected.

Even the federal minister of agriculture acknowledged the success of the initiative. Everyone expected the economy to improve. It didn't. For the 1933 event, the organizers faced the same quandary. Nobody had money. Some circumstances had worsened. Were organizers prepared to go out on a limb again?

They were. Saskatoon held a second free fair. Some changes were made. Admission to the grounds was still free for everyone, but both adults and children had to pay for the evening grandstand show. Many more local musicians were featured in the band for the grandstand show. Ball games, horse shoe tournaments, and other free or very inexpensive entertainments were part of the plan. Still, the number of visitors went down from the previous year.

Excitement on the midway was another story. Shows and rides were a nickel for kids. Entertainment included a camel, exotic dancers at the Garden of Allah, a horse and chimpanzee that were "educated," a mind reader, a minstrel show, an acrobatic tumbler, and performers with daring shows that featured fire and electricity. Not only that, the city of Saskatoon had its film debut. In the area beneath the seats of the grandstand, crowds watched a free two-hour moving picture about their own community. Called *Scenic and Industrial Saskatoon*, the movie had even captured local children on film, and they were thrilled.

Some aspects of the fair were unchanged. Surprisingly, bets on the horse races were up. People placed bets just in case, somehow, they might win, and the win would mean their pockets were no longer so empty. Too, that year, the Kinsman Club held its charity lottery and gave away a DeSoto custom sedan worth about $1500.

The second free fair wasn't as big a success as the previous year, but once again, the idea had worked. However, with still worsening conditions, the fair association had few choices and returned to admission fees in 1934.

General admission remained reasonable throughout the thirties. In 1937, admission to the grounds was 25 cents for adults. Grandstand seats and most rides and shows were 5 cents for children. On bargain Monday, in the evening, grandstand seats were only 25 cents for adults. The rest of the time, grandstand seats were 50 cents, and reserved seating was 75 cents.

The traditional horse races were scheduled. With its 25 year history, the Saskatoon Handicap, which locals claimed was the oldest continuously run race in western Canada, ran as planned. About 250 horses arrived for the various races. Once again, prizes offered by the Kinsmen were outstanding. The raffle winner could choose from an Oldsmobile deluxe sedan, a two-ton Fargo truck, or a John Deere tractor. Second prize was a Bulova gold watch. On the last night, the exhibition gave away a $100 gift certificate, too.

Despite the Depression, at fair time, no one wanted pessimism. Everyone needed and wanted hope. The booster spirit became important, and helped people get through the bad times. The organizers' daring decision to offer a free fair – or at least free admission – in the early thirties had been rooted in community spirit. In 1938, Sid Johns, who managed Saskatoon's exhibition for 21 years, was elected president of the International Fairs and Exhibition Association. It was a fitting acknowledgment of the work of a man who kept the community fair going – even through the hard times.

Kelowna's Festival: From Fizzle and Flames to World Famous

All summer festivities with long histories faced troubles. Some communities, such as Kelowna, managed to deal with the turbulence in a surprisingly positive manner. The Kelowna Regatta survived economic depressions, two world wars, and in recent years, youth riots.

The festival had its roots in early fall fairs and sports days. An autumn agricultural fair was held as early as 1896, but the community had been involved as early as 1891 in the Okanagan regional fair held in Vernon. The Kelowna fair had produce and livestock competitions and displays, but also sailing races and other sports competitions.

The first "official" Kelowna Regatta was held 15 August, 1907. The event was a success, becoming the best summer carnival in the interior. The focus was water sports; the parade was comprised of decorated boats on the lake; and entertainment included such unusual competitions as paddle boat races. By 1910, the events were held in front of the newly constructed grandstand, and the regatta had all the trappings of any other summer festival or fair.

The First World War presented a local, as well as global, challenge. On 4 August, 1914, Canada declared war, but Kelowna determined to carry on its tradition and held its usual two-day regatta on August 12 and 13. There were dramatic attractions. An American pilot gave exhibition flights of the first hydroplane to be seen in the area. Still, the declaration of war had its affect, and attendance was poor. By the next year, so many young men had gone to war, there were few to compete in the events. For the duration of the war, the regatta was reduced to one day of summer fun, but it wasn't cancelled.

Although this Kelowna Regatta photo is dated 1906, the year generally credited for the community's first regatta is 1907. Becoming one of the most important aquatic shows in western Canada, the event gained international renown. Courtesy of Kelowna Museum Archives, 2103.

By the 1930s, the regatta became an enormously popular and successful event, but produce prices had plummeted. The Kelowna Fall Fair was cancelled, a victim of the times. Instead, produce and livestock were entered in displays and competitions at the Interprovincial Fair at nearby Armstrong. As well, fruit and vegetables made great showings in competitions at Vancouver and other major fairs. The efforts of local organizers in Kelowna were re-directed to making the regatta the primary summer festival and the most important water sports competition in the country.

The regatta hosted the provincial championships in diving, swimming, and boating. War canoe races were especially popular. A midway brought rides and concession joints, and a local girl was crowned queen of the lake. Horseshoe matches attracted some to the event, and in 1931, other fun included apple box races and balloon races, baseball games and open-air band concerts,

Diving exhibitions were popular at regattas. In the 1950s, these three divers leapt from the five-tiered dive tower of the Aquatic Club in Kelowna, BC. Courtesy of Kelowna Museum Archives, 3963.

boxing and wrestling matches, evening fireworks and dances.

During the 1930s, Dick Parkinson, who had lived in the Okanagan all his life, was a mover and shaker in terms of organizing the regattas. He became president of the sponsoring association and later took the job of secretary-manager.

Parkinson was a high-energy sports enthusiast with nicknames like Mr. Regatta, Mr. Mayor, Mr. Okanagan, and Mr. Everything. He was instrumental in the direction, development, and contracting of the summer event. Sometimes, the spectacles went off as expected. Other times they were spectacular failures.

In the 1930s, Parkinson and other regatta organizers came up with an idea for a performance that they were sure would leave everyone awe-struck. They contracted Freddie Thompson, a local diver, for a human torch diving routine. That evening, Thompson donned large, heavy overalls. At the top of the tower, his helper douse him in kerosene. All the lights were turned off for the performance. Using a lighter, the helper attempted to set Thompson ablaze. The strong breeze blew out the flame. He tried again and again, but the wind was determined to prevent the blazing human torch from impressing spectators. In the meantime, the audience sat in the darkness. Wanting action, detractors and disbelievers yelled impatiently. City workers tried to turn on the lights, but for some reason, they failed to work. Finally, after ten minutes, the lights were restored, and the act was deemed impossible. The awe-inspiring performance was a fizzle.

Another year, an especially spectacular display of fireworks was planned. The fireworks were donated, and a barge was placed on the lake as a launch area in full view of the grandstand. That night, Parkinson and a large group gathered on the barge. Again, all lights were turned out, and spectators waited for the light show to begin. On the barge, the man responsible for launching the rockets accidentally dropped his lighting torch in the centre of the fireworks. The sudden "Bang" was deafening. Sparks were everywhere, and in seconds, the entire show was over.

During the Second World War, Kelowna was to have one of the strongest and most interesting wartime festivals in the country. Parkinson helped organize the 1940 Win-the-War Regatta, and without doubt, it proved one of the most dramatic shows of community support for the war. Every penny above costs, whether from gate admission, raffle ticket sales, or midway games, was earmarked for the Dominion's war chest. The donation would have no strings attached on how the money should be used.

As usual, the war canoe races were scheduled, but there was a military twist. For one race, two militia units, D Company of the Rocky Mountain Rangers and Squadron C of the BC Dragoons, competed against each other. At one time or another, Parkinson had belonged to both units, so their participation was logical. For the most important night of the event, the military parade was the largest in Kelowna's history, and visiting military and civilian bands came from throughout the area. Most spectacular of all was the Grand Naval Pageant, or sea battle.

"While a British cruiser is conveying a valuable cargo of Bathing Beauties to the contest platform on the lakeshore through a sea infested with mines and submarines, and convoyed by British war ships, it is attacked by an enemy destroyer."[16]

The convoy came to the rescue. The enemy warship was shelled, set on fire and sunk! What more could war supporters want?

The actual highlight of the regatta was burning Hitler, and the event conveyed the intensity of war fever even in smaller communities.

"For years, you have wanted to see 'that man Hitler' frying in the Nethermost Regions with a thousand little devils dancing around prodding him with their three-tine forks to see if he were cooking properly," claimed the advertising for war saving stamps in the *Kelowna Courier.*

For two days prior to the fire to burn "His Demonic Highness," Hitler in effigy was tied to a pole outside the aquatic building. Everyone was encouraged to buy as many war saving stamps as they could afford and add them to the pile intended as fuel for the fire. By burning the stamps, which were redeemable in about seven years with the added value of 3½% interest, sup-

Here Hitler is burned in effigy. War savings stamps were sold to raise money for the troops, and $500 worth of the stamps were used as fuel for the fire. Courtesy Kelowna Museum Archives, 662.

porters made a donation to the government. Best of all, "The world's arch-enemy Hitler [suc-cumbed] emblematically to the righteous wrath of all free peoples."[17]

In 1941, again, Parkinson helped organize the On-to-Victory Regatta, but by 1942, he enlisted. Jack Treadgold, the new secretary-manager, and other organizers continued to focus on the war theme. That year, the community held its Thumbs Up Regatta, but Parkinson would soon be once again in a position to show support for Kelowna's annual event.

At the time, Parkinson was too old for active duty overseas, so after training, he was placed at the Vernon Basic Training Centre, under the command of the camp brigadier. Becoming adju-tant in charge of the sports and entertainment, Parkinson played an important role in organiz-

As part of the opening cere-monies, Brigadier General Keller arrived at the 1945 Kelowna Regatta in a mili-tary amphibian. Courtesy Kelowna Museum Archives, 39.

ing military performances in support of the war effort at civilian locations, too. Bands and "army entertainers" appeared at nearby Penticton, Oliver, Kamloops, and Kelowna.

For the 1943 Kelowna Regatta, the theme was Combined Ops. The feature attraction on the most important evening of the event was a commando raid. The show was advertised as the "thrill of a lifetime as assault boats and amphibious jeeps approached the shore under fire." Commandos landed, met opposition and gave an amazing display of power and skill, all in the interest of raising money for the war.[18]

In 1944, the Kelowna Regatta became the Liberation Regatta, and finally, by 1945 and the end of the war, the Kelowna organizing committee could determine its overall financial commitment to the war effort. From 1940 to 1944 inclusive, the community had raised $10 000 for war-related causes. During the first three years, the money raised had gone directly into the national war chest. With a contribution to the Red Cross, in 1943, money raised at the Kelowna Regatta went to the Prisoner of War Fund. In 1944, the funds raised were given to the Kelowna and District War Veterans Rehabilitation Committee to help local veterans.[19] Throughout the war years, the events staged revealed the imaginative and innovative planning of both the local committee, as well as the co-operative involvement from the nearby armed forces base.

Years later, the community again put on a brave face and survived when the Aquatic Club, the heart of regatta activity, burned to the ground in 1969. Yet, another even more difficult battle was on the horizon.

Shocking levels of mob violence first became associated with the regatta in 1985. For both the Penticton Regatta and the Kelowna Regatta, the mid-1980s brought mob scenes that seemed

The Aquatic Club in Kelowna, BC, burned on June 26, 1969. The problem was compounded when the insurance company would not cover replacement costs. Courtesy of Kelowna Museum Archives, 4166.

unimaginable. In both cases, trying to end the re-occurrence of violence, organizers contemplated suspending the annual events.

During the 1986 Kelowna Regatta, there were about 15 officers patrolling the area when, at about 1:00 a.m., drunken revelers on roof-tops began throwing bottles at them. While three police officers tried to arrest a young man, a crowd of 500 angry youths surrounded them. Given the threatening crowd, the policemen backed into side streets and called for back-up from Vernon and Penticton.

Then, for three hours, the drunken rioters took control, creating a disaster area that some said made downtown streets look like they were the centre of a civil war. The mayor read the Riot Act on four different street corners, advising the young people of the consequences of their behavior.

By 4:15 in the morning, with the extra man-power, police attempted break up the mob. They backed rioters down main street, but as the youth retreated, they smashed windows and looted. Finally, with helicopter spotters giving them directions, police launched tear gas into the crowds.

In the end, 190 people were arrested and 30 went to hospital with injuries. The riot had been brought under control, but property damage was in the hundreds of thousands of dollars.[20]

Forced to address the problems of crowd control and youth drunkenness, organizers found solutions. Careful planning and the determination of organizers and the community curtailed the possibility of future riots and reassured visitors of safety and family fun. The summer festival returned to sun and fun events, with world-class water sports, just as it had always been.

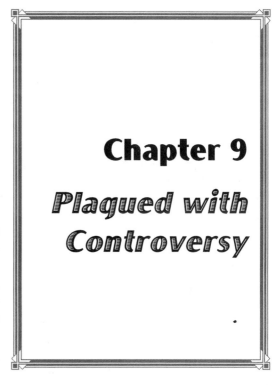

Chapter 9
Plagued with Controversy

Strange Bedfellows: Values, Politics, Law, and Commerce

Western Canadian fairs and festivals have had their dark times, and the range and complexity of issues reflects the range and complexity of the human story. Vastly different than in earlier times, contemporary culture and festivals have successfully solved some problems while others remain potential pitfalls.

A perennial complaint has been that costs for visitors are too high. The blatant commercialism is slammed. Parades and races involve too much advertising by sponsors, protestors claim. They dismiss the fact that most chuckwagon drivers today could not afford their outfits and horses without sponsors. Too, extravagant events are expensive to stage. However, to most critics, more significant than costs and commercialism were issues related to health, safety, hiring, human rights, and societal values.

Today's laws regarding equal opportunity, basic human rights, child labor, labor relations, safety codes, and the inhumane treatment of animals allow those who feel there has been wrongdoing to confront those who are responsible. As a result, the men and women performing in the travelling shows, as well as the competitors and stock on the rodeo circuits, have been dramatically affected. Employees, competitors, visitors, managers, and others have seen the industry revolutionized.

The new laws did affect who might be employed by the travelling midway and show companies. Child and teen labor – whether as carnival workers selling peanuts or performers with circus and rodeo companies – came in for close monitoring, and minimum wages and safety conditions were ensured for employees.

Too, changing values affected midways and shows. Some show performers were labeled and, in fact, advertised as freaks. Then freaks shows fell out of favor. The shows made objects of people, denigrated them, and re-enforced negative stereotypes; they perpetuated attitudes of superiority and inferiority, rather than respecting the intrinsic value and equality of all human beings, claimed reformers. From a philosophical and moral point of view, eradicating the freak show as an "entertainment" was reasonable. Yet, for some who worked in side-shows, their disabilities or special physique limited the jobs available to them. Some limitations were real. Others were needlessly and unjustly based on appearance. When a lack of education was part of the problem, the workers found that losing their midway jobs meant regressing from financial independence to financial dependence. Too, the midway "family" had accepted them, and at times had been the only family they had known.

Also, treatment of livestock used in rodeos and the animal performers of circuses became the source of deep-seated differences and wide-spread controversy. Sometimes, communities made the decisions about what was acceptable use of animals in the shows. At other times, the new laws – such as prohibiting transportation of exotic animals through national parks – made travelling with lions, tigers, and elephants from locations such as Calgary to Revelstoke and points west so cumbersome that it was no longer financially viable. In other instances, the conditions and relationship between people and animals were governed by cowboy associations, pressure from the SPCA, and most certainly, decisions of the courts.

In some ways, First Nations participation became less controversial over the years. In the late 1800s and early 1900s, governments were concerned about encouraging Aboriginals to pitch teepees on fair grounds, participate in parades, and give exhibitions of traditional dances or hunting activities. The festivities might distract them from the agricultural pursuits and way of life that Indian Affairs preferred for them. Later, First Nations participation began to receive unconditional support from governments, but other political activists took issue for different reasons, mostly related to commercialism and stereotyping.

Many other practices that had once caused an uproar became less and less controversial. In recent years, casino gambling in exhibition buildings has failed to raise eyebrows. Too, whereas at one time, serving any alcohol, anywhere, was illegal, and the person who bought boot-legged liquor and came to the grounds drunk was considered a degenerate, today, alcohol flows freely in bar tents on the grounds. Girlie shows are seldom on the midway, but at bars in close proximity to many fairgrounds, the strip shows are far more explicit than the most daring of midway shows prior to the 1960s. Yet, differences regarding issues centred on community values remain.

When touring shows or even contestants came to town, some locals labeled the outsiders potential troublemakers and even crooks. Questions of honesty were usually directed at a poorly-dressed, unshaven carnie. Yet integrity was not always evident in the well-dressed, well-educated organizer or sub-contractor. New laws and greater public awareness has helped shape contemporary festivities. Today, proper financial audits and transparent dealings are the new watchwords for organizers.

First Nations and Fairs

The relationship among fair or rodeo organizers, government employees and officials, and the First Nations people was often a complicated one. To some extent, it was controlled by changing policies of the Department of Indian Affairs. However, over time, both indigenous and Métis people determined their own degree of participation. In terms of rodeo competitions, First Nations and Métis were keen and successful competitors.

White organizers valued the presence of the First Nations, especially when they wore traditional clothes, brought their teepees, erected Indian Villages, performed traditional dances, and rode in parades. Visitors loved seeing the spectacle.

Admittedly, some local whites stood ready to condemn any Aboriginal person who partied to excess. More insidious was government policy that discouraged involvement of the indigenous people in the annual events. First Nations people wanted to enjoy the rodeo or exhibition, like any other visitor. Not only did they want to represent the heritage of their nations, they wanted to encourage their own children to be culturally aware and proud, and one way was to participate in the summer events. Although the indigenous people held pow wows and First Nation gatherings throughout western Canada, the festivals of the larger multi-cultural community offered a special opportunity for showcasing their culture, talents, and successes.

Unfortunately, government policy and spokesmen made an already complex relationship worse. In 1910, concerning Native participation in fairs, D.C. Scott, Superintendent of Indian Schools for the Dominion said, "I think it is the worst thing possible for Indians. They come to the fairs when they should be on their farms and give pow wows and snake dances in their native costumes for prizes."

Likely photographed in the 1940s, this Prairie Chicken Society dancer was participating in a Blackfoot Sun Dance. Such dancers were in demand for fairs, too. Courtesy of Glenbow Archives, NA 667-222.

The superintendent continued to an *Edmonton Bulletin* reporter, "Our purpose in educating the Indians is to make them forget their native customs and become useful citizens of the Dominion."

He wanted First Nations showmanship at the fairs stopped. "...as long as they are applauded by the crowds and given money for acting as their forefathers did they will still keep to their old barbarous ways."

As far as he was concerned, their exhibiting agricultural products at the fairs should be encouraged with special prizes, "But when it comes to encouraging them to act like uncivilized heathens I think it is time to draw the line."[1]

He was not the only government official to vent that point of view. Arther Barner, an instructor at the Indian Industrial School at Red Deer, AB, wrote to the *Edmonton Bulletin* newspaper. He confronted voices that insisted on "treating the Indian like another citizen."

In 1908, he claimed, there had been no special invitation or financial incentive for the Cree at Hobbema to attend the Edmonton Exhibition. Few attended, and a great deal of farm work was completed during the fair days. In 1909, an exhibition agent had visited the reserve and made a financial arrangement with the tribe for their participation at the exhibition. Because of the disruption, instructors managed to get the local Cree to break only a "paltry thirty acres" during fair days, instead of the large acreage the instructors had planned: "...these agents of the various exhibition boards are the chief actors in enticing the Indians away from their work just at the time when their duties call them to be on the job."

To him, exhibition board agents were only interested in the financial stability of the fairs: "...the methods adopted by these men who act as Exhibition Board agents condemn themselves," he wrote.[2]

Instead of going to the First Nations people, they should have gone directly to the Indian Department at Ottawa or to the Indian agent and missionary, who acted as guardians for the indigenous people, he insisted.

Very early on, some communities ignored the government policies and spokesmen, but their motives may have been – at least to some extent – financial.

In Banff, Indian Days dated to the last decade of the 1800s. Not only were First Nations encouraged to participate, they were central to the event that became Banff's most important summer festival. The evolution of the town's celebration was not simply to acknowledge the importance of the First Nations in western Canadian history. As with many decisions that affected the direction of local festivals, money was part of the story. So was the weather, and so was tourism.

Four slightly different versions circulated about the first Indian Days. One year, no one is sure which, there had been such a wet spring season that railway tracks and schedules suffered. Railway passengers – some said a few hundred, other claimed 600 – were stuck in Banff. While they waited for train service to resume, they were lodged at the CPR's Banff Springs Hotel

When Princess Elizabeth and Prince Philip visited, a one hour sampling of rodeo was held in their honor. The October 18, 1951 event was named the Royal Stampede. To answer questions, rodeo champion Herman Linder sat beside the woman who was soon to be queen. Courtesy of Glenbow Archives, NA 4325-14.

W.L. Matthews managed the castle-like hotel in the mountains. Outdoors people, wealthy guests and happy visitors were the norm. This time, he hosted stranded and impatient travellers at the hotel, and he needed spectacular entertainment to keep them happy.

Some said he turned to Tom Wilson. Tom had a good relationship with the people of the Stony Nation at the nearby Morley reserve in the foothills. He understood Matthews' problem, and they came up with an idea. Then, Tom followed government protocol. He approached the Indian agent, asking permission for the band to help him out.

Others said Matthews went to Norman Luxton and the Brewster brothers for help. They knew that the Stoneys were already camped at the foot of Cascade Mountain. Perhaps that first hasty organizing "committee" involved them all. However it actually happened, Indian horse races were quickly organized. Chief Bearspaw led his band closer to Banff, and camp was reassembled.

"They pitched their tents on what is now the buffalo paddock, close to Banff, and the following morning visitors gazed with wide amazement and admiration as the tribes in all their barbaric splendor paraded past the hotel."[3]

It was the inaugural event for one of the most impressive displays of western Canadian Aboriginal culture. With the passing years, it began to share characteristics with other fairs and stampedes. There was a wide variety of novelty races, running horse races, "democrat" races, and rodeo events with significant inter-tribal competition.

In 1947, with both Native and white actors, the signing of the 1877 treaty was re-enacted to a packed, outdoor auditorium at the Banff Springs Hotel. The four-day event also showcased Eddie One Spot of the Sarcee. Guest soloist, he was considered the Frank Sinatra of the plains Indians. Indigenous dances included the deer dance, war dance, and chicken dance, with dancers as young as four and as old as 70.

The successes meant drum rhythms, accompanying Aboriginal voices, dances, tug-of-war contests on horseback, bow and arrow contests, and the spectacle of painted teepees remained a treasured part of Banff Indian Days.

The event was not the first to feature First Nations participation. However, it may have been one of the first to present the Aboriginal culture in such truly grand style to visitors. The involvement of the indigenous people was central, not peripheral, to the event.

Circumstances have changed, but controversy over First Nations involvement in fairs has a new twist. Some believe that First Nations are being "used" by exhibitions, fairs, and rodeos. The traditional dress and housing create an unrealistic view of Native people. Even the correct nomenclature has become a concern. According to the activists, use of the word "Indian" evoked too many stereotyped ideas. Large stampedes such as Calgary's dropped their "Indian Races" but continued to host an Indian Village and eventually crowned an Indian princess.

First Nations women were the first western Canadian women to enter as riders in horse races. Their names were seldom recorded even though the races were highly competitive and required outstanding riding skills. Because they were called "Squaw Races" and there is serious and realistic objection to the negative connotations of the terminology, that story may remain the hardest of all to find and tell.

First Nations will decide their future in terms of participation in the events. They will do it based on what they believe to be best for themselves, but the role of early government policies does have implications in terms of understanding past and present relationships.

Staring at Freaks and Fleshpots

"Sacrilege!" detractors might rail, while others bought tickets to see the "Unborn" attraction. Some listened carefully to the lectures inside the tent. To them, the speaker was providing education, offering important science, or giving insights into pregnancy and the development of the fetus. Many midways carried such shows in the twenties.

"Disgrace," railed some after seeing Althelia, the monkey girl.

"Those poor creatures," was often the response to the talented, armless artist or the unusual seal boy.

On tour with the Johnny Jones Show, these three employees had acts at the Edmonton Exhibition in 1924. In the jargon of the time, the acts were called Fat Shows. The weight of such people was usually 350-475 lbs [159-215 kg]. Courtesy of Glenbow Archives, NA-4282-7

"They shouldn't show such deformity!" a ticket purchaser would proclaim, whether the side show tent had featured a three-legged chicken, two-headed calf, person with no legs, or eight-foot tall woman. Some people simply raised their eyebrows; others were totally uncomfortable.

"My wife and children had to cover their eyes," was a common enough response.

"Amazing!" someone else would marvel.

Reactions to displays commonly known as freak shows were always mixed. American midways featured more of these than Canadian ones. Some believed they should be stopped at the border, and Canadian shows that traded in the degradation of humanity should be outlawed, too.

A founding concept for agricultural fairs had been showcasing progressive ideas in agriculture and superior livestock, grain, and produce. Critics claimed the outstanding displays were degraded by the side shows. Fairs contracting midways that travelled with objectionable shows should be ineligible for funding from national or provincial governments.

Although some targeted the shows, others felt they had positive outcomes. Visitors learned about the diversity of life. They heard from little people, commonly called dwarves; big individuals known as giants or fat people; and physically unique or challenged individuals. Whether they simply possessed more hair than most, had hair in unexpected places, or lived with what most called "abnormalities" or "defects," supporters claimed the show people had taken jobs that invited audiences to see them.

Some visitors entered side show tents out of curiosity. Others went to giggle or laugh, and Bozo, the midget clown, was one of many popular acts. Some with a more serious attitude rationalized the ticket price with ideas and intentions related to Christian charity and moral reform. In fact, show lecturers provided an exposé intended to appeal to those social reformers. Yet inevitably, the crowd always included at least a few hecklers.

These men travelled the western Canada fair circuit in the 1920s with the C.A. Wortham Circus. This 1921 photo was taken by renowned photographer L.B. Foote of Winnipeg. Courtesy of Archives of Manitoba, Foote 361 N1961 1913.

Somewhat less controversial as "entertainment" were mind readers such as Capt. E.L. Mundy, Mme. Zola, and the Hindu and Gypsy fortune-tellers. Also performing at western Canadian exhibitions were the Fire Eating Turk, sword swallowers, snake charmers, and magicians. They did not receive such harsh criticism or negative responses, but they were subject to suspicion.

For the suspicious, the side shows were places where the worst in humanity lured the unsuspecting to see what was commonly perceived as sad or alarming examples of humanity. Nevertheless, year after year, little people and big people, strong men, and hairy man-beasts drew crowds.

Even more fascinating to those who toured the "pike" were the women who were small or large, thin or heavy, bearded or snake-skinned. Conjoined twins, commonly called Siamese twins, inevitably garnered a crowd of the curious. At the Brandon fair, in 1902, Millie Christien was in one of the side shows. She was billed as a double woman, but reporters were skeptical. "At every performance a number were allowed to examine the curiosity and all pronounced it was 'the real thing.' After the show had pulled its tent pegs....a strange transformation...took place whereby she or they were able to navigate alone. No doubt Millie and Christien will grow together in time for the next show."[4]

Commonly, midways had a serpent girl, who was supposedly half woman, half snake. Another popular tent show was The Human Mermaid. In a letter to the editor of *The Nor-West Farmer*, H.V. Clendening claimed fraud or slavery charges should be filed against a show presented at Manitoba's large fairs held in Killarney and Portage la Prairie. At the Wild Woman from Madagascar tent, a black woman was the attraction. The show was billed as having a woman "surrounded by a Thousand Hissing Reptiles from Every Cline." Presumably, she ate and slept where "a dog would not live for an hour."[5]

Considered an erotic freak show, Serpentina: The Serpent Girl was supposedly half woman and half snake. The act travelled with the Johnny Jones Show and appeared at the Edmonton Exhibition in 1919. Courtesy of Glenbow Archives, NA-4282-1.

The hootchy-kootchy girls drew crowds. The later the scheduled show and the more available alcohol was in the community, the larger the male-dominated crowds.

"Scandalous flesh pots, " representatives of women's groups often exclaimed as they stood outside a tent where the banner showed scantily clad young women.

"Lewd and licentious," was also charged by men associated with religious and social reform groups.

Today, many of the X-rated girlie shows on early midways would not even be considered risqué. Others that combined physical deformity with sexuality would cause controversy. Today, they might violate values and sensitivities – if not laws – and social reformers would object to the stereotyping, objectification and degradation of women. In earlier decades, controversy over the girlie shows raged in fairly diverse and wide-spread communities, and guardians of Christian morality fought to close down the shows.

Some girlie shows were open to anyone brave enough to publicly step up and pay the ticket price. Others were advertised "for men only." Adult males did flock to the shows, and boys, some as young as ten, entered the tents. Yet by today's standards, the girls showed a little leg and wore scanty tops or bottoms, although some, such as the 6'8" [203] exotic dancer with Royal American in about 1959, would still be unusual.

The guardians of public morality had other concerns, too. Was pornographic literature – pictures of naked girls, women, and even boys – being circulated and sold in the shows? One photo card available at fairs in Alberta in 1921 caused a furor. The image was of conjoined or Siamese twins Josephine and Rose Blazek and their son. They were well dressed and appeared very respectable. Still, local women's organizations were outraged, most likely because the image implied group sex in order for the boy to have been conceived.

Some were concerned that community girls might be lured into white slavery and degradation. Others worried about the moral effect on men and boys. Theatre inspectors licensed the girlie shows for the provinces. The inspectors and local police then monitored the shows. They did tolerate exotic dances, and they tolerated degrees of undress. Generally, oriental veil dances were more acceptable than the "bumps and grinds." However, a show's passing an inspection did not mean it would go without incident. Too, the performance rating the pass was not necessarily the one shown at subsequent fairs.

Many locals speculated that the girls working the shows were promiscuous. Although prostitutes did book rooms during the fairs, most were independents rather than show girls. In 1919, a local at Wakaw, SK, warned Constable George Maxwell that prostitutes were expected from Winnipeg. On arrival, strangely enough, they had trouble finding accommodation, so they left.

That did not mean there were no sexual thrills. Hall's Circus was playing the same fair. Maxwell discovered books and photos "of a questionable nature" were being sold for 25 cents.

Of one act, Constable Maxwell reported, "...she finished with a disgusting thing that I cannot very well describe."[6] But presumably, the show had passed inspection.

Usually, the after-midnight act, or Midnight Special, meant even greater shocks or thrills. Before they left the tent, some men were induced into paying an extra 25 cents to "see it all." However, the operator was tipped off about the presence of an officer or inspector, and a tame act was substituted.

The girlie shows generated other kinds of trouble, too. Campbell Brothers Show, which played in Saskatchewan in 1920, became the centre of controversies and criminal investigation. At the time, prohibition was in effect. In the town of Earl Grey, a Mountie shut down a show. Accusations by the show's manager attacked the morality of the constable.

The same midway continued to Quill Lake. Problems related to immorality, racism, mob mentality, and public drunkenness erupted.

About ten oil and gas workers were at the event. They were drunk, the show manager told a constable. The drillers had cut the guy ropes holding up the tent that was the women's dressing room. With showgirls in it, down came the tent, all because the men wanted to party with the girls.

"There was an immoral show going on," J. Willson, one of the drillers, told another constable. "We were standing near the ropes and some kids came along and pulled down the ropes, and a coon came along and blamed it on us. He called us some dirty names that we could not stand for and a fight started."

When the tent collapsed, the show manager had politely asked the drillers to leave, he insisted to police. The drillers had used terrible language, and when they wouldn't leave, he had called the other midway workers to protect their property and see that the men scattered.

"Pretty soon the whole show troop came at us, and it was a general fight," claimed Wilson. "None of us were drunk."

The constable taking his statement was skeptical. He knew the men had been drinking. In fact, he had wanted them for liquor violations, but proof was elusive.

Show owners and managers were as concerned as the community when it came to troublemakers, whether from inside or outside the show. Often, they attributed harsh criticism to religious nuts or vested business interests. To them, the carnival was an amusement industry. Trouble meant less profit on a particular contract and fewer contracts. As a result, many had strict in-house rules, and their press agents presented the midways in a positive light. But few years passed without one controversy or another associated with the industry.

There Ought To Be A Law

"Those shady characters are nothing but a bunch of racketeers and grifters."

"I don't trust those smooth-talking carnies."

"They'll take you for every cent you have and they'll try every trick in the book to do it."

All were common enough expressions at fair time.

In more than one community, local stereotypes maintained that, during fairs, law-abiding citizens mingled on the midway with reprobates. To some, the string of gambling joints along the midway were the steep and slippery path to financial ruin. There, honest folks threw away their hard-earned cash.

Rules and laws regarding the gambling joints on fairgrounds varied. Early in the century, if the exhibition association approved, and nothing was clearly illegal, the joints could open, but the local mayor and police might still close them down.

At Calgary in 1905, there was an uproar, even though the same midway had offered games in Edmonton without incident. The Calgary association was paid $500 for the three-day "privilege." Then, when young boys gathered around the gambling booths, a citizen group led by Rev. G.W. Kerby complained. The joints were "fleecing the public," and the goings-on "would make the average tin horn eyes bulge out." Kerby maintained, "men with rolls of 'phoney' money have been displaying their 'bogus' cash and inviting the public to come up and win it."[7] He got the

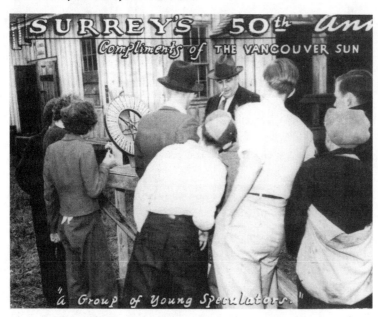

A source of controversy, gambling concessions and race track betting have a long history as part of fair and midway operations. Courtesy of City of Surrey Archives, Photo #40-2-01.

mayor and other citizens on side. Together, they threatened the chief of police with "impeachment" if he didn't arrest and punish those who operated the skin games. Often, such waves of protest came when fairs were ending. Even if arrests were made, the judges simply told offenders to get out of town, and the next year, the same scenario developed.

In 1924, use of gambling wheels that offered significant prizes became illegal. Similarly, shell games, dice games, and others deemed objectionable by police were prohibited. By 1925, fair visitors might gamble if it was only for the fun of it. So wheels were legal at fairs where prizes were small – for the most part worthless – items. Use of cash wheels remained illegal at the fairs, and operators were not allowed to buy back any of the merchandise prizes for cash. In fact, fair midways enjoyed special status. For those playing "still" dates, not associated with fairs, or playing other professional entertainment engagements, gambling remained a no-no.

Within the industry, most owners decided concessionaires could make enough money under the new rules. The wheels and games were designed with odds in the operator's favor. The prizes were inexpensive, and even if joints offered only legitimate games, the summer tours could still be profitable. As businessmen, owners in the carnival industry inevitably adapted to whatever laws and public pressure determined was acceptable or not acceptable, but the public remained suspicious of flimflam artists.

In 1928, following articles in the *Country Gentleman* and *Saturday Evening Post* about crooked midway practices, *Billboard* acknowledged the problems.

"For every show that is trying hard to do the things that will build prestige, confidence and public following, there are two that tear down."[8]

In fact, the industry magazine was prepared to publish its own exposé about midways.

"Do away with gaff joints, shills, 'men only' shows, short-changers, crooked gamblers and gyps of all kinds," claimed *Billboard* in the 4 August 1928 issue.[9]

In December, writing for the magazine, Louis Heminway noted, "The carnival of the future must be clean in every respect and live according to the letter of the law....The day of the 'grifter' and 'grift show' is ended. The people will not stand for it."

He continued, "Clean concessions and clean, moral shows. That's the edict. The men who carried 'rat-eating', raw cooch and blow-off for men only shows have seen their day. These men have done their fellow showmen thousands of dollars of harm…"[10]

By 1929, some provincial governments were withholding grants from any fair association that allowed questionable shows. Small time cheats at some joints, who operated without the knowledge or approval of midway owners, were a still part of the problem.

But grift was an issue at the top, too.

"…shows cannot clean up and stay clean as long as there are crooked local authorities and committees expecting to be greased," claimed *Billboard*.

Likely, many deals that involved at least some "grease" were made at one time or another by individuals who had the power to give or withhold contracts for major events. More common than hard currency were the countless free tickets that went to organizers, their friends, and families.

For at least three years during the Second World War, Patty Conklin made donations of $500 to the Western Canadian Association of Exhibitions. Two of those years, he did not win the concessions or midway for the A Circuit. In 1944, he did win the contract, and he offered his donation at the annual general meeting. As he had in the past, he specified that it was to be put towards the war charity of their choice. Also, he encouraged members to donate $100 each. The donations were made openly and specified for war charities. In fact, many fairs were raising money for the war effort, so the donation was reasonable.[11]

In contrast, a case of fraud was brought against Royal American in 1976. From the late 1940s on, with only a few exceptions, Royal American Shows held a monopoly on contracts for the A Circuit fairs. During the scandal of the mid-seventies, the Edmonton Exhibition manager was also at the centre of the fray, and the fraud case generated headlines in western Canadian newspapers.

By then, Royal American's operation was impressive. The show would have been a strong competitor for A Circuit contracts, no matter which midways were in competition.

The scandal first erupted in 1975. The case was high profile, and police procedure became part of the problem. That year, 120 city police and RCMP raided the Royal American Shows office during Edmonton's Klondike Days. They seized 65 000 documents.

Not only did the police want the documents for their investigation, so did the national tax investigators, who "seized the evidence" from the police. Regarding the original seizure by police, in court defense claimed that there had not been adequate evidence for the provincial court judge to have issued the warrant. The case became more and more complicated.[12]

Along the way, numerous charges were filed. Corruption was alleged against the former general manager of the Edmonton Exhibition Association, Al Anderson, who had been hired in 1956. He was charged with conspiring "to defraud" the exhibition association. Also, he was accused of accepting "secret commissions," and charged with "illegally accepting rewards, advantages or benefits of goods and money" from Royal American between 1956 and 1972. The first charge was dismissed due to inadequate evidence, since the original search warrant had been deemed invalid.

However, neither Edmonton police nor the tax department were prepared to drop the case. So, two Edmonton detectives travelled to Saskatchewan with search warrants and seized documents from the national revenue department in Regina. When they returned, detectives were posted as guards outside the investigator's room at Edmonton Police headquarters, where the evidence was temporarily held.

Finally Anderson faced three charges. One was defrauding the Exhibition Association of $52 000 between 1 July and 31 August, 1972. Another was conspiring with Royal American to defraud the association between 1956 and 1972. The third was accepting secret "commissions."[13]

Charges were also brought against Royal American for fraud and tax evasion. In February, 1977, the courts determined the tax department had been wrong in seizing the evidence from the police. The case was reassigned to agents of the provincial attorney-general. By 1979, most of the Canadian charges had been dropped. With jurisdictional and procedural conflicts, none had resulted in convictions, but in the end, Royal American Shows was barred from doing business in Canada.

The messy scandal spilled into the USA, where there were further charges against Royal American. Investigators from Edmonton City Police and RCMP went to testify for the American government in its own fraud case. There, too, procedural issues came into play. Believing they had been authorized to do so, the Canadian police had used a phone tap, intercepting calls between an American man and his wife in Canada. The USA inquiry found that though done in good faith, "the interceptions were wrongful acts." When Americans with the midway considered filing a civil suit over it, the police returned to their Canadian home, evading the problem.[14]

Although the charges had been dropped, many Edmontonians, especially those who had volunteered thousands of hours of honest work to making the annual exhibition a success, were embarrassed and disillusioned. The scandal was unfortunate for honest midway owners, too. It had confirmed the stereotype that the midways were shady businesses – despite the thousands of honest, hardworking people who were in the industry.

Rodeo, the SPCA, and the King of the Cowboys

Rodeo is a high risk sport both for people and animals. Events have led to serious injury and death. Fans have loyally supported their heroes, whether animal or human. They have claimed that some of the wildest bucking horses, ones that had no place with serious ranchers needing good saddle horses, would have been sent to slaughter houses had they not been so valued in the rodeo ring.

This accident occurred during the Rangeland Derby in Calgary in 1944. Courtesy of Stockmen's Memorial Foundation, SFL 100-01-130.

Bucking horses work five minutes in a year, and they work in ten second spurts, supporters explain. For those few minutes of work, they were given better care and attention than the vast majority of domesticated animals. Talented bucking bulls shared the same good fortune.

But detractors have a long history of protesting rodeo. Historically, one of the most risky events was roping long-horned steers. Contemporary bulldogging, steer wrestling, steer decorating, and calf roping are cousins of the violent steer roping. In today's bulldogging or steer wrestling competitions, during a timed event, the rider drops from his horse to the horns of the steer and twists its head until the steer falls. To some extent, success is a matter of landing at the right place on the animal's neck and shifting weight at the right time. If a cowboy lands too far back on the neck, the event is much harder and more dangerous. The cowboy has only 10 seconds to succeed or fail. Odds are in favor of the running steer and against the cowboy. If there is an injury, it is usually the cowboy on the horns of the steer. For steer decorating, much the same happens, but instead of dropping the steer, a ribbon is put on its horn, with similar risks to the cowboy. For calf roping, to reduce the possibility of injury, there are strict rules about roping and dropping the calf.

Steer roping in days of old could be brutal and became one of the most controversial of sports. Roping a long-horned steer and then wrestling it to the ground was an event deeply rooted in early rodeo traditions. Almost any method that worked to bring the animal down would score.

The steer was roped and stopped as suddenly as possible. Then, with his horse keeping the rope taut, the cowboy wrestled the steer to the ground. Animals were about 1500 to 1800 pounds [680-816 kg]. Their horns were long, as much as 18" [46 cm] or more across.

Newspaper accounts documented some of the injuries to animals. On the first day of the Winnipeg Exhibition and Stampede in 1913, a bulldogging event was scheduled. A long-horned steer ran into the infield. The mounted cowboy, Clayton Banks [reported as Clayton Dacks], rode in full pursuit. He released his rope and it caught one of the long horns. The sudden halting of the steer snapped the horn. The audience gasped as the soft tissue inside bled. Despite the gore, Banks roped the steer once again. The horse stopped, and the rope went taut so suddenly the heavy steer flipped. Half somersaulting, with all four hooves in the air, it thudded against the hard ground. At first it managed to get up, but again, Banks tried to throw it to the ground. In the end, the steer got away.

Alarmed by the violence, the audience considered Banks a hardened and brutal competitor.[15] By the time the Stampede ended, three steers used in the events died from injuries. A horse also died, and both cowgirls and cowboys, including one of the bulldoggers, were injured.

Reaction was mixed. Some claimed Winnipeg audiences loved the competitions, others that they were sickened by the brutality of the steer roping.

Lieutenant-Governor Cameron of Manitoba was in the audience. "We would not think a great deal of a hockey match that was not as rough as [rodeo events]. The work is naturally rough. The people come here to see this very thing and [they] crane forward every time they think there is a possibility of a performer or an animal being injured."[16]

Cowboys in North America were concerned about injuries to both animals and competitors. Many cowboys had been seriously injured, including those who had been enormously competent and successful in the arena. Even the Canada Kid lost sight in one eye after he plunged forward onto a bull's horn.

Finally, rodeo competitors organized into protective and professional associations. They had many concerns. One was the welfare of competitors, but they also wanted competitions that were safe for animals. As a result, they were instrumental in developing and changing rules. The old style of bulldogging, that meant roping long-horned steers, was dropped from almost all rodeos.

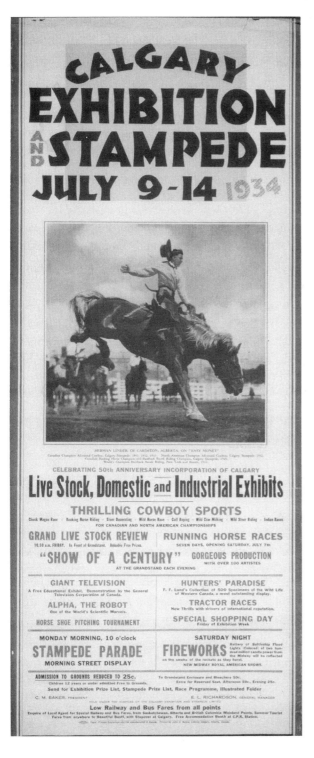

Injuries to both animals and competitors did not end. Horses with broken legs were put down. However, year after year, more and more safety-related regulations made rodeo less risky and violent.

Then, in 1949, the sport of rodeo was put on trial. The court's decision could have ended rodeo throughout Canada and had serious consequences in North America.

On one side was the Vancouver branch of the Society for the Prevention of Cruelty to Animals [SPCA] and on the other was the King of the Cowboys, Herman Linder. Both had a history of service to their causes. Two incidents became the focal point of the court cases and the public outrage on both sides.

Linder started with rodeo in 1924 as a boy. Over the years, the Cardston, AB, cowboy won countless competitions. He competed in most events at one time or another and was seven-time Canadian All Round Cowboy. Four times, he won North American All Round Championships. At Madison Square Gardens, NY, he won the world title for five successive years, and he also competed in London and Australia. By age 32, he retired from competition and became a rodeo judge and later a rodeo manager.

Well aware of the complexities and problems of the rodeo world, Linder was

Rodeo champion Herman Linder appeared on this 1934 stampede poster. Courtesy of Historical Committee, Calgary Exhibition and Stampede.

a member of the Rodeo Cowboys' Association and eventually president of the Canadian Stampede Managers' Association for several years. He produced rodeos in large cities like Edmonton and small towns like Coleman, AB. Few were better known in the business, but to most, he was a friendly, mild-mannered, Mormon rancher and rodeo hero. But because of his international reputation, he was a logical target for social reformers in the animal rights movement.

From May 24-29, Linder was contracted to bring 200 head of stock to Callister Park in Vancouver and produce a rodeo. Sponsored by the Marpole Rotary Club as a fund raiser, rodeo organizers expected a huge crowd, and they got one.

From the first day, the event was in trouble. Advance tickets had been sold, but buyers had not been made adequately aware of how to redeem tickets for actual seats. With the stadium oversold, 10 000 advance ticket buyers were ready to riot when seats weren't available for them. Inside the stadium, 8000 watched the first performance of the stampede, billed as the sixth largest on the continent. For the unfortunate without seats, an extra matinee was scheduled.[17]

Before the event, Linder had met with local officials and the SPCA to agree on rules. During the rodeo, one BC and two Alberta cowboys were hurt. The solution was to take them to the hospital. In contrast, the alleged abuse to a horse and a calf embroiled Linder in lawsuits. The SPCA charged him and four cowboys – three American and one Canadian from Lillooet, BC – with cruelty to animals.

The complaints maintained that one of the bucking horses, Rimrock, had been spurred by a cowboy. Supposedly seriously injured, it had been withdrawn from competition. The second charge was that a calf had been stunned when thrown during the calf roping competition.

"The cowboys involved had already disappeared before we could summon them," said assistant prosecutor A.S. McMorran. "They may have finished their part in the stampede and gone home but it looks strange."[18]

Linder was the rodeo producer, so he was the principal in the case and ultimately responsible. Charged with unnecessarily abusing domestic animals, he appeared in Vancouver police court. He pleaded not guilty to the two charges that would have given him a year in jail and a $500 fine.

For the rodeo, Linder had followed the rules in use at Madison Square Gardens, developed by the Rodeo Cowboys Association and the American Humane Society. In terms of the calf roping, the cowboy was to lasso the calf, jump from his horse, and then throw the calf and tie it. If he roped a calf and jerked it off its feet by the force and sudden stop, the cowboy received a ten second penalty. Any cowboy who wanted a shot at winning – and they all did – didn't purposefully let that happen. Linder had discussed the rules in a "desire to co-operate as far as possible with the SPCA."

David Ricardo, local manager of the SPCA, maintained, "very little co-operation had been given."

The court found Linder innocent of the charge related to the calf. The charge related to Rimrock caused an even greater stir.

The rules for bronc riding declared the cowboy must come out of the chute with both heels high on the animal's shoulder. Spurring was then natural, and it prompted the horse to buck.

According to the SPCA, Rimrock's shoulder had been ripped open by spurring and streamed blood after the event. Also, to make the horse buck more, a bucking strap had been cinched tight under its belly.

"The horse was prancing around Callister Park like a two-year-old colt, and showed no ill effects," testified Harold Ring, the actual owner of Rimrock. He maintained the horse had been bitten by another horse while in transit. As for the event, dull spurs had been used and they had no injurious affect, he added.[19] Other witnesses said the marks were not bite marks.

Speaking in his own defense, Linder claimed the rider's heels could not reach the spot of the injury. Anyway, the spurs were blunted and simply tickled and excited the animals into action.

"The horses must have enjoyed the performances very much," he added to the magistrate.

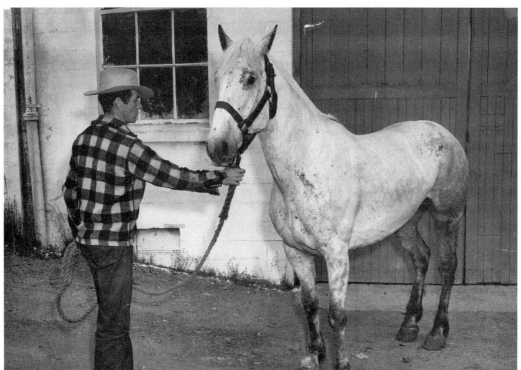

Rimrock was at the centre of the SPCA's suit against Herman Linder. The spot on the horse's front, left shoulder was the injury. Courtesy of Historical Committee, Calgary Exhibition and Stampede.

Judge McInnis didn't believe the injury was a bite. "The torture of animals used as entertainment shows a universality of human depravity," he said.[20]

"The rider should have been arrested right way," he continued. "He would have been sent to jail."[21]

He added, "The very basis of the performance is cruelty because the horse has to be put in a condition of pain, tormented and infuriated by straps and continual spurring."[22] The idea that the spurs simply tickled the animal was an "insult to the horse's intelligence."

Too, he determined, the use of a flank or bucking strap was unnecessary cruelty.

"We all know that humans all over the world get pleasure out of tormenting animals," announced the judge, "but that does not justify it happening here."[23]

The magistrate found Linder guilty. The fine was only $100 or 30 days, because Linder was a principal but had not committed the actual act.

"Spurs, spurs, spurs – that's all they talked about," said a frustrated spectator. "The RCMP uses spurs, the Vancouver Police use spurs, every cowboy uses spurs – if they didn't the horses wouldn't respond."[24]

With the victory, the SPCA prepared to fight all rodeos because they required abuse to animals.

Linder filed an appeal. "If the appeal fails, it means every rodeo in Canada and the US would have to close down," said Linder.[25]

County Court Judge Lennox heard the case in a Court of Appeal.

Rimrock became a star witness. Because of winter snow, bulldozers had to clear a path from Ring's ranch in Wilber, Washington, to the main road. The trip to Vancouver for Ring and his high-strung, 11-year-old gelding took 24 hours.

Once they arrived, while court was in session, the truck holding Rimrock, who Ring described as a "real outlaw," waited outside.

"I would like you to look at this horse," the defense requested of the judge.[26]

"I am opposed to any view," replied SPCA lawyer McMorran, insisting the case was under summary conviction and the court could not leave its place of sitting.

"Then I will have to bring the horse into court," replied the defense.

"It seems so," said Judge Lennox, and he adjourned court.

Later, he decided against bringing the bucking bronc into the court, but moved the county court to the Pacific Meat Company corrals.

Finally, Judge Lennox ruled. The wound had been inflicted by a bite when Rimrock was in transit. However, the use of the flank strap was a problem. The strap, His Honor determined, "does at least excite or irritate bucking, in its struggle to unseat its rider, and is an abuse of the horse."

He added, "It is noted that the strap used on this horse is lined with sheepskin, but that is only to save the horse from being hurt by chafing."

"To abuse is to ill use," he ruled. "To make money by the abuse of the horse is no excuse and is not by any means a defense…showing a necessity for the abuse, and I find that the flank strap was an unnecessary abuse."[27]

An appeal to the British Columbia Supreme Court had to be filed within 30 days. Linder filed another appeal. The case was heard in Victoria by three judges.

Linder won.

Still, the controversy did not completely disappear, and hostilities between the SPCA and Linder surfaced again when he staged a rodeo in conjunction with the Pacific National Exhibition in about 1960.

This time, however, the courts weren't the venue for the dispute. The newspapers were. The PNE decided to add a rodeo to the August 20-27 exhibition. Once again, the SPCA opposed Linder's rodeo, and this time, the war of words between the society and Linder was nasty.

The director of Vancouver's SPCA was Tom Hughes. He complained that he needed nine extra officers to ensure animals at the rodeo were not abused.

"August is our peak month. In past years, we have had to chloroform up to 2000 cats," he added. He would have to apply for a special grant for the officers. "This is police work – we are doing the job for the police, and they should pay."[28]

Linder wasn't troubled by the idea of inspectors.

"If they get butted by a Brahma bull, that's their lookout," he commented.

He didn't stop there. Linder was a cat lover. He had 14 on his ranch and one cow specifically to provide milk for them.

"When my cats have kittens I go out of my way to find good homes for them," he said. "I certainly would not think of destroying them."

That year, Linder planned to produce rodeos at the Canadian National Exhibition in Toronto and also in Winnipeg.

"I've followed rodeos for 30 years all over Canada, the US, in England and Australia, and nowhere else do we run into this type of opposition."[29]

The SPCA spokesman responded that it was not legally constituted in those places, and other humane societies handled objections.

To decide the fate of the Vancouver event, the SPCA and PNE held a meeting closed to the press. Some admitted it was "hot." The stampede won despite SPCA disapproval. The rodeo could go on – with inspections – but the SPCA urged people to boycott the events.

"The best way we can be certain it won't be back is not to go," said Hughes.

George Leask, Sr., from Madden, AB, had a long career as a rodeo competitor. He's seen here in a calf roping contest. Courtesy of Stockmen's Memorial Foundation, CHR 062-Vol. 2.

He admitted he couldn't do anything about the Calgary Stampede in Alberta, but "we have the law behind us in B.C." The society could seize animals as evidence or to prevent cruelty.

Vancouver wasn't the only place where animal rights were seen to conflict with rodeo contests. The Anti-Rodeo Society of Victoria laid a charge that animals were "wantonly bound and abused" during rodeo events of the Cowichan Exhibition.

Linder wrote a letter to the editor maintaining the individuals were "misguided."

"I appreciate and support their program to protect the welfare of our animals. Our rodeos today are conducted according to the rules and regulations of the Rodeo Cowboy's Association Inc. And these rules have been approved by the American Humane Society," wrote Linder.

The 800 American and Canadian rodeos of the time and the thousands of mayors, senators, other officials, and responsible leaders in these communities were not the type to associate themselves with "a recreation which was wantonly cruel and painful to animals," he claimed, adding "Let us recognize rodeo for what it is – a good, clean Canadian sport that is becoming more popular every year."

Chapter 10
Memories

From spring to fall, the popular culture of annual festivals brightened lives. Some people wandered the grounds simply for the thrills and party atmosphere, and others wanted to be educated. Many wanted good family entertainment their children; others went to compete or rally behind competitors; and countless people depended on the summer work.

At fair time, 4-H camps brought farm youth to cities for young farmer classes. For them and their parents, winning agricultural competitions re-enforced career choices and offered encouragement. Farmers went home more confident that they would survive whatever the landscape, political, and economic environment tossed their way. Whether facing droughts, deluges of rain, foot-and-mouth disease, or prairie fires, they would compete at the fair another year.

The thrilling moments of competitive sports were highlights for both visitors and locals. Crowds watched in tense anticipation as competitors participated in foot, bicycle, stock car, and chuckwagon races. The running races for horses, show jumping events, tractor pulls, plowing

Revelstoke, BC, men entered the best beard contest held in 1944 as part of Golden Spike Days. Courtesy of Revelstoke Museum & Archives, P1178.

matches, baseball and lacrosse games all had their fans. They shouted encouragement, waved programs, and stamped their feet with victories. Novelty events such as pig, moose, and buffalo races were cheered with almost equal enthusiasm and with roars of laughter.

Fairs were places where invention and excellence mattered. Technological progress and the man-made world were priorities, too. Industrial components or industrial fairs brought success in some communities and many inventions were seen for the first time by western Canadians when they visited fairs. Even the midways showcased new machines and gadgets. Invented in 1932, Alpha-the-robot was a big draw at fairs in 1934, and it made appearances on the midways of Conklin, Royal American, and World of Mirth. At the same fairs, giant telephone displays heralded a world in which phones and other wonders would become commonplace.

This horse-drawn Red River cart, in the exhibition parade at Red Deer, AB, celebrated one of the earliest modes of transportation in western Canada. Courtesy of Red Deer and District Archives, Mg 32-4-95.

PNE: The Great Industrial Exhibition of the Great West

The great Pacific National Exhibition [PNE] became the most important annual fair in BC. It was very different from strictly agricultural fairs. It started as an industrial fair, an appropriate theme given the shipping, manufacturing, and commerce of the city. The Vancouver Exhibition Association's first president, newspaper man J.J. Miller, had been involved with the Winnipeg Exhibition before becoming president of the coastal fair association, organized in 1908. In fact, he held the reins of the organization for 14 years.

Whether times were good or bad, organizers had to adapt. As this 1929 photo suggests, the gates of the exhibition grounds should lead to fun. Courtesy of Vancouver Public Library, 7925.

By 1910, the Vancouver Exhibition moved to Hastings Park, a public park that had wasted to little more than a race track. Soon, the facility's schedule was filled with festivities and competitions for the regular fair-going public, but a Boy Scouts Jamboree brought an international crowd, too. The timing of the 1910 event was always tricky. This time, the schedule didn't quite work and the conflict resulted in one of those embarrassing moments that most fair organizers eventually faced.

The prime minister was to open the fair – but on the second day. Five thousand people wanted to watch the opening ceremonies, and a crowd thronged through the gates to the grandstand. People pushed. With women being shoved about, two Mounties were called in to help.

Most – but not everyone in the grandstand – wanted to hear Prime Minister Laurier's speech. Unfortunately, races were already in progress when the prime minister was ready to open the fair. The grandstand was filled with a mixed crowd, including a few rowdies, who were watching the races.

"Sit down," they yelled at the prime minister, and continued rooting for the jockeys and horses.

Embarrassing moments aside, the main attraction at this fair was industry. For those who wanted to know what was latest and greatest in technology and industry, there were office furnishings, cash registers, electric hot water heaters, furnaces, pumps, cream separators, chicken incubators, farm implements, gas lights, gas lighting plants, pulleys, and steel shingles. Displays included safes, from small ones to those weighing a few tons. Enthusiasts could inspect the latest wagon or buggy or go the Dominion Car Company display to see vehicles. Booths held the best in home appliances and decoration, including pianos, fine furniture, clothes dryers, and Singer sewing machines. Imported teas, jams, and confections tempted the hungry and thirsty.

At the fair, the midway and concession area was called Skid Road. According to the *Vancouver Daily News-Advertiser*, 16 August 1910, the midway promised a horse with a human brain, a sacred crocodile from the Ganges, burlesque shows, Oriental dancers, and booths where people could buy "nigger babes."

Described in the same article was an African dodger show. The description and event would cause an uproar today, but the newspaper of the time boldly described the show. "Here a dusky negro sits on a board fixed to an iron bar directly over a pool of water. A basketball thrown at the target above the son of Ham's head, springs a trap and allows the seat on which the black man sits to move backward, throwing the occupant head foremost into the water. This device is now one of the most popular on the Road."[1]

The midway of 1910 was entirely different from the world of today in other ways, too. A merry-maker would need at least $5 to enjoy all the rides. If he wanted "to eat a sandwich at each of the stands, drink lemonade at all the booths, or smoke cigars at each tobacconist's stand [he] would require at least another $5 bill," claimed the same newspaper.

During the First World War, the fairgrounds were used for patriotic gatherings. The track was ideal for military parades and training. With the docks and ships nearby, the location was perfect as a mobilization camp, and expanses of open space in the park were filled with hundreds of armed forces tents. The PNE's new role was to inspire people to support the war effort, all the while "maintaining the commercial and social equilibrium of communities in times of danger and unrest."[2]

This exhibit at Regina in 1917 included material about war and "war trophies" from Belgium and North France. Courtesy of Glenbow Archives, NA-1574-6.

When the war was over, more traditional fair activities returned to the spotlight, but horse racing lost some ground to the new auto races. Also, some entertainments reflected educational concerns. At the Vancouver General Hospital tent, people could ask questions about health and health care. Children's health became a focus, too, in the Better Baby Contests and the free check-ups for children.

Years later, the economic and social hardships of the thirties meant many fair buildings across the country were needed to house or feed the unemployed and homeless. At Regina, by 2 July, 1935, the exhibition building had become a soup kitchen to feed between 1000 and 2000 people, many of whom had rioted over jobs and lack of food, and who hadn't eaten in 24 hours or more. The same occurred in Vancouver.

In the forties, the exhibition grounds once again came under the command of a war-time government. During the Second World War, not only were buildings used to feed thousands, they housed thousands. The exhibition association was pulled into what is one of Canada's darkest moments in its treatment of citizens.

The fair was cancelled during this war. Other things were happening on the grounds. With war fever, the large Japanese and Japanese Canadian population on the coast was viewed as a threat. The federal government decided to evacuate them to internment camps, which meant uprooting them from homes. The internees were allowed only the luggage they could carry. From March to September of 1942, more than 8000 were temporarily housed at Vancouver's exhibition grounds. Living conditions were deplorable. Buildings where some were housed had been used as barns. Dust and the smell of manure lingered. In one of the women's buildings, there were ten showers for 1500 internees. At first, toilets didn't have seats or dividers. Mattresses were straw ticks, and internees received three army blankets as bedding, but people were just as likely to hang them between cots in order to have some privacy. The operation was handled by the British Columbia Security Commission, not the exhibition board, but the travesty became part of the history of the exhibition grounds.

By 1946, the Vancouver Exhibition had changed its name and began a new period in its history. Now called the Pacific National Exhibition or PNE, its grounds became Exhibition Park. Growth was accompanied by entertainment extravaganzas and more sports events. The British Empire Games came to Vancouver and the PNE. For the games, Empire Stadium was built on the grounds, and there, in 1954, Roger Bannister became the first man to run a mile in less than four minutes. The games were filled with exciting moments, and in the meantime, Vancouver and the PNE moved centre stage in the national and international arena.

Carnival Atmosphere

On the grounds, a kaleidoscope of faces smiled. There were big people – so big they were giants. There were little people, not only small children but the small adults who performed with shows like the Lilliputian troupe at the Winnipeg Exhibition in 1913. Whether people were fat

For Kelowna and Okanagan Lake, the lake monster Ogopogo might appear at the festivities. In 1958, Heather Watson, who was Lady of the Lake and queen of the Kelowna regatta, moved along the parade route while sitting on the monster's head. Courtesy of Kelowna Museum Archives, 4124.

or skinny, had alligator skin or excessive unwanted body hair, there was a place where they were welcomed, and that was at fairgrounds across the country.

The performers captured the imagination of people in small towns and sophisticated, large communities. Girlie shows captivated the attention of many a young male patron who caught his first glimpse of female anatomy. The shows also attracted married men who preferred that their families, neighbors, and minister didn't know they had visited the hootchy-kootchy shows. Even some young women sneaked a peek in the many tents showcasing what was forbidden or unusual.

"I just loved the side shows. I just loved them," claimed a Calgary woman who grew up in the forties. To her, Royal American was the best midway because of its sideshows. At the Calgary Stampede, she and a girlfriend sneaked into a girlie show. They visited the side shows where human oddities had fascinated her.

On the fairgrounds somewhere, another person was bound to ask, "Did you see the two headed calf?"

"Yes, I hardly believed my eyes!"

Although such animals were often real, other acts were paste, smoke, and mirrors. Yet many who guessed of the trickery and had paid good money for tickets didn't seriously mind the deception. To someone else, even the idea of paying money and gawking at some "poor creature" had been too repugnant to even consider. As the years passed, for many organizers and community members, some shows created too much controversy to be worthwhile. They raised moral questions, ones not easily answered.

Inventor Will Wright travelled the western Canadian circuit. By 1930, still working with Conklin Shows, Wright had created a side show called Death on the Guillotine. No small-time thinker, he had a travelling agent responsible for his invention, and the world became interested. His first "production" appeared in Australia, but he soon placed seven of the shows and then put them on the open market. Although today Death on the Guillotine seems morbid, it wasn't new to show biz or the Canadian fair circuit, where mock hangings had also been popular. Yet compared with today's gruesome and violent games and movies, the entertainments were often lightweights.

In 1926 and 1927, at Fernie, BC and other stops on the western tour, Wright's daughter, Sybil, caused quite a stir. Today, she would cause a controversy. At the time, she was a sensation in the Palace of Illusions. Sybil was 11-years-old. She had been in the show business for seven years and made her first appearance with the Foley & Birk Shows.[3] So for her, packing up the midway in a snow storm that year would have been no real hardship. Contemporary labor and child protection laws would never tolerate the young girl's "career" and other responsibilities placed on her shoulders.

Although times have changed, the love of fair goers for midways hasn't dwindled. Decades ago, little kids rode the steeds on the merry-go-round, flew on the backs of bumblebees, rode elephants and ponies. Young adults roamed everywhere, often anticipating nightfall when they might steal a kiss at the top of the Ferris wheel or in the tunnel of love. Fair-going adults wandered the midway, shook their heads in amazement at the variety and danger of rides. They threw balls at buckets, placed bets on wheel games, tried to stump carnies with their age or weight, and proved their strength with giant hammers. While the hours passed too quickly, midway visitors licked ice cream, drank lemonade or pop, and enjoyed the strange sensation when candy floss melted in their mouths.

Today on the fairgrounds, people enjoy many of the same pleasures. The freak shows have disappeared and so have many of the exotic animal acts. The rides are more sophisticated and daring.

"I thought I was going to be sick," an older person will recall of the wild rides during youth.

"I thought I was going to up-chuck," someone slightly younger might say.

A still younger generation might describe the same feeling in more vivid language. "I thought I was going to puke all over you."

These prairie team-mates were entered into an international plowing competition. Courtesy of Stockmen's Memorial Foundation, SFL 20-02-004.

Whatever it took, midway owners intended to create fun for a price, but companies could have massive overhead and debts. They paid huge sums to purchase some of their rides, most imported from the USA. Eventually, Canadians, as well as immigrants, invented and refined rides, shows, and gaming concessions. More than one mechanical genius worked with the shows, and they adapted their concessions and machines to make them ever more successful –

from the standpoint of the midway's bottom line. New shows and rides were constantly appearing. In 1926, one of the new fun houses was Fun-on-the-Farm. Its manufacturer was a New York firm that sold carnival caterpillar rides, carousels, and over-the-jump rides. In January of 1928, the company plugged its product.

"Grossed 25% of its cost in a single day! ... Fun-on-the-Farm is the flash of the midway – an imposing yellow structure with seven animated ballys to attract the crowds and draw them into its mysterious passageways, where every step is a new type of thrill. It's a repeater, too – [and]played bigger in 1927 than in 1926....It's a low-priced fun house with a high earning capacity."[4]

In the mid thirties, Roll-O-Plane, Fly-O-Plane, Loop-O-Plane and the Octopus came out of the aircraft industry in Oregon. Of course, they would be big hits and big money makers. In 1940, a mountain-type ride called Silver Streak [Himalaya] and an aerial joy ride was being promoted, but the types of rides were affected by ever-changing technology and ideas of fun.

Already in the 9 December 1939 of *Billboard*, 35-year veteran of the industry, Harry Illions commented, "Today the public demands speed, especially the younger generation, and we, therefore, have to speed up our devices if we want to be in the swim....we increased the speed of one [Ferris wheel] to seven revolutions per minute while the other was about 3½. In over a month's time we could not get anybody to ride the slow wheel."

The things to buy and win on midways changed. In the early days, items were small. Today's huge stuffed animals didn't appear on midways until about the 1950s.

Gambling skill games changed. The experience didn't.

"It's rigged. I should have won," cries a loser, who then tries a different game.

In fact, the odds were against those spending their money on the ring tosses, bucket and ball games, shooting galleries and diggers. In contrast, the odds were in the visitor's favor when it came to finding special trinkets to buy, discovering new thrill rides each year, seeing entertaining shows, and indulging in too much cotton candy, pop, mini donuts, or hot dogs.

The Past Meets the Present

In 1941, during war time, Swift Current welcomed Winnie Stonewall Winston, a blue-blooded Bulldog, who became the star of the show. Winnie was a tribute to leader and war time hero Winston Churchill, often considered a "bulldog." The theme for the 1941 annual summer event became Bull Dog Days in the Frontier City.

Year after year, communities held draws for houses, pots of gold, cars, trucks, motor homes, and even tractors. The money went to the association or a good cause, such as the war effort or a children's charity. In Swift Current, instead of having their usual draw for a car, Winnie went up for grabs.

It took serious effort by Hugh Leslie, the publicity chairman for the community fair, to find the star qualities he wanted in a Bulldog, and he searched the Dominion. Finally the choice was clear. In fact, when he arrived as a beautiful little Bulldog pup, Winnie had a pedigree that impressed everyone. With a sire valued at $13 000, he was no small catch. Winnie was the best choice to represent the tenacity of the British during the war. But Swift Current offered more, and organizers attached a $1000 bond to his collar.

To promote the event, Winnie would become "one of the most publicized dogs in the world," claimed the 18 March edition of the *Swift Current Sun*. "He will travel the length and breadth of this province, gaily bedecked as befits a blue blood of the canine world."[5]

Strange things happened at fair time. It was as if Swift Current's concern for the war effort was transmitted through the air, and its support for the war deserved note. At about the same time as the event opened and the draw was made, elsewhere in the world, the H.M.C.S. Swift Current minesweeper was launched, ready to play its part in the war. The draw was made just before midnight June 30.

By another co-incidence that seemed to acknowledge war work, the winner of the Bulldog was a returned soldier, a local man who had served his country and the British Empire in the First World War.

Winnie was destined to have even more symbolic importance. Two weeks later, the Kinetic Club that sponsored the fair bought the dog back from the soldier. The Bulldog had new orders.

Winnie became the mascot for the H.M.C.S. Swift Current. Crowds were at the train station when the dog began his journey to join the navy. On arrival for duty, Winnie was made an able seaman.

Tragedy struck while the minesweeper was still at a Newfoundland port. The bulldog decided to challenge a bull, and he lost the battle. Winnie might have begun his distinguished career with Swift Current's summer fair, but he was buried at sea with full honors. For locals who attended the fair, memories of the dog would mingle with other fond ones of fairs past.

British Columbia's Centennial was another occasion when past and present were fused during special celebrations – many held during at fairs, but stretching into a year-long celebration. Those 1958 festivities clearly demonstrated the diversity of people and resources, the long history of the province, and the industry and business important to the province. The themes for fairs were endless.

During the year, both the province and Vancouver shared the limelight. They staged the province's first International Trade Fair at Vancouver's Exhibition Park. As a trade show, not only

Photographed here in Victoria, throughout 1958, this Centennial Caravan truck stopped at many community fairs. Courtesy of British Columbia Archives, E-07385.

These Mounties continued the RCMP's long history of performing the Musical Ride at special events throughout the summer. Courtesy of Walt Holt.

was it a different in focus from any previous BC fair, it was world class. The goal was to emphasize the role of imports and exports in economic development, and 160 nations attended. As well as participation from foreign governments, 149 companies staged exhibits. For the trade fair, the four large buildings of Exhibition Park were transformed into exhibit areas with eye-catching facades, color, and pools of light.

That year, Vancouver still staged the Pacific National Exhibition, and it attracted 925 000 to the grounds. The RCMP Musical Ride performed and drew audiences totaling 60 000 people.[6] But Vancouver was not alone in staging outstanding events at fairs and exhibitions to celebrate the province's centennial. Almost every community planned something. In large cities, such as in Victoria and Vancouver, special events were scheduled throughout the year. Tiny communities, such as Invermere, entered into the same spirit of the celebration during their annual summer festivals.

The BC Centennial Caravan headed out on the road, taking exhibits to large and small communities. The Centennial committee assisted in funding parades, plays, concerts, barbecues, canoe races, square dance exhibitions, re-enactments, and infra-structure projects on fair grounds. Princess Margaret toured. Even a giant balloon floated in the sky over Victoria.

Yet, the concept of presenting how the real people within the community lived, the diversity of their cultural heritage, and the new ways of earning a living increasingly had devotees who organized countless new festivals that appealed to specific audiences.

The cultural diversity of immigrants played a stronger role in Vancouver than in much of western Canada. Entertainment, and festivals rooted in Asian culture became popular. At first, that happened most clearly in the welcome for Chinese and Japanese acrobats who performed with circuses as fair entertainment. But soon, Vancouver summer festivals celebrated the Asian population. Dragon Boat Races became popular and attracted throngs of people. The Sikh population, which first arrived on the west coast early in the 1900s, celebrated the spring festival of

Baisahki. Like many festivals and fairs, it began with a colorful parade of floats and bands. Later, there were folk songs and demonstrations of traditional dance. In July, the Japanese celebrated the Buddhist Obon Festival, which included religious rites to welcome the spirits of ancestors.

Like Vancouver, Winnipeg has many festivals, including its Red River Exhibition, Championship Regatta, Fringe Festival, Folk Festival, and sports championships. All across the west, large communities have added festivals to the calendar. Most were one-day special events, and some have become very successful, though usually not outshining the traditional fair.

Today's summer festivals celebrate jazz and country music. There are folk festivals, lilac festivals, sun and salsa festivals, Caribbean festivals, and Africa days, to mention only a few. At the same time, fairs and festivals have become more serious about the heritage of early pioneers, and many communities have their Threshing Days in the fall.

The Bunnock Festival in Macklin, SK, is an unusual and recently developed fair. Rooted in the heritage of Russian Germans who immigrated to western Canada, it celebrates the game of Bunnock. Developed in the late 1800s by the Russian military, it makes use of horse bones. In earlier days, the bones were free and readily available when horses died of old age along roads, in fields or on farms. In Siberia during winter, the ground was too hard for driving in the peg needed for horseshoes, So the ankle bone of horses were set in the snow for a tossing game with its own rules and scoring system.

When Germans immigrated to Russia, they picked up the game, and when those immigrants' families moved to Canada, the game came with them. The Bunnock World Championship, held in Macklin, started as a family gathering for the local Stang family. Today, an authentic set of the 52 bones is costly, and not readily available, but for the

Where there are lakes, stunts have included balancing on a log – and in this case, on a chair on a log in a lake. At some regattas, fully clothed men jousted and wrestled on floating logs. Courtesy of Kelowna Museum & Archives, 666.

gathering and games, the family bought the bones from a meat packer.[7] And a new western Canadian festival was "born."

The community was interested. Gatherings grew and became fair-like. With live bands, food booths, balloons, jugglers, midway rides, and an evening dance. The championship sporting competition became like any other fair across the country – despite its unique sporting event and history.

Also, reviving and strengthening their traditional gatherings, First Nations see more and more people attending their pow wows. In 1997, Alberta had at least 11 pow wows, as well as other First Nations festivals. BC hosted at least seven pow wows as well as other festivals, including ones centred on war canoe races. In Saskatchewan, Aboriginal people enjoyed another seven pow wows, and celebrated Back to Batouche Days and Crescent Lake Homecoming Days.[8] At the same time, they remain important participants in the other festivals in their communities.

Numerous traditional exhibitions, rodeos, and regattas have grown into week-long festivities, but even that never seems long enough. Each fair, circus, powwow, rodeo, or regatta had its grand finale. The contest finals, most extravagant stage show, and special presentations were saved for last. Then, the best of the fireworks exploded in the dark sky.

In 1928, for the Provincial Exhibition in Regina, the fireworks display cost $1000 per evening for six nights. As a grand finale each evening, 180 "bomb shells" were fired simultaneously. Courtesy of the Saskatchewan Archives Board, R-E 1994, Provincial Exhibition, 1928.

Staring skyward, the watching crowd gasped. Tiny missiles whistled from the ground high into the air. Sparks mushroom out and down like falling stars. The day was over and the awed but exhausted crowd of men, women, and children make their way home. The most important community gathering of the season had ended. Midway and show companies followed their circuit to the next community, and so did many of the competitors. Local organizers and visitors had to wait until next year for the work and fun to begin again – unless they decided to travel to a neighboring community and share in its celebration. Too, they might head to air shows and trade shows and smaller local events, but none were quite like the most important festival of the summer. There, they discovered something of themselves, something of the culture they shared with others and something of their personal interests.

By the end of the day, most visitors, competitors, workers, and organizers went home happy. There was always so much to remember. With the annual events, memories piled up – year after year. For children and adults, alike, there seemed little to match the excitement, the highs and the lows of those community events. They were summertime days filled with stories that revealed western Canada's history, people, and pop culture, a culture that constantly changed, yet invariably remained the same and relevant through the decades.

SMF – Stockmen's Memorial Foundation Library & Archives, Cochrane, AB

EEA, CEA – Edmonton Exhibition Association, City of Edmonton Archives

GA – Glenbow Archives, Calgary

CPL – Calgary Public Library

CESA – Calgary Exhibition & Stampede Archives

NWE, NWPL – New Westminster Exhibition, New Westminster Public Library

SAB – Saskatchewan Archives Board, Regina

REA, LHR, RPL – Regina Exhibition Association, Local History Room, Regina Public Library

RDMA – Red Deer and District Museum and Archives

SPL – Saskatoon Public Library

MHMAG – Medicine Hat Museum & Art Gallery

Footnotes

Chapter 1 – Days of Delight

1. "Plenty Excitement and Amusement At Third Day of Winnipeg Stampede," *Manitoba Free Press*, 13 August 1913.
2. Nellie McClung. As quoted by Grant MacEwan in *Agriculture on Parade*, Toronto, ON: Thomas Nelson & Sons (Canada) Ltd., 1950, 1.
3. *Saturday News*, [*Edmonton Bulletin*], 6 July 1907. Clippings File, EEA, CEA,
4. "Our Forgotten Past," *Royal City Record*, 5 June 1983, Clipping Files, NWE, NWPL.
5. Grant MacEwan, *Agriculture on Parade*, 8-20. MacEwan suggests the Portage La Prairie fair was the first permanent one in western Canada. New Westminster and Victoria had earlier initial dates, but the fairs did not remain permanent. See Clipping Files, 5 June 1983, NWE, NWPL.
6. "Edmonton's First Exhibition Staged at HBC Fort In 1879," *Edmonton Journal*, 16 July 1955. Clipping File, EEA, CEA.

7. *Kelowna Courier*, 19 September 1912.

8. Newspaper of the Six-day Fair in September, 1922, *The British Columbian*, Clipping Files, NWE, NWPL.

9. "Toronto Fair Has Attendance Record," *The British Columbian*, 11 September 1923. Clipping Files, NWE, NWPL.

10. "Our Forgotten Past," *Royal City Record*, 5 June 1983, Clipping Files, NWE, NWPL.

11. Bud Bargholz, "Big Gap Stampede." Manuscript, SMF, Cochrane, AB. Adapted from "Big Gap Stampede," *The Cattlemen*, January, 1952.

12. Daryl Drew, "Ribstone country 'bank robbers,'" *Western People*, 4 October 1984, WP7.

13. *Billboard*, 13 February 1926.

14. *Billboard*, 17 November 928.

Chapter 2 – Adding Pizzazz

1. "Rushing Work at Exhibition Grounds," *Edmonton Bulletin*, 13 July, Clipping Files, EEA, MS 322, CEA.

2. "Martha Florinne and Her Pets," *Edmonton Bulletin*, 20 August 1910, Clipping Files, EEA, CEA.

3. "Al Barnes' Circus," *Edmonton Bulletin*, 19 August 1910, Clipping Files, EEA, CEA.

4. Minutes, General Annual Meeting of the Western Canadian Association of Exhibitions, 20-22 January 1936. Pamphlets, Exhibitions, SAB. All information re: the attraction committee is from this source.

5. Ibid., 18.

6. Ibid., p. 21.

7. John Robertson, "Rodeo Clowns Don't Laugh To Themselves," [*Winnipeg Tribune*, 1960] Clipping, Herman Linder Scrapbook, CESA.

8. Gail Hughbanks Woerner, *Fearless Funnymen: The History of the Rodeo Clown*, 62.

9. Jerry Connelly, "An Interview With Slim Pickens," *Persimmon Hill*, Vol. 13, No. 2. SMF

10. Correspondence with the Author, Russ Overton, April, 2003. All quotes by Mr. Overton are from this source.

11. R.S. Robertson, "Airship New Westminster, B.C.," *Vancouver Postcard Club Newsletter*, April 1995.

12. *Morning Albertan*, 29 June 1920. As quoted by Bruce Gowans in *Wings Over Calgary*, 79.

Chapter 3 – Putting Together the Pieces

1. This figure appears in dispute. *Grant McEwan's West*, 142, suggests the Territorial Government donated $5000. *Regina* by Drake reports it as $10 000. Also see: "Regina in 1895..." *Saskatchewan History*, VIII, 2, Spring, 1955, 56. Other statistics on the 1895 fair are also from

these sources.

2. "By order, meals 35 cents," *Regina Leader Post*, 4 August 1955. Clipping file, Exhibitions, SAB.

3. Prizes listed are based on [The Official] Canadian North-west Territorial Exhibition Prize List, 1895, Regina, NWT, July 29 to Aug 7. Some information conflicts with other sources.

4. Op Cit.

5. Ibid.

6. "Growth of Exhibition....," *Regina Leader Post*, 18 June 1963. Clipping File, REA, LHR, RPL.

7. Ibid.

8. Spectator, David. *Agriculture on the Prairies 1870-1940*, 130.

9. Information from photo published in *Leader-Post*, 28 August 1942.

10. James Gray, *A Brand of Its Own: The 100 Year History of the Calgary Exhibition and Stampede*, 38.

11. Fred Kennedy, *Calgary Stampede*, 17. He and James Gray do not agree on some statistics. Kennedy suggests the Calgary population in 1912 was 47 000.

12. Lady Ishbel Aberdeen, nee Marjoribanks, *The Journal of Lady Aberdeen: The Okanagan Valley in the Nineties*, 23. Both quotes by Lady Aberdeen are for this source. For further information, see also pp. 21-24, 65-66, 79.

13. As quoted by Michael Dawe and Judith Hazlett in *100 Years of Progress: A History of Red Deer Fairs and Exhibition*, 100.

14. "Parkland's Rube MacFarlane granted fairs' highest honor," [*Red Deer Advocate*] RDDMA, Clipping File, MacFarland, Rube, Exhibition

15. King, Andrew. *Pen, Paper & Printing Ink*, 75.

16. Ibid., 76. See also 85-92 for personal experiences with showmen.

Chapter 4 – Wild West Shows, Rodeo, and the Real West

1. For discussion of first known American rodeos see *The Real Wild West* by Michael Wallis, 136-137.

2. Dempsey, Hugh. *The Golden Age of the Canadian Cowboy*, 121-123.

3. Zack Miller as quoted in *American Heritage*, December, 1969, 50.

4. Elsworth Collings and Alma Miller England. *The 101 Ranch*, 1971, 175.

5. Terrill, Mary. "Reflections from a California Feedlot," *Canadian Cattlemen*, October, 1950, 30.

6. MacEwan, Grant. *Calgary Cavalcade*, 147.

7. For discussion of Ad Day and H.C. McMullen's roles in organizing the Calgary 1912 Stampede and Winnipeg 1913 Stampede, see "Addison P. Day, Rodeo Great," by A.P. Day Junior in *True West Magazine*, September-October, 1978. Also, extensive records on the Day family are held at MHMAG.

8. Calgary Exhibition and Stampede, 1912, Official Program, Pamphlet Files, CPL.

9. Fred Kennedy, *Calgary Stampede*, 22.

10. James Gray, *A Brand*, 39.

11. *Calgary Albertan*, 23 March 1935. See also, Calgary Exhibition and Stampede, Business and Correspondence Papers, 1899-1965, GA, ff 10-14, GA.

12. *Calgary Albertan*, 11 April 1934.

13. Minutes, General Annual Meeting of the Western Canada Association of Exhibitions, Winnipeg, 1936, SAB, Regina, Pamphlets File, Exhibitions.

Chapter 5 – Sporting Competition Anyone?

1. Tony Cashman, *Edmonton Exhibition: The First Hundred Years*, 91.

2. Letter, Western Canadian Fair and Racing Circuit, EEA, CEA, MS 322.

3. Wally Wood, *Thoroughbred Racing in Canada: A Historical Perspective*, Unpublished manuscript, CESA. Although publication of this manuscript is not certain, it was prepared for the Calgary Exhibition and Stampede and seems a more reliable source than the article by Denny Layzel, "The Iceman," *The Canadian Horse*, [clipping, no date], which offers conflicting dates and statistics.

4. Wood, Wally. *Thoroughbred*, 1-2.

5. A.P. Day, Jr., *True West Magazine*, October, 1978, 54. A.P. Day Fonds/files, MHMAG. Additional information on the Day family is available at the Swift Current Archives.

6. *[Calgary] Albertan*, 11 Sept 1912.

7. Kennedy, *Alberta Was My Beat*, 110. See also: *[Calgary] Albertan*, 23 Sept 1912; *Macleod Adviser*, 18 Sept 1912.

8. For a complete discussion, see Hugh Dempsey, *Tom Three Persons: Legend of an Indian Cowboy*.

9. Dee Marvine, "Fanny Sperry Wowed 'em at the First Calgary Stampede," [Magazine Title Not Given]. Calgary Exhibition and Stampede 1912, Pamphlets File, CPL. This article was adapted from the author's biographical novel, *To Chin the Moon*. The book was heavily researched but some details are not consistent with other sources.

10. Ibid.

11. All prize and title winners are as quoted in the Prize List from: Official Program, "The Stampede at Calgary, Alberta, 1912 September 2, 3, 4, 5" CPL Pam File 791.8 CAL [1912].

12. R.H. Imes, "The 1912 Calgary Stampede," *Field, Horse and Rodeo*, February, 1963. Vol. I, No. 8.

13. In "The Death of Barra Lad," *Alberta Was My Beat*, Kennedy gives Louis's age as 16. According to his obituary, *Edmonton Journal*, 26/1/71, he was ten at the time.

14. Kennedy, "The Legend of Pete Knight," [*Calgary Herald*, ca 1950], Linder Scrapbook. CESA.

Chapter 6 – Communities On Display

1. EEA, Clipping Files, *Edmonton Bulletin*, 9 December 1910.

2. *Brandon Mail*, [1891]. As quoted by Coates & McGuinness in *Pride of the Land*, 14.

3. Ibid. News paper source is not given.

4. Editor, *Brandon Sun*. As quoted by Coates & McGuinness in *Pride*, 13.

5. Garry Allison. *100 Years of History: The Lethbridge and District Exhibition*, 12. All related quotes and statistics are from this source.

6. Ibid. Other sources estimate 40 000 admissions.

7. *Manitoba Free Press*, 10 July 1912.

8. *Manitoba Free Press*, 11 July 1912.

9. *Manitoba Free Press*, 12 July 1912.

10. *Manitoba Free Press*, 18 July 1912.

11. *Manitoba Free Press*, 13 July 1912. The sign for the side show advertised, "Hit a coon, win a cigar."

12. *Manitoba Free Press*, 12 July 1912.

13. *Manitoba Free Press*, 18 July 1912.

14. *Manitoba Free Press*, 12 July 1912.

15. *Manitoba Free Press*, 16 July 1912.

16. Ibid., 16 July 1912.

17. _____ "Medals Won by the Province of British Columbia...," Okanagan Historical Society, *Forty-third Report*.

18. *Spokane Review*. [No Date Given]. As quoted by Hume Powley in "Francis Richard Edwin DeHart," Okanagan Historical Society, *Fifty-second Report*, 126.

19. [Charles L. Willis], "List of Awards for the Stettler Exhibition," *Stettler Independent*, August, 1930. All quotes regarding the 1930 fair are from this source. See clipping file: Stettler Museum.

20. [Charles L. Willis], "List of Awards at Stettler Exhibition, " *Stettler Independent*, 6 August, 1931. All quotes for the 1931 fair are from this source.

21. Charles W. Gordon and Jack L. Kerns. *The Alberta Livestock Exhibit: Fifty Years at the Royal Agricultural Winter Fair 1922-1972*, 1.

Chapter 7 – Insider Stories From the Midway

1. John Thurston, Notes on Conklin Shows from *Billboard*, 19 February, 1921, 88. All *Billboard* references are from Mr. Thurston's notes.

2. *Billboard*, 15 September 1923, 102. All references to the 1923 tour are from this source.

3. Western Canadian Exhibition Association Meeting, 1936. All references to this meeting and midway pitches are from this source.

4. Patty Conklin, *Billboard*, 29 August 1936, 77.

5. Oney Martin, Correspondence with the Author, 7 July 2003.

6. Oney Martin, Interview with the author, Calgary, 6 November, 2003.

7. Opt Cit., Correspondence, 7 July 2003

8. Interview, Oney and Doug Martin, 15 November 2003. All further comments by Doug and

Oney Martin are from this source and the above mentioned interview and correspondence.

9. Oney Martin, Interview with the Author, 15 April 2003.

10. Norman Sharein, Interview with the Author, 15 April, 2003. All comments by Norman Sharein are from this source.

11. Hazel Elves, *It's All Done With Mirrors: A Story of Canadian Carnival Life*, 21. All comments by Frank Hall are from this source.

12. Ibid., 70-71. All quotes regarding this circumstance are from these pages.

13. Ibid., 95-96. All quotes regarding this circumstance are from these pages.

Chapter 8 – So, What Could Go Wrong?

1. Kay, Flury, *Let's Go to the Fair: A History of the Weyburn Agricultural Society 1908-1968*, 5.

2. "First Signs of Approaching Storm and Midway After It Struck," *Star Phoenix*, 21 July 1937.

3. "Storm Toll Heavy For 2: Damage Is Dealt Sparks, Conklin," *Billboard*, 15 July 1939.

4. "Edmonton Is Down in Heat," *Billboard*, 2 August 1941.

5. *Morning Albertan*, 2 July 1908. This date gives the capacity of the air bag as 8000 cu feet. The *Daily Herald*, 6 July, 1908 gives the capacity as 800 cu feet. The 8000 figure seems more logical.

6. *Daily [Calgary] Herald*, 6 July, 1908.

7. Coates, *Pride*, 54.

8. *Lethbridge Herald*, 11 July 1911.

9. *Winnipeg Free Press*, 12 July 1912.

10. *Morning Albertan*, 3 July 1917. As quoted in *Wings over Calgary* by Bruce Gowen, 77.

11. "Agricultural Society Formed To Show Federal Officials That 'Area Was Fitted for Cultivation,'" *Saskatoon Star Phoenix*, [1952], SPL, Clipping File, Exhibition 1886. This provides fair history and statistics.

12. *Saskatoon Star Phoenix*, 27 July 1929.

13. "Fair Grounds Undergo Transformation," *Saskatoon Star Phoenix*, 31 December 1930.

14. Ibid.

15. "Profit Made by Canada's First Free Exhibition," *Saskatoon Star Phoenix*, 30 August 1932.

16. *Kelowna "Win-the-War" Regatta, Official Program*, 1940.

17. *Kelowna Courier*, 6 August 1940. All quotes about burning Hitler are from this source.

18. *Kelowna "Combined Ops" Regatta, Official Program*, 1943.

19. *Kelowna International Regatta, Official Program*, 1945.

20. *Calgary Sun*, 27 July 1987.

Chapter 9 – Plagued With Controversy

1. *Edmonton Bulletin*, 9 August, 1910, Clipping File, EEA, CEA. All quotes by D.C. Scott are from this source.

2. "Correspondence: Indians and Exhibitions," Arther Barner, *Edmonton Bulletin*, 22 July 1910, EEA, CEA.

3. "Indians Ready for Banff Invasion," *[Calgary] Herald Magazine*, 13 July 1963. Exactly who made this statement is not clear. The source implies it was W.L. Matthew.

4. Coates, *Pride*, 28. As quoted from an unidentified newspaper.

5. David Jones, *Midways, Judges and Smooth-tongued Fakirs*, 55. As quoted from H. V. Clendening's letter to the editor, "Side-Lights on our Summer Fairs," *The Nor-West Farmer*, 20 December 1907.

6. Jones, 56-57. All references to this incident are from this source.

7. "Row Over Gambling at the Exhibition, *The [Calgary] Daily Herald*, 7 July 1905.

8. "Outdoor Observations," *Billboard* , 16 June 1928.

9. "Outdoor Observations," *Billboard*, 4 August 1928.

10. Louis Heminway, "What's Ahead for the Carnival Midway," *Billboard*, 8 December 1928.

11. Western Canadian Association of Exhibitions, Minutes of the Annual Meeting, 1944, 15. SAB, Pamphlets-Exhibitions.

12. "Ex shows evidence guarded," *Edmonton Journal*, 16 April 1977.

13. "Former Ex chief faces 3 new charges," [*Edmonton Journal*] 10 February 1976, EEA, CEA, Clipping File.

14. "Police flee U.S. to evade summons, [*Edmonton Journal*], 25 August 1979. EEA, CEA, Clipping File.

15. *Manitoba [Winnipeg] Free Press*, 9 August 1913.

16. "Changes Made to Reduce Accidents," *Manitoba [Winnipeg] Free Press*, 13 August 1913.

17. Cliff Faulknor, *Turn Him Loose! Herman Linder, Canada's Mr. Rodeo*, 97. Mr. Linder's rodeo successes, as well as the controversies in Vancouver are detailed in this source.

18. "Rodeo Head, 4 cowboys Face Charges," *[Vancouver] Herald*, 30 May 1949. Linder Vancouver Scrapbook, CESA.

19. "Rodeo Head Denies Charges of Cruelty," *[Vancouver] Herald*, 31 May 1949, Vancouver Scrapbook, CESA.

20. "Horse 'Witness' at Trial," [Newspaper Unknown], Linder Vancouver Scrapbook, CESA. Many of the newspaper clipping in the Linder Scrapbooks do not have clear publication information.

21. "Linder Fined $100 on Rodeo Cruelty Count," *Trail Times*, 4 June 1949. Linder Vancouver Scrapbook , CESA.

22. "Court Move May Peril Other Rodeos," *[Vancouver] Herald*, 4 June 1949. Linder Vancouver Scrapbook , CESA.

23. "Manager of Rodeo Fined $100 for Cruelty," *Vancouver Sun*, 3 June 1949. Linder Vancouver

Scrapbook , CESA.

24. "SPCA May Campaign On Rodeos," [Newspaper Unknown], Linder Vancouver Scrapbook , CESA.

25. "City Magistrate Denounces Rodeo," [Newspaper Unknown], Linder Vancouver Scrapbook , CESA.

26. "Flank Strap 'Cruel,'" [Newspaper Unknown], Linder Vancouver Scrapbook, CESA. All comments from the session are from this source.

27. "Producer Must Pay $100 fine for Abuse of Horse," [Newspaper Unknown], Linder Vancouver Scrapbook, CESA.

28. "SPCA 'Too Busy' Killing Cats," [Newspaper Unknown], Linder Vancouver Scrapbook, CESA.

29. "King of the cowboys bucks off critics," [*Vancouver Sun*], Linder Vancouver Scrapbook, CESA. All of Linder's responses at this time are from this source and the original draft of the letter addressed to Editor, *Vancouver Sun*, 20 September 1954.

Chapter 10 – Memories

1. *Vancouver Daily News-Advertiser*, 16 August 1910. As quoted by Breen, 13.

2. Vancouver Exhibition Association, Bulletin No. 9, 1918. As quoted by Breen, 21.

3. *Billboard*, 26 June 1926.

4. *Billboard*, 9 December 1939.

5. *Swift Current Sun*, 18 March 1941. As quoted by Money Kersell in "Winnie Stonewall Winston city's most famous canine," *Swift Current Sun*, [1971].

6. _____ *The Report of the British Columbia Centennial Committee*. Victoria, BC: British Columbia Centennial Committee, 1959, 169-170.

7. The Bunnock Capital of the World, Maklin, Saskatchewan [pamphlet]. See also Notes for the Author by Gerry Mann, Calgary Chapter, American Historical Society of Germans From Russia.

8. *1997 Pow Wow Calendar*, Compiled by Liz Campbell. Summertown, Tennessee: The Book Publishing Co., 1996.

_____ *1997 Powwow Calendar*. Complied by Liz Campbell. Summertown, Tennessee: The Book Publishing Company, 1997.

Aberdeen, Lady Ishbel, nee Marjoribanks. *The Journal of Lady Aberdeen: The Okanagan Valley in the Nineties*. Edited by R.M. Middleton. Victoria, BC: Morriss Publishing Ltd., 1986.

Allison, Garry. *100 Years of History: The Lethbridge and District Exhibition*. Lethbridge, AB: The Lethbridge and District Exhibition, 1998.

Behak, Pete. "Scars Prove It." [Vancouver] Newspaper Clipping, 1960. CESA, Linder Collection, Scrapbooks.

_____ "Bill Pickett," *American Heritage*, December, 1969. American Heritage Publishing Co., Inc, 1967, 50

Breen, David and Kenneth Coates. *The Pacific National Exhibition: An Illustrated History*. Vancouver, BC: University of British Columbia Press, 1982.

_____ *British Columbia Official Centennial Record, 1858-1958*. Vancouver, BC: Evergreen Press Ltd., 1957.

Byfield, Ted. *Alberta in the 20th Century: The Boom and the Bust, 1910-1914, III*. Edmonton, AB: United Western Communications, 1994.

Campbell, Burt. "Commentary on Okanagan Fall Fairs." Okanagan Historical Society, *Thirteenth Report* (1949) 166.

Campbell, Shirley. *Our Fair: The Interior Provincial Exhibition*. Armstrong, B.C.: Armstrong Spallumcheen Museum and Arts Society, [1999].

Cashman, Tony. "Golden Anniversary of Flight." Edmonton Exhibition Clipping File 1, City of Edmonton Archives.

Cashman, Tony. *Edmonton Exhibition: The First Hundred Years*. Edmonton, AB: Edmonton Exhibition Association, 1979.

Card, Douglas. *Lethbridge Seed Fairs, 1896-1988*. Lethbridge, AB: City of Lethbridge, 1988.

Selected Bibliography

Coates, Ken and Fred McGuinness. *Pride of the Land: An Affectionate History of Brandon's Agricultural Exhibitions*. Winnipeg, MB: Peguis Publishers, 1985.

Collings, Ellsworth and Alma Miller England. *The 101 Ranch*. Norman, OK: University of Oklahoma Press, 1971.

Connelly, Jerry. "An Interview With Slim Pickens." *Persimmon Hill*, 13, no. 2.

Dawe, Michael and Judith Hazlett. *100 Years of Progress: A History of Red Deer Fairs and Exhibition*. [Red Deer]: Westerner Exhibition Association, Centennial Book Committee, 1991.

Day, A. P., Jr. "Addison P. Day, Rodeo Great." *True West Magazine* (September-October 1978).

Dempsey, Hugh. *Tom Three Persons: Legend of an Indian Cowboy*. Saskatoon SK: Purich Publishing, 1997.

Dempsey, Hugh. *The Golden Age of the Canadian Cowboy*. Saskatoon & Calgary: Fifth House Publishers, 1995.

Drew, Daryl. "Ribstone country 'bank robbers.'" *Western People* (4 October 1984).

Eamer, Claire and Thirza Jones. *The Canadian Rodeo Book*. Saskatoon SK: Western Producer Prairie Books, 1982.

Elves, Hazel. *It's All Done With Mirrors: A Story of Canadian Carnival Life*. Victoria BC: Sono Nis Press, 1977.

Faulknor, Cliff. *Turn Him Loose! Herman Linder, Canada's Mr. Rodeo*. Saskatoon, SK: Western Producer Prairie Books, 1977.

Fleming, E.S. "Fall Fairs in the Okanagan." Okanagan Historical Society Annual Report, *29th Report*, 1965, 72-75.

Flury, Kay. *Let's Go to the Fair: A History of the Weyburn Agricultural Society 1908-1968*. [Weyburn, SK: No Publisher or Date Given].

Ford, Theresa, ed. *Western Profiles*. Edmonton, AB: Alberta Education, 1979.

Gabriel, Theresa. *Vernon, British Columbia: A Brief History*. Vernon, BC: Vernon Centennial Committee with Vernon Branch of the Okanagan Historical Society, 1958.

Gordon, Charles and Jack Kerns. *The Alberta Livestock Exhibit: Fifty Years at the Royal Agricultural Winter Fair, 1922-1972*. [Edmonton, AB]: Alberta Agriculture, [1987].

Gowans, Bruce. *Wings Over Calgary 1906-1940*. Calgary, AB: Chinook Country Chapter and Historical Society of Alberta, 1989.

Gowans, Bruce. *Wings Over Lethbridge 1911-1940*. Lethbridge, AB: Historical Society of Alberta & Whoop-up Country Chapter, 1986.

Gray, Art. *Kelowna: Tales of Bygone Days*. Kelowna, BC: Kelowna Printing, [n.d.].

Gray, James. *A Brand of Its Own: The 100 Year History of the Calgary Exhibition and Stampede*. Saskatoon SK: Western Producer Prairie Books, 1985.

Giesbrecht, Vern. "The Racing War Canoes." *Westworld Magazine* (May-June, 1979).

Hanes, Colonel Bailey. *Bill Pickett, Bulldogger*. Norman, OK: University of Oklahoma Press, 1977.

Imes, R.H. "The Calgary Stampede." *Field, Horse and Rodeo*. I, no. 8 (February, 1963)

Jameson, Sheila. *Chautauqua in Canada*. Calgary: Glenbow-Alberta Institute, [ca 1979].

Jones, Jo Fraser, ed. *Hobnobbing with a Countess*. Vancouver, BC: UBC Press, 2001.

Jones, David. *Midways, Judges and Smooth-tongued Fakirs*. Saskatoon, SK: Western Producer Prairie Books, 1983.

Kennedy, Fred. *Calgary Stampede*. Vancouver, B.C.: West Vancouver Enterprises, 1965.

Kennedy, Fred. *Alberta Was My Beat*. Calgary, AB: *The Albertan*, 1975.

Kerkhoven, Marijke. "A Cross-section of Life: Agricultural Fairs in Alberta and Saskatchewan, 1879-1915." *Alberta Museums Review III*, no. 2, (Fall 1986).

King, Andrew. *Pen, Paper & Printing Ink*. Saskatoon SK: Western Producer Prairie Books, 1970.

Laing, F.W. "Okanagan Fall Fairs." Okanagan Historical Society, *Thirteenth Report*. (1949) 162-165.

Layzel, Denny. "The Iceman." *The Canadian Horse*. [clipping, no date]

Leslie, Jean. *Glimpses of Calgary Past*. Calgary, AB: Detselig Enterprises Ltd., 1994.

Livingstone, Donna. *The Cowboy Spirit: Guy Weadick and the Calgary Stampede*. Vancouver/Toronto: Greystone Books, Douglas & McIntyre, 1996.

MacEwan, Grant. *Agriculture on Parade*. Toronto, ON: Thomas Nelson & Sons (Canada) Ltd., 1950.

MacEwan, Grant. *Calgary Cavalcade*. Edmonton, AB: The Institute of Applied Art, Ltd., 1958.

MacEwan, Grant. *Grant MacEwan's West*. Saskatoon SK: Western Producer Prairie Books, 1990.

Mair, Alex. *Gateway City: Stories From Edmonton's Past*. Calgary, AB: Fifth House Ltd., Fitzhenry & Whiteside Co., 2000.

McGowan, Don. *The Green and Growing Years: Swift Current, 1907-1914*. Victoria, BC: Cactus Publishing, [1989].

_____ "Metals Won by the Province of British Columbia...." Okanagan Historical Society, *Forty-third Report*. Vernon, B.C.: Okanagan Historical Society, 1979.

Mikkelsen, Glen. *Never Holler Whoa! The Cowboys of Chuckwagon Racing*. Toronto ON: Balmur Book Publishing, 2000.

Mitchell, David and Dennis Duffy, ed. *Bright Sunshine and a Brand New Country: Recollections of the Okanagan Valley 1890-1914*. Sound Heritage Series. Vol. III, No. 3. Victoria, BC: Provincial Archives, Province of British Columbia, 1979.

_____ Official Souvenir Program, (pamphlet) Calgary, AB: Calgary Exhibition and Stampede, 1962.

Oram, Edna. *Ninety Years of Vernon*. Vernon, BC: Greater Vernon Museum and Art Gallery, [ca. 1982].

Orr, Mary Gartrell. "More Early Fruit Awards." Okanagan Historical Society, *Forty-third Report*. Vernon, B.C.: Okanagan Historical Society, 1979.

Pay, Murray V. with Barbara Kwasny. *On Parade!* Saskatoon, SK: Western Producer Prairie Books, 1990.

Powley, Hume. "Francis Richard Edwin DeHart." Okanagan Historical Society, *Fifty-second Report*. Vernon, B.C.: Okanagan Historical Society, 1988.

_____ "Regina in 1895: The Fair and the Fair Sex." *Saskatchewan History VIII*, no 2 (Spring, 1955)

56-60.

Prytula, Martha. "The Dick Parkinson Story." Okanagan Historical Society Annual Report, *38th Report*, 1974, 105-107.

Prytula, Martha. "The Dick Parkinson Story." Okanagan Historical Society Annual Report, *39th Report*, 1975, 63-67.

_____ *Royal Agricultural Winter Fair Livestock Exhibit 1922 – 1972*. Compiled by Charles W. Gordon & Jack L. Kerns. Edmonton AB: Alberta Agriculture, 1987.

Reksten, Terry. *More English than the English: A Very Social History of Victoria*. Victoria, BC: Orca Book Publisher, 1986.

_____ *The Report of the British Columbia Centennial Committee*. Victoria, BC: British Columbia Centennial Committee, 1959.

Riddell, William. *Regina: From Pile O' Bones to Queen City of the Plains*. Burlington ON: Regina Chamber of Commerce & Windsor Publications (Canada) Ltd., 1981.

Robertson, John. "Rodeo Clowns Don't Laugh To Themselves." [*Winnipeg Tribune*, 1960]. Clipping, Linder Scrapbook, Calgary Exhibition and Stampede.

Robertson, R.S. "Airship New Westminster, B.C." *Vancouver Postcard Club Newsletter* (April 1995).

Savage, Candace. *Cowgirls*. Vancouver/Toronto: Greystone Books, Douglas & McIntyre, 1996.

Seagraves, Anne. *Daughters of the West*. Hayden, Idaho: Wesanne Publications, 1996.

Spectator, David. *Agriculture on the Prairies 1870-1940*. Ottawa, ON: National Historic Parks and Sites Branch, Parks Canada, 1983.

Terrill, Mary. "Reflections from a California Feedlot." *Canadian Cattlemen* (October, 1950).

Terrill, Mary. "'Uncle' Tony Day and the 'Turkey Track'." *Canadian Cattlemen* (June, 1943).

Thirkell, Fred & Bob Scullion. *Postcards From the Past*. Surrey, BC: Heritage House Publishing Ltd., 1996.

Torrence, Colleen, "Remembering Roy Seward." [*Golden Star*] (9 September 1992).

Wallis, Michael. *The Real Wild West: The 101 Ranch and the Creation of the American West*. New York: St. Martin's Press, 1999.

Ward, Tom. *Cowtown: An Album of Early Calgary*. No City: McClelland & Steward West Ltd., 1975.

Gilchrist, Mary, ed. *Western People*. Saskatoon SK: Western Producer Prairie Books, 1988.

Wilkins, Harles. *The Circus at the Edge of the Earth*. Toronto ON: McClelland & Steward, 1998.

Willcocks, George. *A History of Exhibitions and Stampedes in Medicine Hat*. Medicine Hat: The Medicine Hat Exhibition and Stampede Company, 1996.

Woerner, Gail Hughbanks. *Fearless Funnymen: The History of the Rodeo Clown*. Toronto, ON: Eakin Press, 1993.

Zwarun, Suzanne. "Alberta aviatrix honored." *Calgary Herald*, [October, 1984]

Archival, Library, Special Collections & Websites

Calgary Exhibition and Stampede; Linder Scrapbooks, stampede queen collection, competitors' data base, horse racing files. Manuscript: Wood, Wally. *Thoroughbred Racing in Canada: A Historical Perspective* (No record of publication).

Calgary Exhibition and Stampede, Pamphlet File, Calgary Public Library, 791.8.

Canadian Western Agribition www.agribition.com.

City of Edmonton Archives, Edmonton, AB: Edmonton Exhibition Association Fonds, MS 322; MS22.1; EA 45, www.archivesalberta.org.

Conklin All-Canadian Shows www.conklinshows.com.

Glenbow Archives, Calgary, AB, Calgary Exhibition and Stampede, M2160, www.glenbow.com.

Golden Museum, BC: Seward, Roy. P.O. 136.

Hyack Festival, New Westminster, BC: www.hayack.bc.ca.

Kelowna Museum, Kelowna, BC: Kelowna Regatta, Clipping File & Official Programs.

Medicine Hat Museum & Art Gallery, Medicine Hat, AB: Tony Day, M64.4; Chautauqua M87.13.1.

New Westminster Public Library, New Westminister, BC: New Westminster Exhibition, Clipping Files.

Penticton Museum, Penticton, BC: May Day, Penticton Peach Festival & Regatta,

Red Deer & District Museum & Archives, Red Deer, AB: MacFarland, Rub'; [Red Deer] Exhibition, Clipping Files.

Regina Public Library, Regina, SK: Exhibition Clipping Files.

Revelstoke Museum & Archives, Golden Spike Days.

Saskatchewan Archives Board.:[Regina] Exhibitions, Pamphlets Files.

Saskatoon Industrial Exhibition, Local History Files, Saskatoon Public Library.

Stettler Fair, Stettler Town & County Museum, Stettler, AB: Fair Clipping Files

Stockmens' Memorial Foundation [Bert Sheppard...], Cochran, AB. Bargholz, Bud, Manuscript; "We Salute the Cowboys," Canada's First All-Girl championships Rodeo & Race Meet, Official Program, 1962; Rodeo Magazines and Files.

Swift Current Museum, SK: Day, A.P. Sr., [W. Nelson Fonds]; Frontier Days.

University of Oklahoma: Western Heritage Collection, Miller Brothers, 36, 2; 33, 2; 95, 5.

Vernon Agricultural Exhibition, Vernon Racing Carnival, Greater Vernon Museum.

Newspapers

Brandon Mail: [1891].

The British Columbian: 11 October 1894; 12 September 1922; 7 September 1923; 11 September 1923; *Daily Columbian*, 11 October 1894; 14 October 1909

Calgary Albertan [Calgary News Telegram]: 6 Sept 1912; 7 Sept 1912; 9 Sept 1912; 11 Sept 1912; 23 Sept 1912; 11 April 1934; 23 March 1935. *Morning Albertan*, 29 June 1920.

Calgary [Daily] Herald: 7 July 1905; October, 1984; 7 Sept 1912; 8 Sept 1912; 9 Sept 1912; [Calgary] *Herald Magazine*, 13 July 1963.

Calgary Sun: 27 July 1987.

Daily Star [Saskatoon]: 15 July 1926.

Edmonton Bulletin: [*Saturday News*] 6 July 1907, 6 July 1907; 9 December 1910; 13 July 1910; 20 July 1910; 22 July 1910; 9 August 1910; 19 August 1910; 20 August 1910; 21 August 1910; 23 August 1910; 25 August 1910; 26 August 1910, 24 December 1910; 10 January 1911; 10 February 1911; 4 April 1911; 14 January 1915; 16 July 1955; *The Morning Bulletin*, 3 March 1917.

Edmonton Journal: 16 July 1955; 23 July 1960; 8 August 1975; 10 February 1976; 16 April 1977; 25 August 1979.

[Edmonton] Real Estate Weekly: 20 April 1995.

Kelowna Courier: 19 September 1912, 6 August 1940; 3 August 1943; 12 August 1954; 14 June 1969; 16 June 1969; 17 June 1969.

Kelowna Capital News: 20 July 1983; 3 August 1997.

Lethbridge Herald: 11 July 1911.

Manitoba [Winnipeg] Free Press: 10 July 1912; 11 July 1912; 12 July 1912; 16 July 1912; 18 July 1912; 9 August 1913; 13 August 1913.

Macleod Adviser: 19 September 1912.

News Leader [New Westminster, BC]: 25 May 2002.

Red Deer Advocate: 18 July 1934; 10 October 1980; 9 July 1991.

Regina Leader Post: 4 August 1955; 18 June 1963.

The Revelstoke Review: 15 June 1944; 6 July 1944.

Royal City Record: 5 June 1983.

Saskatoon Star-Phoenix: 17 October 1902; 6 February 1903; 2 August 1909; 5 August 1916; 21 August 1903; 10 December 1908; 3 August 1909; 4 August 1909; 27 July 1929; 31 December 1930; 30 August 1932; 30 June 1933; 8 August 1933; [clipping] 1933; 17 July 1937; 19 July 1937; 21 July 1937; 24 May 1941; [clipping] 1952;

Stettler Independent: [unknown date] August 1930; 6 August 1931; 12 October 1933;

Swift Current Sun: 18 March 1941 [reprinted 1970].

Vancouver Daily News Advertiser: 16 August 1910.

[Vancouver] Herald: 30 May 1949; 31 May 1949; 3 June 1949; 4 June 1949.

Vancouver Postcard Club Newsletter: April, 1955.

Vancouver Sun: 20 September 1954.

Vernon News: 14 July 1932.

Winnipeg Tribune: clipping [1960]; 18 April 1960.

Interviews and Correspondence

Martin, Oney. Interviews 6 November 2002. Correspondence 7 July 2003. Doug and Oney Martin. Interviews 20 November 2002, Oney Martin and Norman Cook, 15 April 2003.

Overton, Russ. Correspondence re: brother Ralph Overton. April, 2003.

Thurston, John. *Billboard* Magazine information and quotes are based on the detailed excerpts and notes of Mr. Thurston for the period 1919-1941.

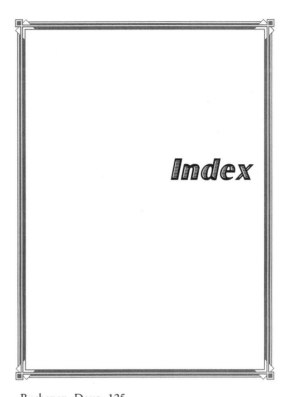

Index